JOURNAL FOR THE STUDY OF THE NEW TESTAMENT
SUPPLEMENT SERIES
144

Executive Editor
Stanley E. Porter

Sheffield Academic Press

The Blind, the Lame, and the Poor

Character Types in Luke–Acts

S. John Roth

Journal for the Study of the New Testament
Supplement Series 144

Copyright © 1997 Sheffield Academic Press

Published by
Sheffield Academic Press Ltd
Mansion House
19 Kingfield Road
Sheffield S11 9AS
England

Typeset by Sheffield Academic Press
and
Printed on acid-free paper in Great Britain
by Bookcraft Ltd
Midsomer Norton, Bath

British Library Cataloguing in Publication Data

A catalogue record for this book is available
from the British Library

ISBN 1-85075-667-8

CONTENTS

ACKNOWLEDGMENTS

This study is a slightly revised and updated version of my PhD dissertation (Vanderbilt University, 1994), which has been written while I have been serving as pastor of Faith Lutheran Church in Jacksonville, Illinois, USA. I am grateful for the unfailing love, support, and encouragement I have received from the congregation.

I would like to thank my wife, Kristina, who has lived with me and my academic pursuits for a decade and a half, and without whose willing partnership this effort would have been impossible. I would like to acknowledge also two friends and colleagues, Arthur Rawlings and Dr Brooks Schramm. I appreciate their encouragement, and their stimulating conversations with me both challenge and delight me.

ABBREVIATIONS

AB	The Anchor Bible
ATANT	Abhandlungen zur Theologie des Alten und Neuen Testaments
BAGD	W. Bauer, W.F. Arndt, F.W. Gingrich and F.W. Danker, *Greek–English Lexicon of the New Testament*
BETL	Bibliotheca ephemeridum theologicarum lovaniensium
BFCT	Beiträge zur Förderung christlicher Theologie
Bib	*Biblica*
BR	*Biblical Research*
BZNW	Beihefte zur Zeitschrift für die neutestamentliche Wissenschaft
CBQ	*Catholic Biblical Quarterly*
CBQMS	*Catholic Biblical Quarterly*, Monograph Series
CurTM	*Currents in Theology and Mission*
HBT	*Horizons in Biblical Theology*
HNT	Handbuch zum Neuen Testament
IDBSup	G.A. Buttrick (ed.), *Interpreter's Dictionary of the Bible*, Supplementary Volume
Int	*Interpretation*
JAAR	*Journal of the American Academy of Religion*
JBL	*Journal of Biblical Literature*
JSNT	*Journal for the Study of the New Testament*
JSNTSup	*Journal for the Study of the New Testament*, Supplement Series
LCL	Loeb Classical Library
LD	Lectio divina
NCB	New Century Bible
NovT	*Novum Testamentum*
NovTSup	*Novum Testamentum*, Supplements
NTS	*New Testament Studies*
SBLDS	Society of Biblical Literature Dissertation Series
SBLMS	Society of Biblical Literature Monograph Series
SBLSCS	Society of Biblical Literature Septuagint and Cognate Studies Series
SBLSP	*Society of Biblical Literature Seminar Papers*
SBS	Stuttgarter Bibelstudien
SNT	Studien zum Neuen Testament
SNTU	Studien zum Neuen Testament und seiner Umwelt

TDNT	G. Kittel and G. Friedrich (eds.), *Theological Dictionary of the New Testament*
THKNT	Theologischer Handkommentar zum Neuen Testament
TU	Texte und Untersuchungen zur Geschichte der altchristlichen Literatur
VT	*Vetus Testamentum*
WBC	Word Biblical Commentary
ZAW	*Zeitschrift für die alttestamentliche Wissenschaft*
ZNW	*Zeitschrift für die neutestamentliche Wissenschaft*
ZTK	*Zeitschrift für Theologie und Kirche*

Chapter 1

INTRODUCTION

Why are the blind, lepers, the poor, and the deaf so prominent in the Gospel of Luke and all but absent in the Acts of the Apostles? The question is not new.[1] Yet the emergence of literary criticism[2] as a tool for biblical exegesis gives us a fresh perspective from which to assess this issue.

The virtual disappearance of the so-called outcast characters from part two of Luke's[3] narrative poses a distinctive problem for Lukan studies because it creates tension between two firmly held consensuses about Luke's writings. The first consensus is that the Gospel and Acts are a unified work. The second is that Luke has a special concern for the poor. A few preliminary remarks about these consensuses will indicate the direction this study will take.

---

1. See L.E. Keck, 'The Poor among the Saints in the New Testament', *ZNW* 56 (1965), pp. 100-29 (108).

2. In this study 'literary criticism' refers to description and analysis of writing using theories and methods developed in the field of literature. 'Literary criticism' understood in this way should not be confused with what biblical scholars have traditionally called 'literary criticism', that is, the attempt to trace a text's written history and to make judgments about the text's authorship. See M.A. Tolbert, *Sowing the Gospel: Mark's World in Literary-Historical Perspective* (Minneapolis: Fortress Press, 1989), pp. 2-3 n. 4; N.R. Petersen, *Literary Criticism for New Testament Critics* (Guides to Biblical Scholarship; Philadelphia: Fortress Press, 1978), pp. 10-11 n. 4. For a relatively recent example of the term 'literary criticism' used in the manner introduced by nineteenth-century biblical scholars, see H. Koester, *Introduction to the New Testament. II. History and Literature of Early Christianity* (Hermeneia Foundations and Facets; Philadelphia: Fortress Press, 1982), pp. 43-59.

3. In this study, the name Luke refers to the implied author of the work Luke–Acts. 'Implied author' is a common literary term designating the textually-expressed, idealized version of the author. The implied author is, therefore, to be distinguished from the real author. While the identity of the author of Luke–Acts is unknown, I will use the name Luke, and masculine pronouns to refer to Luke, as a matter of convenience.

The Consensus regarding the Unity of Luke–Acts

The label 'Luke–Acts', which modern commentators routinely use and which this study will use when speaking of the Gospel of Luke and the Acts of the Apostles, expresses the unanimous view that the two are 'a single literary enterprise'.[4] Frequently cited as evidence of the unity of Luke–Acts are the following points: (1) the work has a single author;[5] (2) parallel motifs appear in both volumes;[6] and (3) Luke–Acts has a unified plot or continuous story line.[7]

These three unifying elements suggest to interpreters that Luke–Acts also has one or more unifying themes,[8] as well as one or more

4.   L.T. Johnson, *The Gospel of Luke* (Sacra Pagina, 3; Collegeville, MN: The Liturgical Press, 1991), p. 1.

5.   See Lk. 1.1-4 and Acts 1.1-2.

6.   Parallel motifs in the Gospel and Acts include stereotypical prefaces (Lk. 1.1-4 and Acts 1.1-2); descents of the Spirit upon Jesus and his followers (Lk. 3.22 and Acts 2.1-4, 24); ministries by Jesus and the apostles of preaching and healing (e.g. Lk. 5.17-26 and Acts 3.1-10; Lk. 6.19 and Acts 5. 16; Lk. 7.11-17 and Acts 9.36-43; 20.7-12); prayer (e.g. Lk. 3.21; 6.12; 9.18, 28-29; 11.1; 22.40-46; Acts 1.24; 4.31; 6.6; 8.15; 9.40); expansive journeys by Jesus and Paul (Lk. 9.51-19.44 and Acts 19.21-28.31); conflicts between Jesus and apostles and religious leaders, and trials before religious leaders (e.g. Lk. 5.17-26; 6.1-5, 6-11; 7.36-50; 11.14-54; 22.1-2, 63-71; Acts 4.1-22; 5.17-42; 7.12, 54-58; 22.30-23.10), and martyrdom (Lk. 23.33-47 and Acts 7.54-59). For lists of parallels between Jesus' ministry and the ministries of Jesus' followers, see R.F. O'Toole, *The Unity of Luke's Theology: An Analysis of Luke–Acts* (Good News Studies, 9; Wilmington, DE: Michael Glazier, 1984), pp. 62-94.

7.   See F.W. Danker, *Jesus and the New Age: A Commentary on St. Luke's Gospel* (Philadelphia: Fortress Press, rev. edn, 1988), p. 1; Johnson, *Luke*, p. 17; R.C. Tannehill, *The Narrative Unity of Luke–Acts: A Literary Interpretation. I. The Gospel According to Luke* (Foundations and Facets: New Testament; Philadelphia: Fortress Press, 1986), pp. 1-2. Prior to the emergence of literary criticism as a tool of biblical scholars, redaction critics drew attention to what they termed Luke's over-arching theological scheme of salvation history, which is, in effect, an appeal to a unified plot. For classic redaction critical treatments of the Gospel and Acts that sketch this picture of salvation history, see H. Conzelmann, *The Theology of St Luke* (trans. G. Buswell; New York: Harper & Row, 1960), pp. 14-17 and E. Haenchen, *The Acts of the Apostles: A Commentary* (trans. by R. McL. Wilson; Philadelphia: Westminster Press, 1971), pp. 96-103.

8.   Among proposed unifying themes are these two samples. F.W. Danker, *Luke* (Proclamation Commentaries; Philadelphia: Fortress Press, 2nd edn, 1987), p. 7: 'Despite defections, Israel's mission as Servant of the Lord and benefactor to the

coherent purposes.[9] Though there is no scholarly consensus as to the exact nature of Luke's overriding purpose in writing Luke–Acts,[10] commentators are agreed that the fundamental purpose for parallels between events in Jesus' ministry recorded in the Gospel and events in the ministries of the Christian missionaries recorded in Acts is to establish Jesus as a model for the ongoing ministry of the church. In this way, the parallels between Jesus and the apostles, the Jerusalem church, Stephen, and Paul serve an ethical purpose. The following quotation from R. O'Toole summarizes the prevailing view:

> These parallels (between Jesus and his followers) remind everyone that Christ continues to work through us, his disciples. All of Jesus' followers are able to continue his salvific activity. As Jesus went about doing good, preaching and endured rejection, yet was innocent, so should we.[11]

The consensus view, then, holds that Lukan theological perspectives and ethical directions will be expressed with consistency and coherence through both the Gospel and Acts. Or, to restate the consensus from another angle, interpreters looking for Luke's theological perspectives and ethical directions are obliged to look for perspectives and directions that can be documented in both the Gospel and Acts.

Expanding interest in the unity of Luke–Acts has corresponded to the increasing use of first, redaction criticism and secondly, literary

world finds fulfillment under the endowment of the Spirit through Jesus and his followers'. Johnson, *Luke*, p. 10: 'Because God had shown himself faithful to the Jews, therefore, the Word that reached the Gentiles was also trustworthy'.

9. Tannehill (*Narrative Unity*, I, p. 2) states this connection between plot and purpose explicitly: 'Luke–Acts has a unified plot because there is a unifying purpose of God behind the events which are narrated'.

10. For a summary of theories about the purpose of Luke–Acts, see R.L. Maddox, *The Purpose of Luke–Acts* (Studies of the New Testament and its World; Edinburgh: T. & T. Clark, 1982).

11. O'Toole, *Unity*, p. 94. See also C.H. Talbert's contention (*Reading Luke: A Literary and Theological Commentary on the Third Gospel* [New York: Crossroad, 1982], pp. 2-5) that Luke–Acts belongs to the ancient biographical tradition and that a key function of biographies that present both the life of the hero and the activities of the hero's successors is to persuade the reader to adopt the values and behaviors of the hero. Like numerous commentators, M. Prior (*Jesus the Liberator: Nazareth Liberation Theology [Luke 4.16-30]* [The Biblical Seminar, 26; Sheffield: Sheffield Academic Press, 1995], pp. 161-62) takes as a point of departure that Lk. 4.18-19 is Jesus' mission and the church's mission. This linkage then propels Prior's (*Jesus the Liberator*, pp. 184-97) chapter on applying Lk. 4.16-30 to today.

criticism in Lukan research. The influence of redaction criticism and literary criticism has produced a reigning scholarly consensus on the unity of Luke–Acts that is in essence a collection of commonly-held working assumptions. These working assumptions form a common ground, which is that interpretation of Luke–Acts should reflect common authorship of both volumes, parallel motifs, coherent plot, unifying themes, and one or more overarching purposes. This common ground is, however, an imprecise common ground because scholars often differ on what they mean by 'authorship', 'motif', 'plot', 'theme', and 'purpose', in addition to differing on what Luke's unifying motifs, plot, themes, and purposes might be. At this point, insufficient attention has been paid to building a theoretical framework for discussion of the unity of Luke–Acts. Connecting literary theory to literary exegesis would make interpretation more persuasive and avoid statements concerning the unity of Luke–Acts that cannot bear their ontological weight.[12] Reader-response criticism does this.

Reader-response criticism locates narrative unity in the audience's narrativity. What matters is not the ontological status of the text, but its status as a discourse heard by an audience. The narrative coheres because its readers actively tie episodes, motifs, and other narrative elements together.[13] From T.M. Leitch comes a concise summary of what constitutes an audience's narrativity. He states the following:

> At its simplest level, narrativity entails three skills: the ability to defer one's desire for gratification. . . the ability to supply connections among the material a story presents; and the ability to perceive discursive events as significantly related to the point of a given story or sequence.[14]

To this I add from W. Iser that narrativity includes the skill of supplying information that the text may hint at but not disclose.[15]

---

12. The field is no longer totally barren. J. Darr takes up the issue from a reader-response perspective in *On Building Character: The Reader and the Rhetoric of Characterization in Luke–Acts* (Literary Currents in Biblical Interpretation; Louisville: Westminster/John Knox, 1992), pp. 29-31.

13. See the discussion in Chapter 3 on W. Iser's concept of 'consistency building'.

14. T.M. Leitch, *What Stories Are: Narrative Theory and Interpretation* (University Park: Pennsylvania State University Press, 1986), p. 34.

15. E.g. W. Iser, *The Implied Reader: Patterns of Communication in Prose Fiction from Bunyan to Beckett* (Baltimore: The Johns Hopkins University Press, 1960), p. 106. See the discussion in Chapter 3 of textual gaps and indeterminacies.

When readers approach a narrative, they assume that the narrative will be understandable and follow a believable sequence. This assumption grows out of common practice and functions effectively because it is a convention shared by writers and readers. Readers conventionally assume that the end of a narrative will be connected to its beginning. When Kino finally flings away the 'pearl of the world' at the end of John Steinbeck's novel *The Pearl*, the reader understands that action as the culmination of a reversal of Kino's point of view about the value of the pearl. The reader's perception of Kino's action is satisfying, at least in part, because the reader's expectation of narrative continuity finds fulfillment. Also, readers of a narrative conventionally expect the narrative world to be consistent or, if changed, that the changes in the narrative world be plausible on the narrative's own terms. Similarly, readers assume that characters will be consistent or, if they change, that character changes will be explainable within the logic of the story.

The conventionality of narrative coherence stretches back to ancient literature and is reflected in the literary guidelines put forth by Aristotle, Horace, and 'Longinus', who are three of the best indicators of conventions for reading and writing in the Hellenistic world. The poetic work imitates an action that has a beginning, a middle, and an end, said Aristotle. 'Tragedy, then, is an imitation of an action that is serious, complete, and of a certain magnitude.'[16] Moreover, Aristotle insisted that character must be consistent, or, if inconsistent, 'consistently inconsistent'.[17] Horace wrote, 'In a word, let your work be what you will, provided only it be uniform and a whole'.[18] 'Longinus' made his point by analogy: 'Among the chief causes of the sublime in speech, as in the structure of the human body, is the collocation of members, a single one of which if severed from another possesses in itself nothing remarkable, but all united together make a full and perfect organism'.[19] Hellenistic literary culture put a high premium on conforming to literary conventions, including conventions regarding consistency and coherence in the poetic work. Luke–Acts is a Hellenistic literary text. It is therefore in keeping with the

16. Aristotle, *Poetics* 6.2.
17. Aristotle, *Poetics* 15.4.
18. Horace, *Art of Poetry* 23.
19. Longinus, *On the Sublime* 40.

literary culture in which Luke–Acts was produced to read it as a coherent work, that is, to build consistency among textual perspectives, relationships between characters, and the like. Stated another way, the assumption of narrative coherence is a convention that would have been shared by ancient readers and writers, including the writer of Luke–Acts and his audience.

The Consensus regarding Luke's Social Consciousness

Luke is broadly considered to be the most socially minded of the Gospel writers.[20] Generally cited in support of this consensus are the following points: (1) Luke has proportionally more material than the other Gospels dealing with the rich and the poor;[21] (2) women play more prominent roles in Luke–Acts;[22] (3) particularly in Luke's Gospel Jesus befriends or makes positive examples of religious and social outcasts;[23] (4) healing the sick and infirm is a leading component of the ministries of Jesus and his followers;[24] and (5) Luke is particularly fond of exhortations to and examples of almsgiving.[25] The general conclusion on the basis of these five points is that Luke considered human dignity and care for the disadvantaged to be important components of the church's ministry.

Of these five points, Luke's material on rich and poor has received by far the most attention, eclipsing the others in discussions of Luke's social ethic.[26] Almsgiving is often integrated into discussions of Luke's

20. E.g. F.B. Craddock, 'Luke', in *Harper's Bible Commentary* (ed. J.L. Mays; San Francisco: Harper & Row, 1988), p. 1014: 'Perhaps the characteristic of Luke's Gospel most commonly known and remarked upon is his attention to and evident concern for the oppressed and marginalized persons in society'.

21. Lk. 4.18; 6.17, 24; 7.22; 12.13-21; 14.15-24; 16.1-31; 18.18-29; 21.1-4.

22. Examples include the roles of Mary in Lk. 1.26-56; Anna in 1.36-38; the women who from their possessions provide for Jesus and the disciples in 8.1-3; sisters Mary and Martha in 10.38-42; the weeping daughters of Jerusalem in 23.27-31; and healings of women in 4.38-39; 8.40-48; 13.10-17.

23. Lk. 7.36-50; 10.29-37; 17.11-19; 18.9-14; 19.1-10.

24. Lk. 4.31-44; 5.12-26; 8.2-3; 9.1-4, 37-43; 10.1-24; 13.10-17; 14.1-4; 17.11-19; 18.35-43; Acts 3.1-11; 9.32-41; 14.8-10; 16.16-18; 19.11-17; 20.9-12.

25. Lk. 11.41; 12.33; Acts 9.36; 10.1-8, 31; 24.17.

26. Studies include R.J. Cassidy and P.J. Scharper (eds.), *Political Issues in Luke–Acts* (New York: Orbis Books, 1978); H.-J. Degenhardt, *Lukas, Evangelist der Armen: Besitz und Besitzverzicht in den lukanischen Schriften: Eine traditions- und redaktionsgeschichtliche Untersuchung* (Stuttgart: Katholisches Bibelwerk,

attitude toward wealth and property.[27] For many commentators, this makes Luke the chief New Testament spokesperson for God's concern for the wellbeing of the poor and God's preferential bias to the poor.

When commentators refer to other disadvantaged or socially outcast groups besides the poor, such as the deaf, the lame, the blind, the captive, the oppressed, lepers, and the dead, they tend to do so in summary fashion, virtually ignoring these other groups or treating them as subcategories under the overarching category 'the poor'. When these marginalized groups are considered collectively, then women, tax collectors, Samaritans, and sinners are generally added to the mix. All together these are said to comprise 'the oppressed and excluded'[28] or 'the neglected mass of humanity'.[29] G.W. Nickelsburg states:

> [Luke's] sympathy for the poor is part of his general concern for outcasts, aliens, and second-class citizens: tax collectors and sinners; Samaritans; women.[30]

1965); J. Dupont, 'The Poor and Poverty in the Gospel and Acts', in *Gospel Poverty: Essays in Biblical Theology* (trans. M.O, Guinan; Chicago: Franciscan Herald, 1977), pp. 25-52; S. Hauerwas, 'The Politics of Charity in Luke', *Int* 31 (1977), pp. 251-62; F.W. Horn, *Glaube und Handeln in der Theologie des Lukas* (Göttinger Theologische Arbeiten, 26; Göttingen: Vandenhoeck & Ruprecht, 1983); T. Hoyt, Jr, 'The Poor in Luke–Acts' (PhD dissertation, Duke University, 1975); R. Koch, 'Die Wertung des Besitzes im Lukasevangelium', *Bib* 38 (1957), pp. 151-69; P. Liu, 'The Poor and the Good News: A Study of the Motif of *Euangelizesthai Ptochois* in Isaiah 61 and Luke–Acts' (PhD dissertation, Fuller Theological Seminary, 1985); D.L. Mealand, *Poverty and Expectation in the Gospels* (London: SPCK, 1980); W.E. Pilgrim, *Good News to the Poor: Wealth and Poverty in Luke–Acts* (Minneapolis: Augsburg, 1981); Prior, *Jesus the Liberator*; D.P. Seccombe, *Possessions and the Poor in Luke–Acts* (SNTU, Series B, 6; Linz: A. Fuchs, 1983).

27. Tannehill, *Narrative Unity*, I, pp. 103-39.

28. E.g. H. Moxnes, *The Economy of the Kingdom: Social Conflict and Economic Relations in Luke's Gospel* (Overtures to Biblical Theology; Philadelphia: Fortress Press, 1988), pp. 119-23.

29. J.A. Fitzmyer, *The Gospel According to Luke I-IX* (AB, 28; Garden City, NY: Doubleday, 1981), pp. 250-51. Similarly, from a social science perspective, Moxnes (*Economy of the Kingdom*, p. 120) states: 'The poor in Luke's Gospel are listed among the sick and the impure; therefore, they are outside the system of social exchange'.

30. G.W.E. Nickelsburg, 'Riches, the Rich, and God's Judgment in I Enoch 92-105 and the Gospel according to Luke', *NTS* 25 (1978–79), pp. 324-44 (341). See

Finally, 'the poor' frequently becomes a catch-all designation for this far larger grouping.[31] Scholarly work has tended, therefore, to define its exegetical task as identifying Luke's (or Jesus') attitude toward the poor, assuming in the process that this attitude is expressed with consistency and is at least part of Luke's intended message to his audience.[32]

Problems with the Consensuses

Luke, then, is understood to have written a unified double work and, by his compassionate attention to the poor, to be an advocate for Christian concern for and ministry to the outcasts of society. These consensuses are plagued by two problems. The first problem has to do with the distribution of the evidence for Luke's preferential concern for the poor. Virtually all of Luke's direct warnings concerning wealth and riches occur in the Gospel alone and are absent from Acts. Moreover, the poor disappear in Acts; the word πτωχός is completely absent. Careful readers of Luke–Acts, such as L. Keck, have noted this disjunction: 'The silence of Acts [regarding the poor] is all the more impressive when we remember that its companion volume, Luke, has a special place for the poverty-stricken'.[33] In addition, gone in Acts are programmatic statements of a ministry directed to the

also M.A. Powell, *What Are They Saying About Luke?* (New York: Paulist Press, 1989), p. 91, and Prior, *Jesus the Liberator*, p. 50.

31. E.g. Fitzmyer, *Luke I-IX*, pp. 250-51; Horn, *Glaube und Handeln*, p. 122; Hoyt, 'The Poor', p. 12; Lui, 'The Poor', p. 8; S. Ringe, *Jesus, Liberation, and the Biblical Jubilee: Images for Ethics and Christology* (Overtures to Biblical Theology; Philadelphia: Fortress Press, 1985), pp. 59-60; W. Stegemann, *The Gospel and the Poor* (trans. D. Elliott; Philadelphia: Fortress Press, 1984), pp. 16-18. In his literary-critical commentary on Luke's Gospel, Johnson (*Luke*, p. 79) writes that 'the "poor" represent not only the economically impoverished but all those who are marginal or excluded from human fellowship, the outcast'.

32. E.g. W. Heard, 'Luke's Attitude toward the Rich and the Poor', *Trinity Journal* 9 (1988), pp. 47-80.

33. Keck, 'The Poor among the Saints', 108. See also J.A. Bergquist, '"Good News to the Poor": Why Does this Lukan Motif Appear to Run Dry in the Book of Acts?', *Trinity Seminary Review* 9 (1987), p. 18-26 (18); E. Bammel, 'Πτωχός', *TDNT*, VI, p. 902. Prior (*Jesus the Liberator*, p. 177) notes the disappearance of πτωχός terminology after Luke 16, but dismisses its significance by pointing to "the alienation of wealth" practiced by early Christians in Acts.

poor, the blind, the lame, and other disadvantaged groups. Gone are proclamations of an eschatological reversal of the fortunes that would seem to show divine favor toward economically marginalized persons.

Not only do the poor disappear in Acts, so also do the captive, the shattered, the leper, the deaf, and the maimed. The blind all but disappear.[34] The table below shows the number of occurrences of the terms under discussion in this study in the Gospel of Luke and the Acts of the Apostles respectively.

	Gospel	*Acts*
αἰχμάλωτος[35] (the captive)	1	0
θραύειν[36] (to shatter)	1	0
τυφλός (the blind)	8	1
κωφός (the deaf mute)	4	0
χωλός (the lame)	3	3
λεπρός[37] (the leper)	3	0
ἀνάπηρος[38] (the maimed)	2	0
νεκρός (the dead)	14	17
πτωχός (the poor)	10	0

With the exception of the lame and the dead,[39] the paucity of references to these groups in Acts is striking. If Luke–Acts is the unified work it appears to be on the grounds of theological themes and interests, why is there this inconsistency? Especially if a significant aspect of the unity of Luke–Acts is parallels between Jesus' ministry and the ministries of the apostles, how do we account for the fact that a prominent facet of Jesus' ministry finds meager expression, at most, in the actions and interests of the apostles?

The second problem with the consensuses is that while Luke's Gospel may be a Gospel for 'the poor', serious disagreement exists among scholars over who 'the poor' are for whom Luke is an advocate. Proposals range from the literally destitute, that is, persons reduced to begging,[40] to the poor as a metaphor, or better, as a cipher for some

34. The only occurrence of τυφλός in Acts is in Acts 13.11. In the scene in Acts 13.4-12, Paul condemns the magician Elymas to temporary blindness.
35. αἰχμάλωτος occurs only once in the New Testament, in Lk. 4.18.
36. θραύειν occurs only once in the New Testament, in Lk. 4.18.
37. In addition, λέπρα occurs twice in the Gospel and never in Acts.
38. ανάπηρος occurs only twice in the New Testament, in Lk. 14.13, 21.
39. These exceptions are treated in Appendix A.
40. Hoyt, 'The Poor'; R.J. Cassidy, *Jesus, Politics, and Society: A Study of*

other group socio-religiously defined, such as pious Jews in a situation of relative poverty,[41] persons called to a special vocational commitment to Christian office-holding ministry,[42] the nation Israel,[43] or persons who fear God and respond to God's word.[44]

Organizing Exegetical Approaches to Luke–Acts

This study will propose a solution to the virtual disappearance of the blind, the lame, the poor, and others from the narrative from a literary perspective, specifically from a reader-response perspective. Some basis for comparing critical approaches to narrative will help to plot the approach of this study in relation to other studies of Luke–Acts. M.H. Abrams's model of literary criticism provides a helpful way to distinguish between and yet show relationships between different exegetical approaches to Luke–Acts.[45]

Abram's model is universally known in literary critical circles and is on the way to becoming well known among biblical interpreters. Abrams orients literary criticisms around three axes and four foci: the work–artist (or author) axis, the work–universe axis, and the work–audience axis. He diagrams his model as follows:[46]

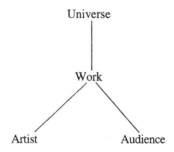

Luke's Gospel (Maryknoll: Orbis Books, 1978).

   41. Horn, *Glaube und Handeln*.

   42. Degenhardt, *Evangelist der Armen*.

   43. Seccombe, *Possessions*.

   44. L.T. Johnson, *The Literary Function of Possessions in Luke–Acts* (SBLDS, 39; Missoula, MT: Scholars Press, 1977).

   45. M.H. Abrams, *The Mirror and the Lamp: Romantic Theory and the Critical Tradition* (London: Oxford University Press, 1953), p. 6.

   46. See H. Adams, 'General Introduction', in *idem* (ed.), *Critical Theory Since Plato* (New York: Harcourt Brace Jovanovich, 1971), p. 2.

Each of these four foci represents a basic critical orientation. Abrams points out that although well-rounded literary theories all account in some way for each of the four foci in the diagram, particular theories may be categorized according to which of the four foci dominates. Thus, theories aimed at evaluating a work based on how well the work discloses the attitudes, the genius, the situation, or the ideology of the author are 'expressive theories'. Theories designed to assess a work according to how well the work represents the real world outside of the text are 'mimetic theories'. Theories that provide means for critiquing the work itself as a self-enclosed entity are 'objective theories'. Finally, theories that judge a work for its effect on the audience are 'pragmatic theories'. Two of the four orientations are comparatively late arrivals into the arena of literary criticism. The work as an expression of the mind of the author did not become a major critical issue until the mid-eighteenth century.[47] Objective criticism as such is essentially unknown prior to the mid-twentieth century, when it came to be identified with the American theoretical movement entitled 'New Criticism'.[48] Mimetic criticism, on the other hand, goes back to Aristotle, Plato, and beyond.[49] Likewise, pragmatic orientations toward literature are as old as the literary criticisms of the classical Greek and Graeco-Roman worlds, as reflected in ancient rhetorical handbooks.[50] Indeed, an audience-oriented approach to literature reflects the educational and cultural disposition of the Graeco-Roman world, a world where rhetoric ruled.[51]

47. See Abrams, *The Mirror and the Lamp*, p. 26 and Adams, 'General Introduction', pp. 5-6.

48. See Abrams, *The Mirror and the Lamp*, p. 26 and Adams, *Critical Theory*, pp. 5, 10.

49. See Adams, 'General Introduction', p. 1; W.A. Beardslee, *Literary Criticism of the New Testament* (Guides to Biblical Scholarship; Philadelphia: Fortress Press, 1970), pp. 15-16.

50. Aristotle, *The Art of Rhetoric* (trans. J.H. Freese; LCL, 193; Cambridge, MA: Harvard University Press, 1926); Demetrius, *On Style* (trans. W. Hamilton; LCL, 199; Cambridge, MA: Harvard University Press, 1932); Horace, *The Art of Poetry* (trans. H.R. Fairclough; LCL; Cambridge, MA: Harvard University Press, 1936); Longinus, *On the Sublime* (trans. W. Hamilton; LCL, 199; Cambridge, MA: Harvard University Press, 1932).

51. See M.A. Beavis, *Mark's Audience: The Literary and Social Setting of Mark 4.11-12* (JSNTSup, 33; Sheffield: JSOT Press, 1989), pp. 18-31; G.A. Kennedy,

Abrams presented his model as a way of illustrating the bases upon which critics evaluate literature. The aim in this study, is not to evaluate the quality of the biblical literature. Rather, the interest is in how in interpret it. With respect to the questions this study is pursuing, Abrams' model can be used then, not for its original purpose, but as a helpful model for discussing the aims of interpretation. Broadly stated, the aim of historical criticism is 'to write a narrative of the history they (i.e. the biblical documents) reveal'.[52] Historical criticism's chief concern is to discern the biblical work's relationship to the universe outside of the text in order, ultimately, to look through the text to the events and persons behind the text. Redaction criticism, aimed as it is at disclosing the theology of the biblical writer, falls along the work–author axis. Up until now, the aims of literary studies of Luke–Acts would place these studies as well along the work–author axis, though the literary analysis itself is largely of an 'objective' or formalist character. This study will bear an affinity to such formalist literary critical work. But the center of gravity for this study will be the work–reader axis because this axis provides the critical perspective from which the textual clues for interpreting the function of the blind, the lame, and the poor in Luke–Acts may be discovered.

Distinguishing Text, Extra-text, and Intertext

In this study, the text is an edited, Greek–language version of Luke–Acts as close to the autograph as modern textual criticism can take us. Whether one understands 'the poor' to mean the literally destitute, pious Israel, or one of the other options, one is constructing that meaning with the help of information coming from outside the text of Luke–Acts. Most biblical interpreters recognize the necessity of applying some context from outside the text itself to the text in order

New Testament Interpretation through Rhetorical Criticism (Chapel Hill and London: University of North Carolina Press, 1984), p. 5; Tolbert, *Sowing*, pp. 41-46; J.P. Tompkins, 'The Reader in History: The Changing Shape of Literary Response', in J.P. Tompkins (ed.), *Reader-Response Criticism: From Formalism to Post-Structuralism* (Baltimore and London: The Johns Hopkins University Press, 1980), pp. 201-32 (201-206).

52. E. Krentz, *The Historical-Critical Method* (Guides to Biblical Scholarship; Philadelphia: Fortress Press, 1975), p. 35.

to reach exegetical decisions. Historical criticism has long insisted that for a competent interpretation of biblical texts it is required at a minimum that the exegete be familiar with the culture and language in which the text was written. Literary critics seeking to anchor their interpretation of Luke–Acts in the text continue this practice of defining historically appropriate circumstances for interpretation. One refinement from the discipline of literature applicable to biblical study is to approach the issue of a text's context as a matter of that text's extra-textual repertoire.[53]

'Extra-text' refers to an expansive cultural and literary competence that the text's audience is expected to possess. J. Darr describes the extra-text presupposed by a text as a variety of elements which can be divided into four overlapping categories: '(1) commonly-known historical facts and figures; (2) classical and canonical literature; (3) literary conventions such as stock characters, type scenes, topoi and so forth; and (4) social norms and structures'.[54] Within this broad extra-textual framework, a text may be related to other particular texts. The audience's engagement in a text-to-text relationship is referred to by literary theorists as 'intertextuality'.[55]

The extra-textual repertoire presupposed by Luke–Acts would include both diffuse general knowledge of the socio-religious world of first-century Palestine and, as this study will demonstrate in Chapter 4, familiarity with another specific text, the LXX. As obvious as it may appear that Luke–Acts presupposes that its audience is familiar with the LXX, the role of the LXX as Luke's intertext has been neglected in studies of 'the poor' in Luke–Acts.

Identifying the captive, the shattered, the blind, the deaf mute, the

---

53. J. Darr, 'Glorified in the Presence of Kings: A Literary-Critical Study of Herod the Tetrarch in Luke–Acts' (PhD dissertation, Vanderbilt University, 1987), pp. 62-68, 79-81, 125-26. For literary theorists' discussions of extra-textuality and intertextuality, see J. Culler, *Structuralist Poetics: Structuralism, Linguistics, and the Study of Literature* (Ithaca, NY: Cornell University Press, 1975), p. 139; W. Iser, *The Act of Reading: A Theory of Aesthetic Response* (Baltimore: The Johns Hopkins University Press, 1978), pp. 53-85; M. Riffaterre, *Semiotics of Poetry* (Bloomington and London: Indiana University Press, 1978), esp. pp. 2-5, 81-86, 109-10, 124-50.

54. Darr, 'Glorified', pp. 125-26.

55. Culler, *Structuralist Poetics*, p. 139. M. Riffaterre, 'Intertextual Representation: On Mimesis as Interpretive Discourse', *Critical Inquiry* 11 (September 1984), pp. 141-62 (141-43).

lame, lepers, the maimed, the dead, and the poor as groups among 'the
oppressed and excluded' or 'the neglected mass of humanity' has often
been based on scholarly reconstructions of social norms and structures
of first-century Palestine. Correspondingly, considerable exegetical
effort has been expended on such questions as: Who were 'the poor' in
first century Palestine or in Jewish religious society? What was the
role of women in Graeco-Roman society? What sorts of people would
first century Judaism have classified as sinners and thus religious
outcasts?[56] These historical and sociological questions assume that the
conceptualizations elicited by the terms 'the poor', 'the oppressed',
'sinners', and so on are provided by the social contours of the
historical situation at the time of the writing of Luke–Acts or perhaps
even at the earlier time of Jesus' ministry.[57]

Historically grounded interpretation of Luke–Acts will, to be sure,
treat the work as a first-century Hellenistic writing. The assumption
that Luke expects his auditors to draw the interpretive context for
references to 'the blind', 'the lame', 'the poor', and so on from the
socio-historical portion of their extra-textual repertoire may, however, lead interpreters to overlook literary factors that may have had
a profound impact on how Luke–Acts was read and, indeed, even how
it was written, in the late first century. Literary conventions do not

56. E.g. P.F. Esler, *Community and Gospel in Luke–Acts: The Social and
Political Motivations of Lucan Theology* (SNTSMS, 57; Cambridge: Cambridge
University Press, 1987); E. Schüssler Fiorenza, *In Memory of Her: A Feminist
Theological Reconstruction of Christian Origins* (New York: Crossroad, 1983);
F.C. Grant, *The Economic Background of the Gospels* (London: Oxford University
Press, 1926; repr.; New York: Russell & Russell, 1973), pp. 111-41; P.
Hollenbach, 'Defining Rich and Poor Using Social Sciences', in K.H. Richards
(ed.), *SBLSP* 26 (Atlanta: Scholars Press, 1987), pp. 30-63; B. Malina,
'Interpreting the Bible with Anthropology: The Case of the Rich and the Poor',
Listening 21 (1986), pp. 148-59; B. Malina, *The New Testament World: Insights
from Cultural Anthropology* (Atlanta: John Knox, 1981), esp. pp. 82-85; B. Malina,
'Wealth and Poverty in the New Testament and its World', *Int* 41 (1987), pp. 354-
67; Moxnes, *Economy of the Kingdom*; D.E. Oakman, *Jesus and the Economic
Questions of his Day* (Studies in the Bible and Early Christianity, 8; Lewiston:
Edwin Mellen, 1986); Prior, *Jesus the Liberator*, esp. pp. 172-76; W. Stegemann,
The Gospel and the Poor; E. Tetlow, *Women and Ministry in the New Testament*
(New York: Paulist Press, 1980); W.E. Moltman, *The Women Around Jesus* (New
York: Crossroad, 1982), esp. pp. 142-44.
    57. Malina, 'Wealth and Poverty', p. 354.

necessarily mirror social circumstances.[58] Numerous scholars have recognized, for example, that '[t]he Pharisees in Luke's Gospel are not so much figures representing actual persons as they are stereotypes'.[59] This insight into the characterization of the Pharisees has not, to this point, been extended to the blind, the lame, the poor, and others.[60]

As Chapter 5 of this study will show, the LXX offers a distinct literary picture of the captive, the shattered, the blind, the deaf mute, the lame, the dead, and the poor, especially with respect to their inability to shape their own future. This study will exploit the direct relationship between Luke–Acts and the LXX in terms of the LXX as part of the extra-textual repertoire of the auditor envisioned by Luke.

Thesis

The point of departure for this study is the observation that since two of Jesus' programmatic statements about his ministry in Luke's Gospel (4.18 and 7.22) draw together the captive, the shattered, the blind, the deaf mute, the lame, lepers, the maimed, the dead, and the poor, readers would evaluate together texts that refer to these characters.

> Opening the book, he found the place where it was written: 'The Spirit of the Lord is upon me, because he anointed me to announce good news to the poor. He sent me to proclaim release to the captives and recovery of sight to the blind, to send the shattered into release, and to proclaim the acceptable year of the Lord' (Lk. 4.17b-19).

58. Tolbert, *Sowing*, p. xii.

59. Moxnes, *Economy of the Kingdom*, p. 152. Though he is not completely pessimistic about the historical value of New Testament evidence regarding the Pharisees, Jacob Neusner (*From Politics to Piety: The Emergence of Pharisaic Judaism* [Englewood Cliffs: Prentice–Hall, 1973], p. 72) states that throughout the New Testament Gospels and Acts, the Pharisees 'serve as a narrative convention'. Note also R. Kysar's (*John, the Maverick Gospel* [Atlanta: John Knox, 1976], p. 57) remarks about 'the Jews' in John's Gospel: 'The Jews are stylized types of those who reject Christ. The Jews are a type of person for the evangelist, and it is that which motivates his strange category. They lose their specific ethnic characteristics in the Fourth Gospel. It is no longer a religious body of persons designated by this term, because John has so used it as to make them simply a type, not a specific person.'

60. S. Moyise's work, *The Old Testament in the Book of Revelation* (JSNTSup, 115; Sheffield: Sheffield Academic Press, 1995) came to my attention too late to be take into account in this study. Moyise discusses intertextuality and biblical stereotypes.

> Then answering them, he said, 'Go, report to John what you saw and
> heard: the blind see again, the lame walk, lepers are cleansed, and the deaf
> mute hear, the dead are raised, the poor are preached good news'
> (Lk. 7.22).

The captive, the shattered, the blind, the deaf mute, the lame, lepers,
the maimed, the dead, and the poor are initially identified together as
direct beneficiaries of Jesus' ministry. Such a grouping then seems to
be a natural one prompted by these texts, particularly 4.18, which is
the first reference to these characters encountered by the reader.
Moreover, that these characters are mentioned several times in
groupings (see also 14.13, 21) would prompt readers to presume that
there is a common thread linking them all even if the lists are not
exactly identical in every case.

This study intends to demonstrate several related points. The first
point is that the captive, the shattered, the blind, the deaf mute, the
lame, lepers, the maimed, the dead, and the poor should be understood
together as a set of types. Tax collectors and sinners, it will be noted,
do not belong initially in the set with the captive, the shattered, and so
on. The second point is that for the captive, the shattered, the blind,
the deaf mute, the lame, lepers, the maimed, the dead, and the poor to
be understood as Luke intended, these types should be interpreted in
the context of the LXX rather than on the basis of extra-textual
historical or social constructs. The third point is that these types need
to be studied with respect to their narrative placement in order to
ascertain their intended rhetorical effect on Luke's auditors.

Proceeding from these points, this study will conclude that the
captive, the shattered, the blind, the deaf mute, the lame, lepers, the
maimed, the dead, and the poor function rhetorically in Luke's narrative to make the christological point that Jesus is God's unique eschatological agent of salvation. Correspondingly, their christological
function explains the peculiar fact of their prominence in the Gospel
of Luke and virtual disappearance from the Acts of the Apostles.

Procedure

Chapter 2 will survey interpretations of 'the poor' in Luke–Acts,
including treatments of 'the poor' in recent literary critical commentaries on the Gospel of Luke. Chapter 3 will offer a more detailed
explanation of the literary-critical method this study employs: an
audience-oriented, sequential reading of Luke–Acts. Chapter 3 will

also propose constructing an authorial audience based on linguistic and literary competence implied by Luke–Acts, and will argue that this approach to constructing an authorial audience is specifically appropriate for a study of the captive, the shattered, the blind, the deaf mute, the lame, lepers, the maimed, the dead, and the poor in Luke–Acts. Chapter 4 will demonstrate that the authorial audience of Luke–Acts is familiar with the LXX, and argue that the discourse of the first four chapters of Luke's Gospel directs the audience to characterize the captive, the shattered, the blind, and the others on the basis of the LXX. Chapter 5 will take the next logical step, which is to survey the captive, the shattered, the blind, the deaf mute, the lame, lepers, the maimed, the dead, and the poor in the LXX. Chapter 6 will offer exegesis of passages in Luke's Gospel involving the captive, the shattered, the blind, the deaf mute, the lame, lepers, the maimed, the dead, and the poor along the methodological lines set out in Chapter 3 and using the insights gained in Chapter 5. Chapter 7 will make interpretive observations based on the exegesis of Chapter 6 and suggest possible avenues of further study. A brief appendix will look at the function of these character types as they appear in Acts.

Chapter 2

HISTORY OF SCHOLARSHIP

Historical Critical Backdrop

In order to position this study of the captive, the shattered, the blind, the deaf mute, the lame, lepers, the maimed, the dead, and the poor within Lukan scholarship, this study will look at how discussions of the poor have unfolded during the past century. This chapter intends to show that scholarly discussions of the identity of poor in Luke–Acts have reached an impasse. Second, this chapter intends to show that Lukan scholarship has not yet provided an adequate explanation for the disappearance of the poor from Luke's narrative.

Turn of the century scholars anticipated some of the conclusions reached by post-World War II redaction critics about Luke's social consciousness. Questions of source criticism and the history of religions dominated their efforts. Nevertheless, they commented on Luke's frequent mention of the poor. Typically, interpreters in this period considered the poor to be one socially-marginalized group among others named in the Gospels. As one would expect, the leading question in source-critical research treating Luke's social consciousness was whether Luke's material about the poor and about property stemmed from Jesus, from some other written source, or from the evangelist himself. Nevertheless, scholars engaged in source-critical research assumed that Luke incorporated material about the poor because of Luke's own interest in the poor. At the same time, history of religions research became interested in comparing early Christianity with contemporary religions and cultural currents. One of its central goals was to sift the transcendent essence of the Christian religion from its cultic and cultural expression. The transcendent essence of the Christian religion could then be expressed in generalized teachings. Accordingly, Luke's mention of the poor came to be viewed as evidence of a voice expressing an early Christian concern for all socially-marginalized groups, including the sick, tax collectors, and sinners. Holding such a view was Herman Jacoby, who commented that Luke had a major interest in Jesus' acceptance of sinners and despised persons.[1] Likewise, Adolf Jülicher stated that particular characteristics of Luke's portrait of Jesus include friendly compassion toward despised persons and heartfelt sympathy for all in need.[2] H.J. Holtzmann added that Luke presented poverty and the absence of possessions, along with almsgiving and prayer, as the model for spiritually mature Christians.[3] Reflecting the interests of source criticism and the history of religions, the reigning scholarly position in the late nineteenth and early twentieth centuries held that Luke, consciously or unconsciously, combined an early Jewish Christian tradition that lifted up poverty as a spiritual ideal with Luke's own world-denying tendencies and utopian vision of Christian 'love-communism', under the influence of Cynic philosophy and escapist Hellenistic religion.[4] Up to a century later, redaction critics, who turned from questions about the origins of Luke's theology to questions of Luke's theological intentions, would nevertheless echo the views of Jacoby, Jülicher, and Holtzmann. As will become apparent, the echoes are pronounced. They continue to reverberate

1.   H. Jacoby, *Neutestamentliche Ethik* (Königsberg: Thomas & Oppermann, 1899), pp. 414-48.

2.   A. Jülicher, *Einleitung in das Neue Testament* (Grundriss der Theologischen Wissenschaften, 3.1; Tübingen: Mohr [Paul Siebeck], 6th edn, 1921), p. 292.

3.   H.J. Holtzmann, *Lehrbuch der historisch-kritischen Einleitung in das Neue Testament* (Freiburg: Mohr [Paul Siebeck], 3rd edn, 1892), p. 390.

4.   The term 'love-communism' (*Liebeskommunismus*) appears to have been coined by K. Kautzky (*Der Ursprung des Christentums: eine historische untersuchung* [Stuttgart: Dietz, 1908]). See Grant, *Economic Background*, pp. 116, 117 n. 1, and Horn, *Glaube und Handeln*, pp. 25-26. The most heated debate in this arena concerned whether *Jesus* preached and practised communism. The chief proponents of the case for the communist Jesus were E. Renan (*La vie de Jesus*, 1863) and Kautzky. Renan and Kautzky appear to be the hidden opponents stimulating much German-language reconstruction of the historical Jesus and early Christianity, including M. Hengel, *Eigentum und Reichtum in der frühen Kirche* (Stuttgart: Calwer Verlag, 1973); ET *Property and Riches in the Early Church: Aspects of a Social History of Early Christianity* (trans. J. Bowden; London: SCM Press; Philadelphia: Fortress Press, 1974). See also the unelaborated rejection of *Liebeskommunismus* in L. Schottroff und W. Stegemann, *Jesus von Nazareth: Hoffnung der Armen* (Stuttgart: Kohlhammer, 3rd edn, 1990), p. 152, and the redefining of *Liebeskommunismus* in R. Albertz, 'Die "Antrittspredigt" Jesu im Lukasevangelium auf ihrem alttestamentlichen Hintergrund', *ZNW* 74 (1983), p. 204.

because the turn-of-the-century extra-textual paradigm for interpreting 'the poor' from a socio-religious perspective has solidified over the decades.

In the era of form criticism following World War I, M. Dibelius substantially affirmed the nineteenth and early twentieth century consensus and incorporated it into a definite socio-religious framework, namely that of 'messianic pietists' of the first century.[5] Dibelius's socio-religious sketch of these 'pious poor' may be considered the classic description of what other New Testament interpreters identify as the Jewish *anawim*.[6] Dibelius writes,

> The later development of the Christian community in Jerusalem, which assumed some of the features of legalistic Judaism (Acts 21.18ff), shows that this community obtained recruits from other circles. The words of Jesus provide further information. When he greets the poor as the heirs of the Kingdom (Lk. 6.20)... and when he speaks about the preaching to the poor (Matt. 11.5; Lk. 7.22), he is presupposing the faith which Isa. 61.1ff so vividly depicts—viz., that the messianic era will bring salvation to the needy (*ani*). At the heart of Jesus' preaching stands the apocalyptic conception of the Kingdom of God. But as a result he directed himself first of all to the people who yearned for the appearance of the Kingdom of God... people who wanted to be pious but whose sins prevented their hope for salvation from becoming confidence in salvation... *These messianic pietists were the heirs of the ardor of the Poor at the time of Jesus.*[7]

According to Dibelius, references to 'the poor' in Luke's Gospel emanate from this Jewish piety, namely, this *Armenfrömmigkeit*. These references reflect a religious movement consisting of those who, imitating Jesus, live 'apart from active involvement in the economic functions of the world because [they] foresee the end of this world'.[8] Drawing from Dibelius's work on the Epistle of James, the second

---

5.   M. Dibelius, *James: A Commentary on the Epistle of James* (trans. and rev. H. Greeven; Hermeneia; Philadelphia: Fortress, 1976), p. 41.

6.   Though he refers to studies of the Hebrew Bible that treat the *anawim*, Dibelius himself does not designate his class of pious poor as the *anawim*. Other interpreters soon do, most notably R. Bultmann (*History of the Synoptic Tradition* [trans. J. Marsh; New York: Harper & Row, rev. edn, 1963], p. 126). See also W. Sattler, 'Die Anawim im Zeitalter Jesu Christi', in *Festgabe für A. Jülicher* (Tübingen: Mohr, 1927), pp. 1-15.

7.   Dibelius, *James*, p. 41.

8.   Dibelius, *James*, p. 43.

most prominent form critic of the New Testament, R. Bultmann, concluded that even though 'a liking for the poor and the despised'[9] is a favorite theme of Luke's, it is more accurate to see this theme 'as an expression of the piety of the Anawim'[10] than as a tendency of the author.[11]

Dibelius and Bultmann clearly located the context for understanding the poor in Luke–Acts in a cultural-historical setting, or in other words, in the cultural extra-text of Luke's Gospel. Interestingly, they concluded that this setting was foreign to Luke. That is, Luke included traditions about the poor, but these traditions do not reflect Luke's historical setting or specific theological concerns. While this conclusion arrived at by Dibelius and Bultmann contrasts with earlier, turn-of-the-century scholarship with respect to Luke's own interests and role in preserving traditions about the poor, it also reasserts the basic societal and cultural arena for identifying the poor.

Matching 'the poor' to a particular manner of Christian social grouping, as form critics Dibelius and Bultmann did, is not only consistent with their form critical methodology, it is practically inevitable because of their methodology. The threefold task of form criticism is to classify individual units of tradition within the biblical Gospels on the basis of their pre-literary form; assign each form to a *Sitz im Leben* (setting in the life) of the early church, and trace the history of the tradition.[12] Form critics, then, postulate Christian communities to match the various traditions, communities that would have preserved

9.   Bultmann, *Synoptic Tradition*, p. 367.
10.   Bultmann, *Synoptic Tradition*, p. 367.
11.   Thus, *anawim* designates religious Jews living in relative poverty and, in their poverty, recognizing their total dependence on God. For Dibelius and Bultmann, the outstanding characteristic of these pious poor is their eschatalogical fervor. Later interpreters tend to omit or downplay the intensely eschatalogical dimension; e.g. O'Toole (*Unity*, esp. p. 110) and T. Schmidt (*Hostility to Wealth in the Synoptic Gospels* [JSNTSup, 15; Sheffield: JSOT Press, 1987]).
12.   Reference here is to form criticism as it is still widely practised. Methods and purposes of form criticism are now in flux, but a discussion of the development of the discipline lies outside the scope of this study. See K. Berger, *Formgeschichte des Neuen Testaments* (Heidelberg: Quelle & Meyer, 2nd edn, 1984), and 'Hellenistische Gattungen im Neuen Testament', in H. Temporini and W. Haase (eds.), *Aufstieg und Niedergang der Römischen Welt: Geschichte und Kultur Roms im Spiegel der Neueren Forschung* (Berlin: de Gruyter, 1984), II.25.2, pp. 1031-1432.

and transmitted the traditions reflected in the pre-literary forms. This methodological predisposition explains why a form critic looking at the Gospel of Luke would tend to look past references to the blind, the lame, lepers, the captive, the shattered, the deaf mute, the maimed, and the dead. In comparison to these other groups, the designation 'the poor' could more easily be applied a community of believers with particular religious beliefs, that is, precisely the type of community form critics sought to discover.

When redaction criticism developed after World War II, the critic's goal became to discover the theology of the author of the Gospel. In his major redaction critical study, *The Theology of St Luke*, H. Conzelmann adopts the stance of Dibelius and Bultmann regarding Lukan references to the poor. For example, of the famous first Beatitude in Jesus' Sermon on the Plain, Conzelmann writes,

> The 'Ebionism' of Luke vi, 20 comes from the source, and is not developed as a theme by Luke. We cannot speak of an ideal of poverty either in the Gospel or in Acts.[13]

With his redaction-critical work on the Gospel and Acts, Conzelmann kindled interest in narrative flow and development. He treated Luke–Acts as a single work. His proposal for a tripartite division of the plot of Luke–Acts into eras—the time of Israel, followed by the time of Jesus, followed by the time of the church—shows an appreciation for the linear character of narrative. Nevertheless, for Conzelmann the theological unity of Luke–Acts is ultimately the theological unity of Luke's thinking, and not the theological unity of the text. Conzelmann appears to assume that an Ebionite[14] tradition lies behind Luke 6.20.[15]

13.   Conzelmann, *The Theology of St Luke*, p. 233.

14.   Conzelmann's label 'Ebionism' is probably anachronistic. In the fourth century, Epiphanius wrote of a second-century ascetic Jewish Christian sect called the 'Ebionites', a name that is derived from a Hebrew word that can be translated 'the poor'. Whether such a sect can be traced back to the earliest Jerusalem church is doubtful. In any case, Conzelmann is assuming a socio-religious group like the pious poor proposed by Dibelius. See Keck, 'Poor', *IDBSup*, p. 674.

15.   Again one could note in passing that diametrically opposed conclusions regarding Luke's attitude may be reached without interpreters who reach opposing conclusions calling into question the extra-textual context invoked to identify the poor of Luke–Acts. According to Conzelmann, the delay of the parousia decisively impacted Luke's ethical thinking such that Luke would present a discipleship that adapts itself to the social circumstances of the day. Thus, whereas the history of religions scholarship of the turn of the century concluded that Luke was world-denying, Conzelmann's

Therefore, because his method assumes that Luke's theology is most clearly shown by the changes Luke made to his source material and by the seams Luke wrote to link his narrative together, Conzelmann has little to say about this traditional material. As a result, Conzelmann mentions the poor only in passing, when he mentions them at all. Sometimes his silence about the poor is striking. For example, when commenting on εὐαγγελίζεσθαι, Conzelmann states that Lk. 4.18 is a programmatic passage describing Jesus' ministry.[16] Yet in the course of that discussion, Conzelmann never mentions that the passage specifies that the promised good news is to be announced to the poor. Though his approach to the Lukan material prevented Conzelmann from pursuing the relationship between the reign of God and the poor in the LXX, had he done so he would have strengthened his conclusion that in Luke–Acts 'the Kingdom has appeared in Christ'.[17]

To use M.H. Abrams's model, redaction criticism marks a shift in the direction of interpretation from the world behind the text, which is the aim of the form criticism of Dibelius and Bultmann, to the author behind the text. This shift begins an evolution in Lukan study that ultimately compels us to question the socio-religious context for interpreting the poor in Luke–Acts. As long as Lukan references to the poor could be assigned to tradition and therefore judged to be secondary to Luke's interests, form and redaction critics would not be troubled by the lack of mention of the poor in Acts in contrast to the frequent mention of the poor in the Gospel.[18] Indeed, Dibelius, Bultmann, and Conzelmann could remain confident of their socio-religious, extra-textual referent for 'the poor'. In the years since Conzelmann's epoch-making study of the Gospel, however, greater appreciation for the freedom Luke used in choosing and shaping his material has progressively weakened interpretations of Luke's theology that rely on distinctions between tradition and redaction. Author-centered interpretation that recognizes Luke's command of his material has been the driving force behind attempts to identify and explicate the unity of Luke–Acts. Eventually, then, the question of how to

Luke is world-affirming.
  16. Conzelmann, *The Theology of St Luke*, p. 221.
  17. Conzelmann, *The Theology of St Luke*, p. 125.
  18. Consider, for example, this statement by E. Bammel ('Πτωχός', p. 907): 'The word πτωχός is not important to Lk. It does not occur in the redactional material, cf. the absence in Ac.'

relate the unity of Luke–Acts to Luke's presentation of the poor had to surface.

As mentioned, studies treating Luke's presentation of the captive, the shattered, the blind, the deaf mute, the lame, lepers, the maimed, the dead, and the poor reduce themselves, as a rule, to analyses of the poor or of possessions. After surveying several studies, I will suggest a reason for this narrowing. Though not usually lending themselves to simple categorization, the studies to be surveyed orbit around one or two of three foci: (1) poverty as a physical-economic situation that followers of Jesus are called upon to alleviate or challenge; correspondingly, the poor are persons to be assisted, comforted, or liberated from their poverty; (2) poverty as a religious ideal, and at the same time an economic circumstance; the poor may be involuntarily poor or voluntarily committed to an ascetic lifestyle; and (3) poverty as a purely religious state; the poor are those with an acute consciousness of their need for God. The following discussion is a selection of significant contributions to Lukan scholarship on the poor categorized according to these foci. Several of the contributions could be placed in two categories, as will become evident below.[19]

The studies surveyed below belong to the post-Conzelmann era of Lukan interpretation. That is, Conzelmann's conception of the grand design of Luke–Acts is critically addressed and to a greater or lesser extent challenged, but *that* there is an overall design underlying Luke–Acts into which the author has kneaded previously existing materials and his own contributions is taken for granted.

The Poor as Objects of Mission

Richard J. Cassidy, in *Jesus, Politics, and Society* sets out to delineate Jesus' social and political stance as depicted by Luke. The Lukan Jesus' attitude toward the poor is a central feature of Jesus' social stance, according to Cassidy. Cassidy concludes that 'in his teaching and ministry, Jesus in Luke espouses a concern for persons and groups

---

19.   The studies are not presented below in chronological order, but rather in the order one might place them in if the three foci were placed along a continuum from focus one through focus three. Listed chronologically, by date of original publication, they run Degenhardt (1965), Johnson (1977), Cassidy (1978), Schottroff and Stegemann (1978), Pilgrim (1981), Seccombe (1982), Horn (1983), and Bergquist (1987).

from all social levels and backgrounds, but especially for the poor and the sick, for women and Gentiles'.[20] Beyond this general statement, Cassidy argues that in Luke, Jesus' stance vis-à-vis the poor, sick, women and Gentiles brought Jesus into conflict with the political and economic structures of his day. In particular, the Lukan Jesus (1) chastised the rich for accumulating surplus possessions instead of sharing them with the poor and hungry; (2) threatened the existing social order by recognizing the value of women, which was greater than that normally accorded them in prevailing social patterns; and (3) in response to oppression and injustice espoused 'a new social order based on service and humility'.[21] Cassidy does not attempt a systematic description of the poor. Rather he treats as self-evident that the poor in Luke's Gospel represent materially destitute persons. Cassidy concludes that 'Luke describes Jesus as having a definite sympathy and concern for those who are poor and hungry'.[22]

Cassidy's aim is to provide social guidance for present Christians. For Cassidy, such guidance is to be drawn from Jesus' actions as well as his words. Says Cassidy, 'When we refer to Jesus' "social stance", we mean the response that Jesus made, through his teachings and conduct, to the question of how persons and groups ought to live together'.[23] Implicit throughout Cassidy's book is the call for Christians to imitate Jesus' social and political stance. Cassidy interprets Jesus' beneficent acts for the poor and infirm as evidence of Jesus concern for the poor and infirm.[24]

At the very least, Cassidy demonstrates the inadequacy of Conzelmann's view that Luke tried to portray Roman authorities in positive terms and thereby encourage a rapprochement between Christians and governing authorities. Cassidy does this, in large measure, by putting at the forefront of discussion Lukan passages and themes that Conzelmann de-emphasized by attributing them to tradition. For Cassidy, concern for the poor is one such theme that suffers under Conzelmann's treatment. But if concern for the poor, which is seen by Cassidy as an attitude of Jesus that brings Jesus into conflict with civil authorities, is intended by Luke to show persons and groups how to

20. Cassidy, *Jesus*, p. 77.
21. Cassidy, *Jesus*, p. 34.
22. Cassidy, *Jesus*, p. 24.
23. Cassidy, *Jesus*, p. 20.
24. Cassidy, *Jesus*, p. 140.

live together, then there ought to be evidence in Acts of the success or failure of Jesus' guidance on this concern. Cassidy bypasses this issue.

Since Cassidy's study is an analysis of the Jesus of Luke's Gospel, he ignores the problem of relating his findings to the second half of Luke's narrative.[25] The problems with relating Cassidy's conclusions about Luke/Jesus' concern for the poor to Acts become more evident in the light of the study by Walter Pilgrim, *Good News to the Poor: Wealth and Poverty in Luke–Acts.* In large measure, Pilgrim echoes Cassidy in that he, too, regards the poor as impoverished and marginalized persons in Jesus' society,[26] and he attributes to Jesus a special message of hope for the poor.[27] Pilgrim adds that Jesus 'belonged to the poor, economically and socially'.[28] Because they abandoned everything to follow Jesus, Jesus' disciples 'were poor by deliberate choice and by virtue of their call on behalf of the kingdom'.[29] Moreover, says Pilgrim, the common denominator among other people attracted to the movement begun by Jesus is that 'they comprised the lowest stratum of society'.[30] According to Pilgrim, constituent groups of this 'lowest stratum of society' are the multitudes, tax collectors and sinners, prostitutes, the poor, beggars, crippled and other handicapped persons, and the *anawim*.[31]

When Pilgrim turns his attention from characteristics of the (presumably historical) Jesus movement 'the distinctive Lukan presentation of Jesus' ministry', he adopts 'good news to the poor' as his thematic focus.[32] Included among the poor are those in dire need because of

---

25.   It appears that Cassidy limited his study as he did out of methodological ambivalence. The study hovers between being a redaction-critical study of Luke's social and theological perspective and a quest for the historical Jesus. In spite of the disclaimer that whenever he speaks of 'Jesus' social stance', he means 'the social stance Luke describes Jesus as having' (Cassidy, *Jesus*, pp. 140-41 n. 4), Cassidy's work is framed by an argument for the historical trustworthiness of Luke's writing (chapter 1) and the closing comment (chapter 6): '[We are] inclined to hold that the stance Luke attributes to Jesus corresponds to the stance that Jesus actually had' (Cassidy, *Jesus*, pp. 85-86).

26.   Pilgrim, *Good News to the Poor*, pp. 41-46.

27.   Pilgrim, *Good News to the Poor*, pp. 48-49.

28.   Pilgrim, *Good News to the Poor*, p. 46.

29.   Pilgrim, *Good News to the Poor*, p. 48.

30.   Pilgrim, *Good News to the Poor*, p. 56.

31.   Pilgrim, *Good News to the Poor*, pp. 51-56.

32.   Pilgrim, *Good News to the Poor*, p. 64.

poverty and disease, who at the same time exist at the edge of society;[33] impoverished believers, that is, Christian *anawim*;[34] and outcasts and sinners,[35] whom Pilgrim specifically states 'should be included under Luke's concept of the poor'.[36] In short, 'good news to the poor' summarizes the Lukan Jesus' ministry to 'those living on the margin of society, socially, ethically, and religiously'.[37]

Unlike Cassidy, Pilgrim discusses Acts as well as Luke's Gospel. It appears to be precisely this effort to find consistency between the Gospel and Acts that leads Pilgrim away from an analysis of Luke's characterization of the poor to a discussion of the proper use of possessions. Part II of the book moves into a discussion of wealth and poverty, or more accurately, a discussion of Luke's presentation of the correct disposition toward and use of possessions. Pilgrim summarizes Luke's message regarding wealth and poverty around three themes: (1) a call to total surrender of possessions; (2) warnings about the dangers of wealth; and (3) instructions and exhortations on the right use of one's wealth.[38] Regarding these themes, Pilgrim concludes that Luke intended for total renunciation of possessions to be an ethic limited to Jesus' time.[39] He contends, however, that the remaining two themes continue to be valid guidance for Christians.

Like Cassidy, Pilgrim quite explicitly considers application for a modern Christian social ethic to be at stake in interpretation of the poor and possessions in Luke–Acts.[40] So, consistent guidance from the Gospel and Acts is what he seeks.

> If the picture of the early church in Acts regarding possessions stood in conflict with the gospel tradition, we would be forced to make a hard choice over which portrait to follow, the gospel or Acts.[41]

Pilgrim contends that 'the Lukan attitude toward wealth and poverty expressed in the gospel finds its fullest confirmation in Luke's des-

33. Pilgrim, *Good News to the Poor*, pp. 73-74.
34. Pilgrim, *Good News to the Poor*, pp. 74-80.
35. Pilgrim, *Good News to the Poor*, pp. 80-82.
36. Pilgrim, *Good News to the Poor*, p. 80.
37. Pilgrim, *Good News to the Poor*, p. 73.
38. Pilgrim, *Good News to the Poor*, p. 86.
39. Pilgrim, *Good News to the Poor*, p. 101.
40. Pilgrim, *Good News to the Poor*, pp. 15-16.
41. Pilgrim, *Good News to the Poor*, p. 147.

cription of the life of the early church'.[42] Thus, Pilgrim maintains that no essential discontinuity exists between Luke's Gospel and Acts. Rather, claims Pilgrim, Luke continues in Acts to press for social justice and to urge a willingness to share with the poor and care for the weak.[43]

There are several reasons why Pilgrim's book is important. First, because Pilgrim lays out in detail the interpretation of Luke–Acts that seems to be most widely represented in recent general commentaries on the Gospel. Secondly, Pilgrim rightly senses the need to interpret what is meant by 'the poor' with the aid of the Old Testament.[44] Indeed, following the book's introduction, Pilgrim devotes 20 pages to an over-view of 'The Poor in the Old Testament and in the Intertestamental Period'.[45] Yet with only two exceptions, he does not make use of the Old Testament background to give meaning to the term 'poor' in Luke–Acts. Those exceptions are his portrayal of the development of the concept of the *anawim* and his discussion of Isaiah 61 in con-nection with Lk. 4.16-21, 7.18-23 and 14.13, 21. Pilgrim's discussion of the Old Testament, and of the intertestamental literature for that matter, is out of proportion to the use he actually makes of the Old Testament and of the intertestamental literature in his interpretation of the poor in Luke–Acts. Therefore his study seems unintentionally to call for another that will make broader use of the Old Testament. Thirdly, Pilgrim's book is important because it underscores how, in studies to date, the center of attention has had to shift from 'the poor'

42.   Pilgrim, *Good News to the Poor*, p. 147.

43.   Pilgrim (*Good News to the Poor*, pp. 172-75) closes his book with 'four simple suggestions' for present-day Christians living in affluence: adopt the Zacchaeus principle for sharing wealth; simplify the way they live; become advocates for the poor; and oppose systems that perpetuate social injustices and inequalities. Though out of my own Christian convictions I concur with Pilgrim's suggestions, his hermeneutical path from the Gospel and Acts to these suggestions is not clear. He seems to pick and choose Lukan emphases and, in these suggestions, apply the emphases in ways that appear to me to be palatable to reasonable people even if the suggestions stretch the average Christian to be more generous and more politically active than he or she currently is.

44.   The designation 'Old Testament' is used without prejudice in this study as a label for the writings of the Hebrew Bible. Using the designation 'Old Testament' allows us to set aside for the moment the question of whether interpreters of Luke–Acts ought to look to the Hebrew Bible or to the LXX as the Lukan intertext.

45.   Pilgrim, *Good News to the Poor*, pp. 19-38.

to 'possessions' in order for the interpreter to find continuity between the Gospel and Acts. Consequently, his conclusions regarding the poor in the Gospel and Acts are less than convincing because he slides over the absence in Acts of the term 'the poor'.

Discontinuity between the Gospel and Acts with respect to reference to the poor is the starting point for the little known but insightful article by James A. Bergquist, '"Good News to the Poor": Why does this Lucan Motif Appear to Run Dry in the Book of Acts?' Bergquist uses standard redaction criticism to establish the centrality of the motif of 'God's gracious concern for the poor and oppressed'[46] in the Gospel of Luke. He then observes that Acts lacks comparable emphasis. A few passages in Acts touch on the sharing of wealth and on service to those in need. But, as Bergquist says, 'none of these passages has anyone outside the young Christian community in mind'.[47] Moreover, the vocabulary in the Gospel for the poor and the rich is lacking in Acts, as are the prominent themes of mission among the poor, fruits of repentance in terms of justice, reversal between rich and poor, and table fellowship with outsiders.[48] Bergquist clearly recognizes the inevitable question. As Bergquist puts it: 'If for other reasons we may observe a literary and theological unity in Luke–Acts, why is the theme of the Gospel as good news to the poor also not a clear point of unity in both the Gospel and Acts?'[49]

Nevertheless, Bergquist holds that there is a theme into which Luke's material on the poor fits, a transcending theme that does indicate the unity of the Gospel and Acts. Bergquist starts by identifying the poor with 'outsiders'.[50] Thus, in the Gospel, the poor function as outsiders to whom the message of salvation is offered. Bergquist concludes that 'in Acts the term "Gentile" (ἔθνος) replaces the characteristic Gospel term for outsiders'.[51] The consistent theme expressed through good news to the poor in the Gospel and good news to the Gentiles in Acts, says Bergquist, is the continuation of salvation: salvation expresses itself through liberation of the oppressed, on the one hand, and through mercy for all people, that is, total inclusiveness, on

46. Bergquist, 'Good News to the Poor', p. 18.
47. Bergquist, 'Good News to the Poor', p. 21.
48. Bergquist, 'Good News to the Poor', pp. 21-22.
49. Bergquist, 'Good News to the Poor', p. 19.
50. Bergquist, 'Good News to the Poor', p. 19.
51. Bergquist, 'Good News to the Poor', p. 23.

the other hand. As with Cassidy and Pilgrim, Bergquist believes the mission of the church today is what is at stake here.[52] Bergquist's final point is that neither dimension of salvation is reducible to the other, and that the church ought to pursue with equal vigor ministry with poor and the Great Commission.[53]

What makes his brief study especially interesting is that Bergquist sees the issue clearly and steers toward a solution that neither turns 'the poor' into a cipher for some other extra-textual group defined socially or religiously nor dissolves the characters, 'the poor', into the theme 'the right use of possessions', as so many other interpreters do. Bergquist maintains the unity of Luke–Acts amid the apparent discontinuity resulting from the absence of the term 'the poor' in Acts by finding another character group in the narrative that, in his reading, serves the same function in Acts that he assigns the poor in the Gospel. The linch pin in Bergquist's argument is his classification of the poor as 'outsiders' along with tax collectors and sinners. In Bergquist's scheme, it is the role of the poor as outsider that relates the poor of the Gospel to the Gentiles of Acts. As I look more extensively at the characterization of the poor in the Gospel, however, it will be seen that the equation 'poor equals outsider' does not accurately describe the function of the poor in the Gospel.

The Poor as a Religious and Economic Combination

The earliest attempt to treat 'the poor' in the Gospel of Luke comprehensively and to account for the relative paucity of material in Acts referring to rich and poor or possessions is Hans-Joachim Degenhardt's *Lukas: Evangelist der Armen*. The book is a landmark in the study of the poor in Luke–Acts because Degenhardt is the first scholar to discuss every text relating to the poor while attempting to draw a conclusion within which the Gospel and Acts cohere.

The problem Degenhardt addresses is the one Pilgrim would later take up, namely the juxtaposition of material calling for the total renunciation of possessions and material urging the right use of possession. Degenhardt opts for a two-tier ethic. He maintains that there is a distinction in the Gospel between λαός and μαθητής such that λαός corresponds to believers in general in the Christian community and μαθητής

52. Bergquist, 'Good News to the Poor', p. 22.
53. Bergquist, 'Good News to the Poor', p. 25.

corresponds to the community's office-bearers. In Degenhardt's model, then, the Lukan poor are the μαθητής of the Gospel who, by renouncing all for the sake of following Jesus (Lk. 18.28), are a reflection of office-bearers in the church of Luke's time. The poverty of the μαθητής is material deprivation, but it is voluntary asceticism out of religious conviction. Crucial to Degenhardt's interpretation is his perception of a shift in the definition of μαθητής from the Gospel to Acts. In the Gospel, μαθητής refers to the close circle of Jesus' followers, that is, those whose 'manner of life had exemplary significance because in them, being connected to Jesus is realized in a visible, sign-bearing manner'.[54] Correspondingly, in the Gospel the λαός are Jesus' general hearers and less intimate followers. In Acts, by contrast, such intimate association with Jesus is no longer possible. Therefore, says Degenhardt, μαθητής takes on in Acts a more general character: 'disciples' are all those who believe. General believers, then, exercise charity and communal spirit through their care for their office-bearers.

Degenhardt's contention that Luke uses a narrow definition of μαθητής in the Gospel and adopts a different definition in Acts is the weakest part of his argument. The evidence does not support the view that in the Gospel μαθητής refers only to a small inner circle of followers.[55] Nor does the evidence support simple identification of the poor with these disciples.[56] Since Degenhardt's overall scheme of discipleship in Luke–Acts is unsustainable, it does not provide an adequate explanation of the lack of references to the poor in Acts.

In *Glaube und Handeln in der Theologie des Lukas*, Friedrich W. Horn calls for a return to 'purely historical' research in the wake of what he considers to be uncritical harmonizations based on current interest in applying Luke's ethic to social debates today. Thus, he seeks to reverse the hermeneutical trend among interpreters of the poor in Luke–Acts such as Cassidy, Pilgrim, Bergquist, and Degenhardt. The principal task as Horn sees it is to separate tradition from redaction and then coordinate the two in a coherent scheme.[57] He follows with a two-stage reconstruction of early Christianity relative to 'the poor'. As a result, Horn's study stakes out two of the three foci mentioned above. On the one hand, traditional material depicts poverty as an

---

54. Degenhardt, *Evangelist der Armen*, p. 32. My translation.
55. See Lk. 6.17.
56. See Lk. 6.17, 24.
57. Horn, *Glaube und Handeln*, p. 32.

involuntary economic circumstance elevated to a religious ideal. On the other hand, according to Horn, redactional material urges Christians to charity.[58]

To begin with, Horn posits an Ebionite tradition. Much like the position advanced by Dibelius, Horn's view is that this tradition reflects the social setting and ideology of poor Jewish Christians who considered their poverty to be proof of their religious disposition and who anticipated heavenly reward. The underside of this Ebionite tradition, says Horn, is a polemic against rich Jewish opponents. Horn does not attempt to tie this Ebionite tradition to Jesus himself. For his purposes, it is sufficient to assign the tradition to a segment of early Christianity.

Lukan redactional activity, on the other hand, emphasizes an ethic of charity and a fellowship marked by almsgiving to meet the needs of others within the fellowship, according to Horn. Though he speaks of 'einem unausgleichbaren Hiatus'[59] between the two planes of tradition and redaction, Horn contends that Luke anchors the Ebionite tradition so deeply in a parenetic context that its original objective no longer carries weight. Thus, the tradition is made serviceable, and subordinated to Luke's redactional interest.[60]

Horn possesses an impressive grasp of the history of Lukan scholarship and acknowledges his debt to his predecessors. It is precisely this allegiance to past scholarship which allows Horn to be so confident in (1) a rather facile separation of tradition and redaction, often with little or no support other than an apparent inconsistency in Luke's attitudes, and (2) his ability to posit a community or socio-religious group behind the recovered tradition. Moreover, his methodology relies on the supposition that Luke treated his sources conservatively. Horn recognizes that Luke's references to the poor serve a christological purpose, but his historical method limits his ability to explain how that purpose is served in the Gospel.[61] Horn has no interest in explaining Luke–Acts as a coherent narrative work. Rather, his method compels

58. Essentially the same conclusions are reached by David L. Mealand (*Poverty and Expectation in the Gospels*). The conclusions are not new, having been put forward 60 years earlier by F. Hauck (*Die Stellung des Urchristentums zu Arbeit und Geld* [BFCT, 2.3; Gütersloh: Gerd Mohn, 1921]). See also Conzelmann, *Theology of St Luke*, p. 233.
59. Horn, *Glaube und Handeln*, p. 169.
60. Horn, *Glaube und Handeln*, p. 169.
61. See e.g., Horn, *Glaube und Handeln*, p. 174.

him to fragment the text for the purpose of constructing a coherent narrative of the history of Christianity behind the text.

Like Horn, L. Schottroff and W. Stegemann make separating tradition and redaction central to their program in chapters 1 and 2 of *Jesus von Nazareth: Hoffnung der Armen*. The authors discuss Jesus, but they define 'Jesus' cautiously. The authors discount the possibilities, first, of uncovering many details about Jesus other than the obvious facts of his execution and, secondly, of ferreting out individual, so-called genuine words or sayings of Jesus. Yet they are far from pessimistic about speaking of Jesus. Rather, Schottroff and Stegemann assert that general knowledge about Jesus is obtainable, and that Jesus can and should be understood in the context of the Judaism of his time and in continuity with his followers.[62] Therefore, they conclude, historically speaking, we ought to speak of the oldest Jesus movement, while at the same time, theologically speaking, we can confidently refer to this as 'Jesus'.[63] Schottroff and Stegemann surmise that the oldest

62. Schottroff und Stegemann, *Hoffnung der Armen*, pp. 9-10. In the introduction of the book, Schottroff and Stegemann offer that Schottroff is the primary author of chapters 1 and 2 and Stegemann is the primary author of chapter 3. Yet they add that the book should be considered as a whole, the joint project of both of them.

63. Authors' quotation marks; Schottroff und Stegemann, *Hoffnung der Armen*, p. 10. Though questions about methods for reconstructing 'Jesus' are beyond the scope of this study, I would note quickly the irony in the way Schottroff and Stegemann bypass the difficulty E. Käsemann, echoing R. Bultmann, addressed regarding continuity/discontinuity between the historical Jesus and the Jesus movement, and adopt a stance reminiscent of M. Dibelius in the way they aim toward the social setting of the earliest Christian communities. Schottroff and Stegemann are certainly correct that one cannot get a representative picture of Jesus by isolating him from Judaism and from his disciples. But their alternative illustrates that historical Jesus research has not substantially progressed since reactions to R.H. Fuller's and N. Perrin's outlines of criteria for authentic Jesus material, which popularized and gave methodological shape to Bultmann's and Käsemann's direction, highlighted the inevitably distorting effect of the criterion of 'distinctiveness' (Fuller) or 'dissimilarity' (Perrin). See R. Bultmann, *Synoptic Tradition*, p. 205; E. Käsemann, 'The Problem of the Historical Jesus', in *Essays on New Testament Themes* (trans. W.J. Montague; London: SCM Press, 1964; repr.; Philadelphia: Fortress Press, 1982), esp. p. 37; M. Dibelius, *From Tradition to Gospel* (trans. B.L. Woolf; New York: Charles Scribner's Sons, 1935); M. Dibelius, *Jesus* (Philadelphia: Westminster Press, 1949); R.H. Fuller, *A Critical Introduction to the New Testament* (Naperville: Allenson, 1966), pp. 91-104; N. Perrin, *Rediscovering the Teaching of Jesus* (New York: Harper & Row, 1967), pp. 15-49.

Jesus movement consisted of people who were socially poor and lowly, and who exhibited humility before God. The authors call them the 'little people' (*kleine Leute*).[64]

Chapter 3 of Schottroff and Stegemann's work shifts to an interpretation of the Gospel of Luke and Luke's social message. According to Luke, say Schottroff and Stegemann, renunciation of possessions for the sake of the kingdom of God is the proper response to the presence of the kingdom. The kingdom is present in the person of Jesus, and therefore renunciation of possessions is an essential component of discipleship in the presence of Jesus. The disciples are poor as a result of renouncing possessions.[65] So, the Beatitudes reflect that 'the poor disciples of Jesus are blessed, for they receive a share of the reign of God in the present'.[66] In other words, 'voluntary poverty, being a disciple of Jesus, and present participation in the kingdom of God belong together'.[67] Schottroff and Stegemann distinguish between what they see as voluntary poverty (*freiwillige Armut*) and what they see as involuntary poverty (*schicksalhafte Armut*) displayed in Luke–Acts.[68] According to Schottroff and Stegemann, Luke intends for the involuntarily poor to benefit from the possessions given up by the voluntarily poor. This spirit of generosity is supposed to continue in Luke's community, say Schottroff and Stegemann, even though the demand that disciples renounce *all* possessions is intended by Luke to reflect a form of discipleship confined to the past when Jesus walked the earth.[69]

To Luke's readers, say Schottroff and Stegemann, the voluntary poverty of Jesus' disciples is a literary ideal that serves as criticism of wealthy Christians who are in danger of succumbing to greed.[70] The

---

Schottroff and Stegemann's 'theological Jesus' (my term) is not simply a new version of M. Kähler's (*The So-called Historical Jesus and the Historic Biblical Christ* [trans. C. Braaten; Philadelphia: Fortress Press, 1964]) biblical Christ. Schottroff and Stegemann are crafting 'Jesus' through historical reconstruction and thus looking through the New Testament to a historical essence behind it.

64. Schottroff und Stegemann, *Hoffnung der Armen*, pp. 55-88 and *passim*.
65. Echoed by, among others, Tannehill, *Narrative Unity*, I, p. 121.
66. Schottroff und Stegemann, *Hoffnung der Armen*, p. 101. My translation.
67. Schottroff und Stegemann, *Hoffnung der Armen*, p. 102. My translation.
68. Schottroff und Stegemann, *Hoffnung der Armen*, p. 105.
69. Schottroff und Stegemann, *Hoffnung der Armen*, p. 101. So also Pilgrim, *Good News to the Poor*, p. 101.
70. Schottroff und Stegemann, *Hoffnung der Armen*, pp. 105, 108-109, 113-19.

community Luke envisions is composed of neither the upper class nor the class of beggars, but does include wealthy persons alongside poorer persons, such as tax collectors and day laborers.[71] Luke's message to the well-to-do Christians of his day is that fruits of repentance ought to include renunciation of half of one's wealth, almsgiving (that is directed toward non-Christian poor), and generous acts of love, including material support, within the Christian community.[72]

This work by Schottroff and Stegemann, in its early editions and in an English translation, is universally cited in subsequent studies of the poor in Luke's Gospel. Overlooked by these commentators who draw on Schottroff and Stegemann's work, however, is the observation by Schottroff and Stegemann that in Luke's Gospel, Jesus does not call the involuntarily poor into his circle of disciples.[73] Furthermore, Schottroff and Stegemann differentiate the poor, whom they classify as beggars, from the 'little people' of Luke–Acts, that is to say, people belonging to the lower classes of society who respond to Jesus' call.[74] Schottroff and Stegemann themselves do not pursue this observation. Their interest is in Luke's warning and guidance to wealthy Christians in his community. As is so often the case in studies of the poor in Luke–Acts, in Schottroff and Stegemann's work the consequence of a significant observation about the characterization of the poor is lost as the authors move to the issue of Luke's teaching about the proper Christian attitude toward and use of wealth. Moreover, as has been seen in the case of Pilgrim's work, when 'the poor' are dissolved into the theme of the correct Christian stance toward wealth and possessions, the absence of 'the poor' in Acts is forgotten.

The positing of two groups of 'the poor' in Luke–Acts—one group voluntarily poor and the other involuntarily poor—rests on the contention that 'the poor' in Lk. 6.20 refers to poor disciples.[75] Only if the blessed poor are disciples may one identify disciples as 'the poor'. Without this interpretation of the poor in Lk. 6.20, the term 'the poor' consistently fits Schottroff and Stegemann's classification of the involuntarily poor. Just how significant the lack of volition is as a characteristic

71. Schottroff und Stegemann, *Hoffnung der Armen*, pp. 149, 153.
72. Schottroff und Stegemann, *Hoffnung der Armen*, pp. 137-48.
73. Schottroff und Stegemann, *Hoffnung der Armen*, p. 105.
74. Schottroff und Stegemann, *Hoffnung der Armen*, p. 105.
75. See Schottroff und Stegemann, *Hoffnung der Armen*, pp. 30-32, 91-95, 100-101.

of the Lukan poor will become clear when the poor are profiled as a character type.

'The Poor' as a Metaphor

D.P. Seccombe's study, *Possessions and the Poor in Luke–Acts*, is significant for its breadth of analysis and its extraordinary conclusion as to the meaning of 'the poor' in Luke–Acts. The book brings together longstanding scholarly interest in the eschatology of Luke–Acts and more recent attention to Luke's portrayal of the poor and possessions. Two features stand out. First, Seccombe spends a goodly amount of time probing possible Hebrew roots for insight into expressions used by Luke either in quotation or narration. Specifically, Seccombe looks to *ani* and *anaw* for insight into πτώχος.[76] He seems, in fact, to consider the Hebrew text of the Scriptures to be a more appropriate guide to interpreting Luke–Acts than the Greek text of the LXX. When he finds an idea supporting his argument missing from the LXX, Seccombe dismisses the significance of this, saying, 'although we cannot postulate direct influence of the LXX on Luke, it is quite possible that the Hebrew text of Zechariah could have contributed to a Judeo-Christian understanding of the poor as the downtrodden remnant of Israel in the last days'.[77] Despite his questionable dismissal of the LXX, Seccombe rightly concludes that 'the argument for the identity of the poor and the pious is... misconceived'.[78] Seccombe's alternative is that 'the poor' is a traditional characterization of suffering Israel.[79] Applying this alternative definition of the poor to Luke–Acts is the second noteworthy feature of Seccombe's study. Building on the traditional definition of the poor as suffering Israel, says Seccombe, Luke uses 'the poor' to represent eschatological Israel, or Israel in need of salvation.[80]

Discovering the referent for 'the poor' is not Seccombe's only interest. As the title of his book shows, Seccombe also seeks to clarify Luke's ethical perspective on possessions. Despite his inventive inter-

76. Seccombe, *Possessions*, pp. 25-27.
77. Seccombe, *Possessions*, p. 40. On the contrary, as I shall show in Chapter 4, the LXX is demonstrably more relevant than the Hebrew text for interpreting Luke–Acts.
78. Seccombe, *Possessions*, p. 28.
79. Seccombe, *Possessions*, p. 94.
80. Seccombe, *Possessions*, pp. 95-96.

pretation of the poor in Luke–Acts, Seccombe's conclusion about possessions is surprisingly commonplace: Luke urges not poverty per se, but 'a fundamental evaluation of possessions in light of the kingdom',[81] that is to say, not asceticism, but ideological detachment from possessions.

Seccombe's study is difficult to characterize and assess briefly. On the one hand, as I mentioned earlier, Seccombe displays exceptional breadth of familiarity with Lukan scholarship. On this basis alone, the book deserves consideration. On the other hand, Seccombe's exegesis is plagued by nagging inconsistencies. At times, Seccombe makes his point by appeal to the *Sitz im Leben Jesu*,[82] even though he dismisses the relevance of the *Sitz im Leben Jesu* for his interpretations, which he claims are to focus on Luke's literary context.[83] Second, by insisting that 'the poor' equals 'Israel in need of salvation' in Lk. 4.16-30, and that the synagogue-goers in Nazareth represent Israel,[84] Seccombe gives us an episode in which, in effect, 'the poor' reject Jesus. Yet acceptance and rejection of Jesus are critical to Seccombe's method of identifying in Lk. 6.20-22 who are the poor and who are the rich respectively.[85] Along similar lines, one must wonder why, according to Seccombe, the mighty and the satisfied of Lk. 1.52-53 are oppressive heathen,[86] but the rich and satisfied of Lk. 6.24-26 are those of Israel who prefer the present order to salvation proclaimed by Jesus.[87] Finally, an additional weakness in Seccombe's argument is that he assumes that Hebrew antecedents to πτώχος are significant guides to Luke's use of the term. Seccombe does not demonstrate that this assumption is valid, and in practice he partially undermines the assumption when he appeals to the *Psalms of Solomon*, which are in Greek. When the difficulties with Seccombe's argument are considered cumulatively, it becomes evident that the poor in Luke's Gospel are not a metaphor for Israel in need of salvation.

Nevertheless, Seccombe is the first Lukan interpreter to look to the Old Testament for an intertextual definition of the poor. While his

81. Seccombe, *Possessions*, p. 223.
82. E.g. Seccombe, *Possessions*, pp. 89, 103-104, 111-12.
83. Seccombe, *Possessions*, p. 107.
84. Seccombe, *Possessions*, p. 67.
85. Seccombe, *Possessions*, pp. 91-92.
86. Seccombe, *Possessions*, p. 79.
87. Seccombe, *Possessions*, pp. 95-96.

specific solution fails, Seccombe shows the potential for an interpretive paradigm that draws on the Old Testament and yet breaks free from the evolutionary model associated with Dibelius. My own study differs from Seccombe's both in method and conclusions. But like Seccombe's work, this study intends to recover a convincing definition of the Lukan poor from the Old Testament.

Luke T. Johnson's *The Literary Function of Possessions in Luke–Acts* departs from the studies mentioned thus far in that he calls his endeavor a 'literary analysis'. Johnson's book is a landmark study both in terms of method and methodological presupposition.

> A literary analysis presumes more than the simple recognition that the work as a whole bears a uniformity of style; it presumes that the writer was more than a collector and collator of sources, was in fact an author in the fullest sense.[88]

Consequently, Johnson occupies himself less with questions of tradition and redaction than do the others surveyed above.[89] He seeks a pattern (or patterns) to the story into which dialogue or action concerning possessions may fit.

Johnson finds the governing pattern of Luke–Acts to be the theme of 'the Prophet and the People'. 'The figure of the "Prophet like Moses" has provided Luke with the basic framework for his understanding of Jesus.'[90] According to Johnson, the question raised by Luke's story is whether the People (and ultimately the reader) will accept or reject the Prophet.

According to Johnson, the language of possessions in Luke–Acts expresses symbolically the People's response to the Prophet. The poor function as metaphors for those who, though themselves culturally rejected and outcast, accept the Prophet. They are those who fear God and respond to God's Word. The rich function metaphorically as those who are self-confident, enjoy earthly favor, and express no need for God's comfort. In both cases, there is 'not an economic designation, but a designation of spiritual status'.[91] In addition, Johnson states that

---

88. Johnson, *Literary Function of Possessions*, p. 13.

89. In this light, Johnson's proposal to treat uniquely Lukan material differently from minimally altered traditional material is curious. See Johnson, *Literary Function of Possessions*, p. 131.

90. Johnson, *Literary Function of Possessions*, p. 95.

91. Johnson, *Literary Function of Possessions*, p. 139.

positively, possessions are a sign of conversion; by selling possessions and giving alms, a man shows that he is responding to God's visitation. . . Luke sees the way a man handles possessions as an indication, a symbol, of his interior disposition.[92]

Johnson concludes that the rich and poor are metaphors corresponding to rejection and acceptance of the Prophet. This conclusion is, however, in keeping with much past scholarship in that Johnson implies that the terms have something of a double meaning when he says, for example, that 'Luke employed the language about possessions not only literally, but also metaphorically, or symbolically'.[93] Thus, the most controversial point of Johnson's study may be his conclusion that the Prophet–People pattern dominates Luke–Acts rather than his specific conclusions regarding possessions.

Johnson has laid valuable methodological groundwork for the type of literary exegesis to be undertaken be this study. But this study diverges methodologically from his at two key points. First, 'possessions' as a focus of study overlaps but is not coterminus with a study of character types. This new focus on character types can provide insights into Luke–Acts not brought to light by Johnson. Secondly, this study will delve more deeply into the matter of the narrativity of Luke–Acts than Johnson did. Interpretation following a more conventional approach to reading narrative will not formulate a pattern from Acts and then superimpose that back onto the Gospel, as Johnson does.

Summary of Studies on the Poor in Luke–Acts

This survey of scholarly contributions covers the range of views presented by New Testament interpreters. The scholarly perspectives overlap. Sometimes they overlap considerably. But they never overlap entirely. In his assessment of research on the rich and poor in Luke–Acts, John Donahue makes two observations. Early in his article Donahue states that there is 'no consensus on the translation and interpretation of the term *ptōchos*. . . used almost exclusively in Luke and the New Testament for the poor'.[94] Later Donahue concludes, how-

---

92. Johnson, *Literary Function of Possessions*, p. 148.
93. Johnson, *Literary Function of Possessions*, p. 170.
94. J. Donahue, 'Two Decades of Research on the Rich and the Poor in Luke–Acts', in D. Knight and P. Paris (eds.), *Justice and the Holy* (Scholars Press Homage Series; Atlanta: Scholars Press, 1989), pp. 129-44 (135).

ever, that 'there is growing consensus that these terms (for the poor) also describe real social conditions'.[95] These seemingly contradictory observations are paradoxically both true, though there is no indication that Donahue intended them to be paradoxical. Not even Johnson and Seccombe want to abandon some socially defined referent for the poor. Yet no two authors quite concur on who the poor of Luke's Gospel are and what the significance of Lukan references to the poor is for Luke's theology.

The history of interpretation shows that as long as exegetical methods put a premium on separating tradition from redaction, the question of the inconsistency between the Gospel and Acts with regard to attention to the poor was not an issue. Author-oriented interpretation has eroded the importance of separating tradition and redaction to interpret Luke–Acts. At the same time, author-oriented redaction criticism interprets the poor in terms of the theme 'right use of wealth and possessions'. The exceptions to this thematicizing of the poor are few.

The tendency to move rapidly from characters to theme grows out of the goal of redaction criticism and the lack of methodological attention to characterization in narrative. Redaction criticism seeks to answer the question: what is Luke's theology? Theology is expressed in terms of ideas, ideas which come to the fore as themes. Therefore, the goal of redaction criticism leads the redaction critic to conceive of the narrative more in terms of themes than in terms of characters and actions. As a result, the subject of the poor as a character group in the narrative is left underdeveloped.

The Poor in Literary-Critical Commentaries on the Gospel of Luke

The subject of the poor as a character group in Luke's narrative would appear to be a matter literary-critical commentaries would address. Several commentaries on the Gospel have appeared that treat it from a literary perspective: *The Narrative Unity of Luke–Acts: A Literary Interpretation*. I. *The Gospel According to Luke*, by Robert Tannehill published in 1986; *Reading Luke: A Literary and Theological Commentary on the Third Gospel*, by Charles H. Talbert, published in 1982; *Jesus and the New Age: A Commentary on St Luke's Gospel*, by Frederick W. Danker, published revised and expanded in 1988; *Luke*,

---

95. Donahue, 'Two Decades of Research', pp. 142-43.

by David Tiede published in 1988; and *The Gospel of Luke*, by Luke Johnson published in 1991.

For the most part, these literary commentaries on the Gospel of Luke have little to say about the poor. What they do offer echoes the interpretive results of form and redaction critics. All maintain that the poor are among those powerless groups of people who are rejected or oppressed within first-century Palestinian society.[96] All five literary commentaries claim that the poor in Luke's Gospel display at least an element of piety or acceptance of Jesus.[97] Though he does not cite the work of Dibelius or other historical-critical studies, Talbert repeats without reservations the theory, formulated by historical critics, of the socio-religious evolutionary development of the term 'the poor' into 'the type of one who is pleasing to God, that is, one who recognizes his total dependence upon God'.[98] Talbert expresses what others seem to have in mind but leave unsaid. As is the case with historical-critical interpreters of Luke–Acts in general, literary critical commentators may consider the spiritual connotation of 'the poor' to be the dominant one[99] or the economic–social connotation to be the dominant one.[100] In the main, however, the literary commentaries published to date steer a middle course in interpretation—a course along the lines of the interpretations offered by Pilgrim and Schottroff and Stegemann—and provide traditional readings of texts involving the poor.

The most developed portrait of the poor presented by a literary commentary is drawn by Luke T. Johnson. Though Johnson's perspective as introduced in *The Literary Function of Possessions in Luke–Acts* has already been discussed, taking a few minutes to review his discussion of the poor in his commentary on the Gospel will help to clarify further the need for and the direction of this present study. I will look first at how Johnson invokes the Old Testament and Qumran

96. Danker, *Jesus and the New Age*, pp. 165, 271; Johnson, *Luke*, pp. 22, 79, 106, 225; Tannehill, *Narrative Unity*, I, pp.103, 127. D.L. Tiede (*Luke* [Augsburg Commentary on the New Testament; Minneapolis: Augsburg, 1988], p. 106) implies this, as does Talbert (*Reading Luke*, p. 72).

97. Danker, *Jesus and the New Age*, p. 106, 139; Johnson, *Luke*, pp. 22, 106, 225, 281, 287; Tannehill, *Narrative Unity*, I, pp. 121, 122, 130, 208; Tiede, *Luke*, 141; Talbert, *Reading Luke*, pp. 71, 72, 157.

98. Talbert, *Reading Luke*, p. 71.

99. E.g. Talbert (*Reading Luke*, p. 71).

100. E.g. Tannehill (*Narrative Unity*, I, p. 208).

literature to characterize the lame and the blind. Then I will raise
objections to Johnson's expansive definition of the poor in the Gospel.
At the head of Johnson's interpretation is an all-encompassing definition
of the poor.

> The poor stand for all those who have been rejected on the basis of human
> standards, but are accepted by God; they in turn accept the Prophet. Among
> them are the crippled, the lame, the blind and deaf, the sexually mutilated,
> and all those ritually excluded from full participation in the life of the
> people. The religiously unrighteous are also included, the 'sinners and
> tax-agents', as well as those women who by virtue of their gender always
> took a second place within the ritual life of the Jewish community.[101]

In comments on Lk. 14.13, Johnson appeals to Lev. 21.17-21, a text
which forbids the lame, the blind, and the crippled from becoming
priests, to point out that these are marginalized people.[102] He adds that
at Qumran these conditions further excluded those so afflicted from
'the Holy War of the end-time' and 'from participation in the eschatological banquet'.[103] They are among the poor, says Johnson, for 'Luke
uses "poor" as a blanket term for all those marginalized in the
people'.[104] Yet Johnson does not explain why Lev. 21.17-21 is the
singularly relevant Old Testament reference to the lame, crippled, and
blind. Nor does Johnson explain why the Qumran literature is pertinent
to the discussion of Luke's meaning. Clearly, Lev. 21.17-21 fits the
model Johnson proposes—the lame, the crippled, and the blind are
second-class citizens in the Jewish community. Yet singling out this
reference gives it undue influence in the interpretation of Luke 14. The
implicit premise for including Qumran writings in the discussion is
that there was a consistent cultural and religious perspective regarding
'the poor' and others within which both a Lukan community and
the Qumran community operated. But this premise overlooks the
obvious difference in the language each used, and it overlooks the radi-
cally different theological frameworks of Luke–Acts and the literature
of Qumran.

    101. Johnson, *Luke*, p. 22. Johnson (*Luke*, p. 125) goes so far as to say that
'"rich" in Luke effectively equals "Pharisee/lawyer," and "poor" equals "sinner/tax-
agent"'.
    102. Johnson, *Luke*, p. 225.
    103. Johnson, *Luke*, p. 225. Tiede (*Luke*, p. 265) applies Lev. 21 and Qumran
citations in a similar way to his interpretation of Lk. 14.7-14.
    104. Johnson, *Luke*, p. 225.

The limited way the Old Testament is brought into the discussion of the lame, the blind, the crippled, and the poor clearly affects Johnson's view of how Luke 14 is to be read. More sweeping than this in its implications for broader interpretation of the poor in Luke–Acts is the expansive definition Johnson gives to the poor and the character trait this definition invests in the poor.

For Johnson, 'the poor' are the socially rejected and/or economically deprived; yet they are also those who, in these conditions, accept Jesus. In the narrative, says Johnson, the presence or absence of possessions and the right or wrong use of possessions function as indicators of a character's stance toward Jesus. That is, says Johnson, those who accept the Prophet, that is, respond favorably to Jesus, devalue wealth and share their possessions. What emerges is that Johnson's expansive definition of the poor allows for the conclusion that in effect 'the poor', namely, those marginalized in a variety of ways by human standards, share their possessions with the needy. Because his discussion of the poor veers into the theme of the right use of possessions, Johnson winds up with 'poor' who may not be poor. The following syllogism is oversimplified, but close enough to the truth of Johnson's thematic construct to illustrate the problem with its logic.

> The poor are all those marginalized who accept the Prophet;
> Those who accept the Prophet are those who share their possessions with the less fortunate;
> Therefore the poor share their possessions with the less fortunate.

The root problem with this syllogism is that Johnson assigns a key characteristic to 'the poor' that does not fit οἱ πτωχοί: acceptance of the Prophet. Nowhere in Luke–Acts do οἱ πτωχοί show or say that they accept Jesus. Without expanding the definition of 'the poor' to include tax collectors, sinners, and others, the narrative material would not support the claim that 'the poor' respond favorably to Jesus.

The absence of a connection between the Holy Spirit and οἱ πτωχοί further shows the weakness of Johnson's conclusion. According to Johnson, the poor, as expansively defined, become part of the restored people of God. The restored people of God, Johnson points out, accept the Prophet and 'manifestly "have" the Holy Spirit'.[105] It must be recognized as significant, therefore, that nowhere in Luke–Acts are οἱ πτωχοί said to be of the Holy Spirit, led by the Spirit, or filled with

---

105. Johnson, *Luke*, p. 17.

the Spirit. In short, two vital characteristics of people who accept the Prophet, namely, that they share possessions and they have the Holy Spirit, cannot be observed in οἱ πτωχοί.

Literary analyses of Luke–Acts, including the literary commentaries on the Gospel, have contributed to our appreciation of the Gospel as narrative. They have taught us to find new exegetical treasures in the narrative by treating it as a narrative whole. They have made us more attentive to literary aspects of the Gospel, such as narrative plot and settings. They have turned our attention to rhetorical devices at work in the Gospel, such as irony and repetition. This study intends to build on their beginnings and take the a next step, which is to apply literary insights into the process of characterization to the captive, the blind, the poor and the others in Luke–Acts.

The Path Forward

Two new elements of interpretation are needed in order to be more precise when talking about 'outcast' or 'marginalized' persons in Luke–Acts. The first is a fresh look at how the Old Testament may be applied to the interpretation of the blind, the lame, and the poor in Luke–Acts. The second is an approach to characterization in narrative that is appropriate to the poor in Luke's Gospel. This study intends to provide both of these elements.

While the socio-religious image of the poor popularized by Dibelius has persisted over the decades, alternative proposals have shown that this image is not adequate. In the process, interpretation of 'the poor' has reached an impasse. All the constructions of the poor surveyed in this study assume that the referent for the poor is a group to be socio-religiously located in the first-century world. Yet the available socio-religious data about the world behind Luke's Gospel cannot adjudicate between the competing claims for the role and significance of the poor in Luke–Acts. Nor have studies searching for an extra-textual referent for 'the poor' in the cultures and proposed Christian communities of first-century Palestine been able to explain convincingly the disappearance of the poor from Acts.

Scholarly constructions of 'the poor' in Luke–Acts diverge not only because there is insufficient knowledge of Luke's cultural extra-text or there are insufficient controls on our application of Luke's cultural extra-text. Constructions diverge also because in Luke's Gospel the term 'the poor' lacks descriptive content and intratextual definition. Chapter 3 presents a method for interpreting the poor in Luke–Acts that is particularly suited to this exegetical situation. Whereas scholarship to date has assumed that in the case of the poor the reference is from text to world, this study suggests that the reference is from text to text, that is, it is an intertextual reference, and that the intertext implicated by Luke's narrative is the LXX.

Chapter 3

AN AUDIENCE-ORIENTED LITERARY APPROACH
TO READING LUKE–ACTS

Chapter 1 introduced two scholarly consensuses about Luke–Acts:
(1) that Luke–Acts is a unified work and (2) that the writer of the
third Gospel is the most socially minded of the Gospel writers, particularly in his concern for the poor. Chapter 1 then drew attention to
the tension between these two consensuses because of the absence of
references to the poor and the other marginalized groups in Acts, and
because of the lack of consensus about who 'the poor' are in the Gospel.

Chapter 2 surveyed interpretations of 'the poor' in Luke–Acts.
Virtually all scholars interpret the poor in Luke's Gospel by reference
to extra-textual historical or social contexts, but scholars are unable to
reach a consensus on the identity and function of the poor in Luke's
work. Consequently, study of 'the poor' in Luke–Acts has reached an
impasse. Chapter 2 also showed that literary commentaries on the
Gospel have not yet made a fresh contribution to interpretation of 'the
poor' in Luke–Acts that would break the impasse. Let me add that
monographs treating the poor in Luke–Acts from a literary perspective
have not appeared.

It is not merely the lack of literary-critical work on the poor in
Luke–Acts that justifies the study undertaken here. The captive, the
shattered, the blind, the deaf mute, the lame, lepers, the maimed, the
dead, and the poor need to be studied on the basis of a reader-response
or audience-oriented literary approach for several reasons. First, the
blind, the poor, the lame, and so on appear to be characters in the
narrative. Therefore, treatment of them requires some understanding
of characterization in ancient literature, and the study of characterization is a standard part of literary analysis. Secondly, Luke signals to
the audience how to understand these characters and an audience-
oriented literary approach leads interpreters to recognize those signals.

In the case of these characters, the author points the audience to the extra-textual context that defines the character types in the narrative and an audience-oriented literary approach is specifically suited to handle this extra-textual context. Thirdly, an audience-oriented literary approach is especially sensitive to the effect that the narrative placement of a given episode within the overall sequence of narrative episodes has on the audience and to the effect on the audience of the manner in which characters are introduced into the narrative and later employed by the narrative. Understanding the narrative placement of episodes involving the blind, the poor, the lame, and so on and the manner in which these characters are introduced and later employed by Luke is crucial to understanding the role they play in the Gospel.

This chapter will sketch the reader-response criticism adopted for this study. It begins with an overview of reader-response criticism. This is followed by discussions of three facets of this study's methodological approach that are especially important for analysis of the blind, the poor, and the lame in Luke–Acts. These three facets are the nature and ramifications of sequential reading; the construction of an authorial audience; and character types as a form of characterization.

Reader-Response Criticism

This study will use the words 'reader' and 'audience' interchangeably. Similarly, 'reader-response criticism' is synonymous with 'audience-oriented criticism'. Literary critics have tended to use the word 'reader', but as this study progresses it will prefer the word 'audience' because 'audience' better expresses the oral character of ancient reading.[1]

Reader-response criticism is rooted in a philosophical approach to language that evaluates language on the basis of its function in the speech act. It is not the interest of this study to describe speech act

---

1.   Aristotle, *Art of Rhetoric*, 3.1407b. The oral nature of ancient reading is well recognized. See J. Balogh, 'Voces paginarum', *Philologus* 82 (1927), pp. 84-109, 202-31; G.L. Hendrickson, 'Ancient Reading', *Classical Journal* 25 (1929), pp. 182-96; G.A. Kennedy, *Classical Rhetoric and its Christian and Secular Tradition from Ancient to Modern Times* (Chapel Hill: University of North Carolina Press, 1980), p. 111; E.S. McCartney, 'Notes on Reading and Praying Audibly', *Classical Philology* 63 (1948), pp. 184-87; W.B. Sedgwick, 'Reading and Writing in Classical Antiquity', *Contemporary Review* 135 (January–June 1929), pp. 93-94.

theory in detail. Rather, a few basic aspects of speech act theory will be sketched to provide a theoretical framework for understanding the audience-oriented criticism to be pursued in this study. As explained in the writings of speech act theory's two most well-known thinkers, J.L. Austin and J. Searle, language has an instrumental character and performs successfully because people use language according to complex linguistic rules.[2] In addition, what is communicated by a unit of speech has to do not simply with the denotative sense of the words involved.[3] What is communicated has to do also with the way the utterance is being used, such as whether the utterance expresses a question, a command, a warning, a promise, or some other type of address.[4] Moreover, saying something to someone has consequential effects on the person addressed[5] All three factors—what is said, the use for which it is said, and the effects elicited by what is said—constitute the speech act. For example, consider the sentence, 'I know where you live'. That sentence may be uttered by a friend who has been phoned with an emergency plea for help and who is reassuring the caller that the friend will come with help immediately. These circumstances would combine to create one speech act. On the other hand, that sentence may well be uttered as a threat by one person to another person in an effort to discourage the second person from doing something the first person disapproves of. This second example constitutes a totally different speech act, even though it involves identical words.

R. Jakobson provides a ready vocabulary for discussion of the speech act.[6] In everyday communication, says Jakobson, an *addresser* sends a

2.   See primarily J.L. Austin, *How to Do Things With Words* (Oxford: Oxford University Press, 1962) and J.R. Searle, *Speech Acts: An Essay in the Philosophy of Language* (Cambridge: Cambridge University Press, 1969). See also M.L. Pratt, *Toward A Speech Act Theory of Literary Discourse* (Bloomington: Indiana University Press, 1977) and J.R. Searle, *Intentionality* (Cambridge: Cambridge University Press, 1983).

3.   The denotative or propositional side of the speech act is termed by Austin the 'locutionary act'. See Austin, *How To Do Things With Words*, pp. 98-101.

4.   See Austin, *How To Do Things With Words*, pp. 98-101. Austin's term for the issuance of a question, a command, a warning, a promise, etc. is 'illocutionary act'. The illocutionary act establishes the speaker's relationship to the way the propositional utterance is used.

5.   See Austin, *How To Do Things With Words*, p. 101, on 'perlocutionary acts'.

6.   R. Jakobson, 'Closing Statement: Linguistics and Poetics', in T.A. Sebeok (ed.), *Style in Language* (Cambridge, MA: Technology Press, 1960), pp. 350-77.

message to an *addressee*.[7] The addresser, the message, and the addressee
are the three 'fundaments' of communication. According to Jakobson,
each of these three fundaments corresponds to a function of language:
emotive, referential, or conative. The emotive function reflects the
attitude, situation, and emotional state of the addresser. The referential
function pertains to the various aspects of the message, such as the
speech situation and the linguistic code of the discourse. Finally, the
conative function of language corresponds to the anticipated effect of
the utterance upon the addressee.

These central features of Austin's and Searle's speech act theory and
Jakobson's communication model point us in the direction of a reader-
response criticism appropriate for interpreting Luke–Acts. With the
help of Austin, Searle, and Jakobson, it can be clearly seen that interpreting human discourse is far more than a matter of applying
dictionary definitions to words. Even the simplest conversation may be
successful because a complex array of factors is in place, even though
those enabling factors are largely invisible to the participants in the
conversation. Especially pertinent to this study is the insight that the
addressee's role in the speech act is integral to what constitutes the
speech act. In other words, one cannot speak adequately of the meaning
of a linguistic unit without taking into account the effect that uttering
that linguistic unit has on a hearer.

Just as no message is complete without an audience, no story is complete without a hearer; no narrative comes to life without a reader. In
her study of narrative dynamics, S. Lanser has adapted Jakobson's
model to describe the 'narrative act' as an elaborate exchange involving
the author, the text, and the audience.[8] A speech act is the complex
exchange of a message, with its mix of propositions, images, and
attitudes, from a speaker to a person spoken to. Analogously, reading

---

Citing Jakobson in connection with Austin and Searle is not intended to imply that
the three belong in the same philosophical camp. Nevertheless, Jakobson's linguistic
model lends itself to speech act theory and, as will be seen below, to literary theory.

7.   Jakobson's own model presents the constitution of the message as a combination of context, contact, and code. It is not necessary to discuss Jakobson's
model in detail because my interest is in aspects of his model that contribute to the
development of the reader-response approach of this study. The 'message' portion of
Jakobson's diagram will be replaced by the 'narrative' when the discussion shifts to
literature.

8.   S.S. Lanser, *The Narrative Act: Point of View in Prose Fiction* (Princeton,
NJ: Princeton University Press, 1981), p. 71.

a narrative generates the complex exchange of a story, with its mix of conventions, symbols, and descriptions, from an author to an audience.[9]

Reader-response critics propose to interpret the literary work from the work's relationship to its reader or readers. Yet reader-response criticism is not a single method. Rather, it is a perspective within literary criticism that focuses the interpreter's attention on the reader, specifically on the reader's role in the production of a text's meaning and, correspondingly, on the text's effect on the reader.[10]

Despite their differences, reader-response critics tend to agree that narratives function rhetorically and that it is the critic's task to identify the reader's response to the text as well as the textual means by which responses are evoked. Yet reader-response critics differ on the degree of control over the production of the work's meaning they grant to the reader and the text respectively. At one end of the spectrum, interpreters speak of a textually inscribed reader who appropriates the objective meaning of the text. Such is the case with W. Gibson's 'mock reader'.[11] Though Gibson introduced his mock reader in 1950, his article still accurately describes the textually-inscribed reader some biblical interpreters now propose for New Testament study forty years later.[12] Gibson distinguishes two readers. The first is the individual who actually reads the literature, that is, the real reader. The second is a fictitious reader, that is, the mock reader, 'whose mask and costume the individual takes on in order to experience the language'.[13] The

9. Lanser, *The Narrative Act*, p. 118.

10. S.R. Suleiman ('Introduction: Varieties of Audience-Oriented Criticism', in S.R. Suleiman and I. Crosman (eds.), *The Reader in the Text: Essays on Audience and Interpretation* [Princeton, NJ: Princeton University Press, 1980], pp. 3-45 [6-7]) distinguishes six varieties of audience-oriented criticism: rhetorical, semiotic and structuralist, phenomenological, subjective and psychoanalytic, sociological and historical, and hermeneutic. Suleiman is quick to add that these approaches are neither monolithic nor mutually exclusive. See also R. Fowler, 'Who is "the Reader" in Reader-Response Criticism?' *Semeia* 31 (1985), pp. 5-23; V.B. Leitch, 'A Primer of Recent Critical Theories', *College English* 39 (October 1977), pp. 138-52; J.P. Tompkins, 'An Introduction to Reader-Response Criticism', in Tompkins (ed.), *Reader-Response Criticism*, pp. ix-xxvi.

11. W. Gibson, 'Authors, Speakers, Readers, and Mock Readers', in Tompkins (ed.), *Reader-Response Criticism*, pp. 1-6.

12. E.g., M. Powell, *What is Narrative Criticism* (Guides to Biblical Scholarship; Minneapolis: Augsburg-Fortress, 1990).

13. Gibson, 'Authors, Speakers', p. 2.

mock reader possesses the values and assumptions the author wants the reader to possess, and, lacking sophistication, uncritically accepts the attitudes the author wishes to impart. Gibson's mock reader is purely a property of the text. It exerts no influence on the meaning of the text, but rather adds a new dimension to literary analysis.

The major shortcoming of Gibson's model is that it overlooks that the mock reader is a product of interpretation and not something independent of or prior to interpretation. Therefore, while the model does draw attention to the effects of the text on readers, it avoids the issue of the real reader's role in creating the mock reader. Despite this shortcoming, Gibson's distinction between the real reader and a construct of a reader implied by the text remains a basic tenet of literary analysis of narrative, even though the distinction is modified by later literary theorists.

In his article, 'Interpreting the *Variorum*', S. Fish represents the other end of the reader-response spectrum.[14] Fish dissolves the text into the reader. Or one may say that according to Fish, the reader writes the text as he or she reads. Fish puts it simply: 'It is my thesis that the reader is always making sense (I intend "making" to have its literal force)'.[15] Interpreters agree on the profile of an optimal or ideal reader and therefore on an author's intention: in Fish's words, 'by becoming a member of a community made up of those who share interpretive strategies'.[16] According to Fish, even the most formal

14. S. Fish, 'Interpreting the *Variorum*', *Critical Inquiry* 2 (Spring 1976), pp. 465-85 (reprinted in Tompkins (ed.), *Reader-Response Criticism*, pp. 164-84). Deconstruction may be considered a reader-response theory, and if so considered would necessitate an additional discussion of the status of the text and of the reader in deconstructive criticism. Yet this study is concerned with the surface structure of the text and with making sense of the text. Since deconstruction is not equipped to make sense of a text and raises questions more appropriate to inquiry about a text's deep structures than about its surface structure, this study will not discuss deconstruction. See also S. Mailloux's comments (*Interpretive Conventions: The Reader in the Study of American Fiction* [Ithaca, NY and London: Cornell University Press, 1982], pp. 57-58 n. 32, and pp. 60-61 n. 39) about why he chose to exclude deconstruction from his discussion of reader-oriented approaches.

15. Fish, 'The *Variorum*' (repr.), p. 175.

16. Fish, 'The *Variorum*' (repr.), p. 174. See also Fish's discussion ('The *Variorum*' [repr.], pp. 182-84) of interpretive communities.

aspects of a text are in reality 'a function of the interpretive model one brings to bear'.[17]

Fish's lasting contribution to literary critical discourse is to draw into the center of discussion the question 'How do readers construct meaning?' Moreover, the exploration of interpretive communities, or text-receiving communities, may prove even more fruitful in biblical study than previous form-critical inquiries about text-generating communities. Unfortunately, Fish leaves no room in his model for scholarly attempts to read narratives from the perspective of a reading public that is not the scholar's own contemporary reading public. In other words, stripping the text of all authority in the reading process leaves interpretation without a model of reading that is historically mindful of ancient texts. Luke–Acts is an ancient text, produced and first read in a foreign literary culture. Consequently, a model of reading is required that is more amenable to historical investigation of narrative and rhetoric. A second objection to Fish's theory is that by effectively denying the text any objective status, such a theory rules out the possibility of a communication act, or a narrative act, in the sense of a transaction between a writer and readers.

I am seeking a model of reading that steers a middle course between the formalism of Gibson and the constructivism of Fish. Such a model would allow the interpreter to speak meaningfully of interpreting Luke–Acts against the background of its Hellenistic literary milieu, and at the same time recognize the role of the reader in the construction of textual meaning. The model of reading that this study adopts owes its substance to the work of W. Iser.

In the course of reading, the reader is introduced to various textual perspectives or vantage points: the narrator, the characters, the plot, the narratee. The reader's role, then, 'is to occupy shifting vantage points that are geared to a prestructured activity and to fit the diverse perspectives into a gradually evolving pattern'.[18] The 'gradually evolving pattern' evolves as the reader connects and arranges the various perspectives. In other words, the pattern evolves as the reader builds consistency into his or her reading. Thus, meaning may be spoken as the effect the text has upon the reader as the reader engages in 'the process of actualization' of the text.[19]

17. Fish, 'The *Variorum*' (repr.), p. 176.
18. Iser, *Act of Reading*, p. 35.
19. Iser, *Act of Reading*, p. 18.

Shifting perspectives, Iser explains, create gaps or blanks in the internal structure of the text. The reader is forced by the reader's own inclination to read the work as a coherent whole to fill the gaps. That is, the reader is prompted to use her or his imagination to connect the shifting textual perspectives of the narrator, the characters, and so on. Imaging a unified whole is not a random process by the reader, however. The reader's imagination, though it is triggered by gaps, is nevertheless restricted by the textual perspectives.

Luke 9.18-22 may serve as an illustration of gaps and how they function. This episode presents the reader with Jesus' perspective, the crowd's, then Peter's, then Jesus' again. At the beginning of the episode, Jesus is praying. This mention of Jesus' posture is more than the narrator's statement of fact. Coupled with other references to Jesus engaged in prayer, this statement communicates Jesus' high assessment of the value of prayer. When his disciples interrupt him, Jesus asks, 'Who do the crowds say that I am?' To this the disciples respond with the perspective of the crowds (seen, of course, through the eyes of the disciples), namely, the view that Jesus is John the Baptist, Elijah, or some other prophet. Between the perspective of Jesus and the perspective of the crowds there is a disjunction, a gap. We recognize the gap's existence when we begin to consider basic exegetical questions: Is there a connection between Jesus' practice of prayer and the crowd's view of who Jesus is? If so, what is the connection? How is it made? The text suggests these questions and provides data on Jesus and the crowds that can be used to formulate answers to these questions. But the text is sufficiently silent so as to require readers to draw their own conclusions. We the readers make the connection between Jesus' practice of prayer and the crowd's views of who Jesus is by pulling together what we know of the narrative from the perspectives of Jesus, the crowds, the narrator, and others as we have encountered them up to this point in the narrative.[20]

The reader of Luke–Acts builds consistency among various textual

20. For a well-presented example of Iser's notion of gaps, applied to an interpretation of Mk 1.1-15, see P.J. Sankey, 'Promise and Fulfillment: Reader-Response to Mark 1.1-15', *JSNT* 58 (1995), pp. 3-18. Sankey's treatment of this passage is especially noteworthy for my purpose because he uses Old Testament contexts to fill in gaps in the Markan passage. Note, however, that Sankey ('Promise and Fulfillment', p. 10) assumes, but does not demonstrate, that Mark's implied reader is familiar with the Old Testament in Hebrew.

perspectives, among successive episodes of the narrative, and among the actions that create and define characters. In this way, the reader makes sense of the narrative and makes the narrative cohere. Note, moreover, that narrative coherence is maintained by the reader as the reader progressively integrates perspectives and actions presented by the text.

The Nature and Ramifications of Sequential Reading

It is the nature of narrativity to head somewhere, but to delay the arrival, that is, to be teleological yet discursive.[21] A given unit within the narrative, be it a speech, an apophthegm, or a parable, is not only a part of the greater whole, but is also a moment along the way that moves toward and yet holds off complete understanding. Narrativity promises that each episode, because it is not the final episode, will contribute to future understanding and itself be understood differently later in the course of reading. An audience-oriented analysis of Luke–Acts will, therefore, be guided by two questions that stem from the nature of narrative: What is the immediate effect on the reader during the reading process? and, What is the rhetorical significance of the placement of episodes and the sequence of events in the narrative? These questions raise to the level of methodological reflection the linearity of the reading process.

In short, reading is a temporal experience of discovery. The reader is led to experience such things as moral judgments, social structures, and theological claims. Audience-oriented criticism focuses on the 'series of activities forced on the reader'[22] through which discovery is made.[23]

The series of activities performed by the reader may be described in terms of memory and expectation.[24] Memory has two aspects. One aspect is the reader's recollection of what has already transpired in the

21. See T.M. Leitch, *What Stories Are: Narrative Theory and Interpretation* (University Park: Pennsylvania State University Press, 1986), pp. 83-104; S. Rimmon-Kenan, *Narrative Fiction: Contemporary Poetics* (London and New York: Methuen, 1983), p. 125.
22. S. Mailloux, *Interpretive Conventions*, p. 73.
23. See also R. Alter, *The Art of Biblical Narrative* (New York: Basic Books, 1981), p. 11.
24. See Iser, *Act of Reading*, pp. 111, 115.

narrative. Everything that has preceded a given narrative moment serves as background for what is unfolding, but often a narrative feature at a given moment will trigger recollection of a particular past narrative moment. For example, words, phrases, actions, themes, and characters encountered by the reader initiate the recollection of prior episodes in the narrative. Such is the function, say, of intratextual allusion. Alluding to an earlier point in the narrative brings that point forward to condition, direct, nuance, or complicate the reading in some way.[25]

Prior episodes provide a context for the present reading moment. But prior episodes are also themselves given new meaning in the present scene as expectations raised in prior episodes are fulfilled, frustrated, or revised. Memory revises the reader's perception of what has preceded.[26]

Memory also involves invoking reader competences beyond the text itself, that is, mentally calling up the reader's extra-textual repertoire.[27] Of the various elements that make up the extra-text implied by Luke–Acts, most important for this study is the LXX, an 'intertext'.

I noted in Chapter 1 that within the audience's extra-textual repertoire an intertext may be identified. In M. Riffaterre's words, 'An intertext is a corpus of texts, textual fragments, or textlike segments of the sociolect that shares a lexicon and, to a lesser extent, a syntax with the text we are reading (directly or indirectly) in the form of synonyms or, even conversely, in the form of antonyms'.[28] When such a corpus of texts, textual fragments, or textlike segments is implicated by the text being read, the reader must then connect the two and make

---

25. Consider the parable of the Good Samaritan (Lk. 10). Jesus' identification of one of the characters in the parable as a Samaritan recalls the reference to the Samaritans at the end of ch. 9. The rejection of Jesus by Samaritans makes the meaning of Jesus' portrait of a Samaritan as the hero all the more pointed.

26. For example, the dying Stephen's echoing of Jesus' words from the cross (Acts 7.59-60) not only makes Stephen's death a death parallel to the Lord's, but also makes Jesus' activity at his death a model for his followers. In other words, Jesus' dying assumes in light of Stephen's a certain paradigmatic character in addition to what it meant in Lk. 23.34-46.

27. Memory as the invoking of reader competences beyond the text itself is not contained in Iser's discussion of memory per se, but it is implied in his overall vision of the reader's participation in the creation of meaning. On 'extra-textual repertoire', see Chapter 1 above.

28. Riffaterre, 'Intertextual Representation', p. 141.

sense of the text at hand by means of the intertext.

Intertextuality, as the term will be used in this study, refers to the audience's application of the text-to-text relationship. As Riffaterre says, intertextuality 'refers to an operation of the reader's mind, but it is an obligatory one, necessary to any textual decoding'.[29]

In his book, *Let the Reader Understand*, R. Fowler appears to be using the term 'intertextuality' in a different sense, one that comes across as problematic for his purpose of helping New Testament interpreters learn 'to read with an ear attuned to the rhetoric of Mark's Gospel'.[30] Because intertextuality as defined in this study is crucial to its thesis, and because Fowler's book is likely to be widely read by New Testament interpreters interested in literary analysis of the New Testament Gospels, a few words are needed to clarify the contrast between Fowler's use of the word 'intertextuality' and that of this study.

Fowler states, 'Intertextuality is the recognition that no text is ever truly autonomous; no text is ever produced or read apart from other texts'.[31] This notion of intertextuality sounds more like deconstruction than reader-response criticism. Fowler's terminology implies an abstract interdependency among texts, rather than a surface structure writing and reading strategy. He goes on to speak of the 'interweaving' of Mark's text and the Jewish Scriptures. Such an interweaving, says Fowler, serves to make Mark's text 'the proper reading grid through which not only the Jewish Scriptures are to be read but also all of history'.[32] Yet this grid is hardly a grid at all. For in Fowler's scheme, the interweaving of Mark's text and the Jewish Scriptures multi plies interpretive options to infinity: 'Mark's openness to the Jewish Scriptures is alone sufficient to render the experience of reading Mark inexhaustible'.[33] This comment about the relationship between intertextuality and the inexhaustibility of the reading experience is itself peculiar, and appears to be at odds with Fowler's later comment on intertextuality: 'That is,. . . the experience of reading one text shapes or constrains the way we view another one'.[34]

---

29. Riffaterre, 'Intertextual Representation', p. 141.

30. R. Fowler, *Let the Reader Understand: Reader-Response Criticism and the Gospel of Mark* (Minneapolis: Fortress Press, 1991), p. 4.

31. Fowler, *Let the Reader Understand*, p. 88.

32. Fowler, *Let the Reader Understand*, p. 88.

33. Fowler, *Let the Reader Understand*, pp. 88-89.

34. Fowler, *Let the Reader Understand*, p. 233. One further aspect of Fowler's

Intertextuality, as used in this study, explicitly constrains interpretation inasmuch as it is a gap-filling activity. When the readers apply the intertext to their reading, the intertext guides interpretation, that is, it narrows the range of likely effects that the text being read will have on its readers.

The gap-filling character of intertextuality becomes more evident when the matter of characterization in narrative is considered. It is worthwhile to quote Riffaterre at length here.

> There are. . . literary representations almost devoid of descriptive content, or so vague and so skimpy that their object cannot be analyzed or rationalized in sensory terms. Criticism is hard put to explain why readers feel compelled to evaluate them. And yet these texts not only lend themselves to interpretation but they are especially apt to trigger and control the reader's hermeneutic. In short, the represented object eschews referentiality yet refuses to vanish altogether, becoming instead the verbal vehicle of an interpretive activity that ends up making the object subservient to the subject.
>
> Critics fail to explain this paradox because they stick to referentiality as the only law governing representation and assume that the reference on which the mimesis is based is from words to things, from the verbal to the nonverbal domain. I propose that reference in such cases is from words to words, or rather from texts to texts, and that intertextuality is the agent both of the mimesis and of the hermeneutic constructions on that mimesis.[35]

In Luke–Acts, the captive, the shattered, the blind, the deaf mute, the lame, lepers, the maimed, the dead, and the poor are in fact 'literary representations almost devoid of descriptive content, or so vague and so skimpy that their object cannot be analyzed or rationalized in sensory terms'. Yet interpreters are compelled to explain them. Moreover, the abundance of diverse explanations of particularly the poor in Luke–Acts shows that, indeed, the object of interpretation, namely, 'the poor', has become subservient to the interpreting subject. At the same

discussion of intertextuality is troublesome. According to Fowler, the reader's experience of reading the Gospel of Mark 'fills full' the Scriptures as the reader recognizes allusions to, quotations from, and echoes of the LXX (Fowler, *Let the Reader Understand*, pp. 88-89). Here it appears that Fowler is referring to a process by which reading Mark reinterprets the LXX for the reader of Mark. Yet it is not clear in Fowler's discussion how recognizing allusions, quotations, and echoes accomplishes this. Moreover, might it not also be true, for example, that the experience of reading Mark's Gospel subverts the Jewish Scriptures for some readers who fit Fowler's definition of 'informed reader' rather than filling them full?

35. Riffaterre, 'Intertextual Representation', p. 141.

time, the possibility of text-to-text referentiality has been overlooked in scholarship.[36] As I fill this gap in scholarship, a new assessment of the blind, the lame, the poor, and so on in Luke–Acts will emerge, along with a fresh perspective on their function in the narrative.

I move now from memory to expectation. Expectation is a frame of reference out of which future plot and character developments appear inevitable or at least consistent with the narrative to this point. Thus, a given narrative moment gains meaning by how it fulfills, alters, or frustrates expectations the reader has developed. These expectations may be thematic, as in the angel's prediction (Lk. 1.32) that Jesus will be called the son of the Most High.[37] Or they may be structural, as when the pattern of the annunciation to Zechariah (Lk. 1.11-23)— angelic appearance, beholder's surprise, angel's reassurance, angel's announcement of forthcoming birth—sets up a pattern over against which the annunciation to Mary is viewed.[38]

Therefore, linearity means that the reader is continually synthesizing memory, present narrative moment, and expectation. This process is a distinctive characteristic of the reading of narrative discourse. Yet the synthesizing process resists absolute objectivity. Judgments must be made that are not clear cut. An interpreter has to weigh relative degrees of plausibility when considering items such as whether an allusion is an allusion, a parallel a parallel, a word play a word play, or a connection a connection. We are in a better position to explain interpretive decisions if we specify what audience these decisions assume.

36. The lone exception is the work of Seccombe. See above, ch. 2.

37. See B.C. Frein's ('Narrative Predictions, Old Testament Prophecies and Luke's Sense of Fulfillment', NTS 40 [January 1994], pp. 22-37) discussion of 'narrative predictions', such as the angel Gabriel's prediction of the birth of John the Baptist (Lk. 1.13-17); Simeon's prediction that Jesus will be 'a sign spoken against' (Lk. 2.34-35); and John's prediction that Jesus will baptize with the Holy Spirit and fire (Lk. 3.16). Frein's interest is 'the relationship between the fulfillment of Old Testament prophecy and the fulfillment of these narrative predictions' (Frein, 'Narrative Predictions', p. 22).

38. Points of narrative design and literary character are not unknown to historical critics. Conzelmann notes instances of foreshadowing, or what is termed 'a pointing forward' of certain narrative events. For example, the Transfiguration, says Conzelmann (*The Theology of St Luke*, p. 59), 'points forward to the events in Jerusalem'. Correspondingly, Conzelmann (*The Theology of St Luke*, p. 81) mentions later, 'The disciples sleep out of sorrow, which is an echo of the sleeping at the Transfiguration'.

Constructing an Authorial Audience

Luke–Acts has had innumerable actual audiences. Once written, a work is available, in theory, to anyone who can read the language or understand it read aloud. It is possible to posit any number of potential actual audiences, and to speculate about reactions of these audiences. So, one may ask: How would Hellenistic Jews of first-century Palestine have read Luke–Acts? How would first-century residents of Rome have read Luke–Acts? How would followers of Hillel have reacted to Luke–Acts? Or members of the court of Domitian? Or wealthy gentile Christians? Or poor Jewish urbanites? Each actual audience provides researchers with another angle from which to view Luke–Acts.[39] Literary competences vary widely among actual audiences.

The authorial audience is more limited.[40] Every author, P. Rabinowitz writes, 'cannot write without making certain assumptions about his readers' beliefs, knowledge, and familiarity with conventions'.[41] Interpreters may construct a work's authorial audience in one of two ways.[42] The first way is to build an audience inductively from existing social and historical knowledge of the culture at that time. A second way is to extrapolate a reader from the reader's role given in the text and the competencies required to fill that role. This study adopts the latter way as its route.[43] Yet the two ways are not mutually exclusive. More informed judgments about Luke's authorial audience may be arrived at when outstanding, typical characteristics of ancient readers are recognized.

The foremost difference between ancient reading and modern reading

---

39. So R.A. Culpepper, *Anatomy of the Fourth Gospel: A Study in Literary Design* (Foundations and Facets; Philadelphia: Fortress Press, 1983), p. 210.

40. Actual audiences are social phenomena and study of actual audiences requires the use of tools of sociological research. Sociological models may help to identify some characteristics of authorial audiences as well, but because sociological models are designed to reconstruct actual audiences, they are not well suited for this study.

41. P. Rabinowitz, 'Truth in Fiction: A Reexamination of Audiences', *Critical Inquiry* 4 (1977), p. 126. See also, W. Ong, 'The Writer's Audience is Always a Fiction', *Publications of the Modern Language Association of America* 90 (1975), pp. 9-21.

42. Cf. Iser, *Act of Reading*, p. 28.

43. F.W. Danker leads the way among Lukan scholars in constructing one or more audiences inductively from cultural artifacts. See, Danker, *Luke*, pp. 20-21.

is that ancient reading was done aloud. Consequently, ancient authors composed for the ear rather than for the eye. Correspondingly, ancient audiences were skilled listeners. Children educated in Greek would have been exposed to fundamentals of rhetoric at the outset of their instruction.[44] Rhetorical education began in primary school with training in spelling, punctuation, grammar, and figures of speech and with practice in oral reading. Secondary schooling devoted itself to rhetoric, and it was in secondary schools that the five components of rhetoric were taught:

> . . . *invention*, which deals with the planning of a discourse and the argu-
> ments to be used in it; *arrangement*, the composition of the various parts
> into an effective whole; *style*, which involves both choice of words and
> the composition of words into sentences, including the use of figures;
> *memory*, or preparation for delivery; and *delivery*, the rules for control of
> the voice and the use of gestures.[45]

Lectors, that is, persons who read literary works aloud, would be especially skilled listeners. Skilled listening was not, however, limited to literate persons. D.E. Aune observes that the Graeco-Roman population was in large measure a rhetorically-attuned population.

> The literary conventions and styles of the upper classes percolated down
> to lower levels, and they occur in attenuated and simplified forms in popu-
> lar literature. For elevated literary forms and styles were not locked away
> in the libraries and salons of the rich and educated, they were on public
> display. During the first and second centuries CE, public performances of
> rhetoricians were in great demand. . . Listening to the public recitation of
> literary works was also a popular form of entertainment. All levels of the
> population of the Roman world were exposed to the variety of structures
> and styles found in rhetoric, literature, and art that were on public display
> throughout the Empire.[46]

In such a literary environment, aural factors, such as verbal repetition, alliteration, and anaphora, created rhetorical impact. At the same
time, rhetorical tropes could not be overly subtle, since hearers cannot

---

44. On education in the Hellenistic world, see Beavis, *Mark's Audience*, pp. 20-
31; and Kennedy, *New Testament Interpretation*, pp. 8-10. The classic study in the
field is H.I. Marrou, *A History of Education in Antiquity* (London and New York:
Sheed & Ward, 1956).

45. Kennedy, *New Testament Interpretation*, pp. 13-14.

46. D.E. Aune, *The New Testament in Its Literary Environment* (Library of
Early Christianity, 8; Philadelphia: Westminster Press, 1987), pp. 12-13.

pause to study or review text the way silent, solitary readers can.[47]

To summarize, ancient Greek readers were, to state it more aptly, hearers. Furthermore, they would expect stories to display the rhetorical skill of the writer. Indeed, the persuasiveness of discourse, even narrative discourse, depended not only on the truth of the discourse, but also, to no small degree, on how artistically the writer delivered the truth.

Taking into account this broad culturally-drawn image of a Hellenistic audience, we may turn to Luke's narrative for more specific characteristics of the authorial audience. The author's imagined audience, the audience for whom the narrative is designed, will possess literary competence corresponding to literary conventions employed by the author in the narrative. The authorial audience is comprised of the knowledge, beliefs, and linguistic and literary competences the writer assumes his or her readers possess. Note that ancient listeners could acquire linguistic and literary competences as hearers, without necessarily being able to read and write.

We cannot read the mind of the Evangelist. Yet the narrative itself provides clues as to what Luke assumed about those expected to hear the work. Actual audiences may or may not match the writer's assumptions, even though writers naturally try to keep the gap between their authorial audience and real audiences as narrow as possible.[48]

Though reader-response criticisms may be portrayed as promoting a shift from attention to what one needs to know to understand a work to how one actually reads,[49] these are two sides of the same coin. How an audience reads or hears a narrative is contingent upon what the audience knows. In order to draw conclusions about how an audience reads or hears, certain assumptions must be made about the audience. In particular, it is necessary to consider what conditions are needed or what conditions provide the means for a given reading. This study will not separate reading competence and the act of reading. It will

---

47. Kennedy, *New Testament Interpretation*, p. 5.

48. C. Perelman and L. Olbrechts-Tyteca, *The New Rhetoric: A Treatise on Argumentation* (trans. J. Wilkinson and P. Weaver; Notre Dame: University of Notre Dame Press, 1969), pp. 19, 20, and Rabinowitz, 'Truth in Fiction', p. 130. Cf. W.S. Vorster, 'The Reader in the Text: Narrative Material', *Semeia* 48 (1989), pp. 21-39 (35-36).

49. J.R. Knott, Jr, '*Paradise Lost* and the Fit Reader', *Modern Language Quarterly* 45 (June 1984), pp. 123-43 (125).

ask, with respect to the authorial audience, what competence does the
work expect its audience to possess, and then, how does such an
audience read Luke–Acts?

Numerous factors may be taken into consideration in constructing
the authorial audience. In his discussion of the narratee of John's
Gospel, A. Culpepper identifies five areas that may 'characterize the
narratee's knowledge or lack thereof':[50] persons or characters, places,
languages, Judaism, and events.[51] Other areas could have been included,
as Culpepper acknowledges, but these appear to him to be key in John's
Gospel. Such areas can be identified when constructing characteristics
of the authorial audience of Luke–Acts. Most fruitful for this study,
focusing as it does on the character types, is to pursue the authorial
audience's knowledge with respect to linguistic and literary competence.

Linguistic competence refers to the language or languages the audience is expected to know. Literary competence refers to an audience's
familiarity with literary works. In *The Poetics*, for example, Aristotle
assumes that his readers know Greek. Linguistic competence in Greek
is so self-evident, since Aristotle wrote *The Poetics* in Greek, that its
significance may be overlooked. But the importance of this observation appears, for example, when the reader reaches Aristotle's comments on the origin of the label 'comedians' (3.1448a) or his discussion of poetic rhythm (22.1458b). On the other hand, Aristotle does
not assume his audience knows, say, Hebrew. Therefore, the linguistic
competence of the authorial audience of *The Poetics* includes Greek
but does not include Hebrew.

Similarly, Aristotle regularly assumes that his readers have read or
heard Homer. This can be easily demonstrated by an illustration taken
from the *Nicomachean Ethics*:

> Our attitude toward pleasure should be the same as that of the Trojan elders
> was toward Helen, and we should repeat on every occasion the words
> they addressed to her. For if we dismiss pleasure as they dismissed her,
> we shall make fewer mistakes.[52]

---

50. Culpepper, *Anatomy*, p. 212.

51. Culpepper further subdivides Judaism into the areas Old Testament, Jewish
institutions and festivals, and Jewish practices and beliefs. Culpepper, *Anatomy*,
pp. 219-22.

52. Aristotle, *Nicomachean Ethics* 2.9.1109b (as translated by Martin Ostwald in
Aristotle, *Nicomachean Ethics* [The Library of Liberal Arts; Indianapolis and New
York: Bobbs-Merrill, 1962], pp. 50-51).

Clearly, one must know from the *Iliad* what the Trojan elders said in order to follow Aristotle's advice. Therefore, works of Homer fall within the literary competence of the authorial audience of the *Nicomachean Ethics*. Determining the literary competence of the authorial audience means demonstrating what background writings a work assumes its readers know. Again, real audiences may or may not possess the literary competence presumed by the text.

The primary distinction to keep in mind, then, is the distinction between real, flesh-and-blood readers and the authorial audience assumed by the text.[53] The second basic distinction deserving brief comment is not discussed by Rabinowitz, but is implicit in his model: the distinction between the literary competence of the author and the literary competence of the authorial audience. This is, in the case of Luke–Acts, the distinction between what the researcher can reasonably conclude the Evangelist knew and what audience knowledge the Evangelist's work appears to assume. When, for example, a writer copies from another writer, does the borrower assume his or her readers will know the antecedent work? Or does he or she assume, and even hope, that they will be ignorant of it? The point is, that the authorial audience's literary competence ought not be assumed to be equal to the author's literary competence.[54]

Character Types

'Characters are a central element of the story world.'[55] Yet in the

---

53. For more developed discussions of hierarchically-related levels of readers, see Culpepper, *Anatomy*, p. 6; Lanser, *The Narrative Act*, esp. p. 144; Rabinowitz, 'Truth in Fiction', pp. 121-41; Tolbert, *Sowing*, pp. 92-93.

54. W. Bauer ('Introduction', BAGD, p. xxiv) recognized in 1955 the different perspectives of the writer and the reader: 'When Paul speaks of sacrifice, of the wrath of God or the δικαιοσύνη τοῦ θεοῦ, it is quite correct to understand his words from Judaism. But what about his public, who have heard these words before but with different connotations and associations? His hearers certainly did not feel themselves challenged to make an eschatological decision as often as the apostle summoned them to it. With this in mind we might conclude that sometimes there are two meanings for the same passage, one from the standpoint of the writer and another which becomes evident when one puts one's self in the place of the recipient, intellectually and spiritually.' One may quarrel with Bauer's remarks about Paul's hearers, but his overall methodological point is sound.

55. D. Rhoads and D. Michie, *Mark as Story: An Introduction to the Narrative*

fictive world of narrative, not all characters are created equal. E.M. Forster introduced what have become standard categories of characters: round and flat.[56] Yet, as Forster points out further, these are more accurately aspects of a continuum. 'In their purest form, they (i.e. flat characters) are constructed around a single idea or quality: when there is more than one factor in them, we get the beginning of the curve towards the round.'[57] Other descriptive terms may be added as ways of differentiating the relative complexity with which a character is presented, such as static character, dynamic character, or stock character.[58] Yet the principle poles of flat and round are sufficiently descriptive at the beginning of our discussion.

A helpful way to compare characters for their relative roundness or flatness is to explain characters in terms of their character traits and point of view. Rounder characters display a greater number and more varied array of character traits, as well as a more developed point of view. Flatter characters, by contrast, lack character traits and point of view.

Character traits may be assigned to a character by direct definition, as when the (reliable) narrator labels Elizabeth and Zechariah righteous (Lk. 1.6) or when the angel (a reliable character) declares that Jesus will be great (Lk. 1.32).[59] Character traits may also be assigned by indirect presentation, when a trait is not mentioned but must be inferred by the reader from the display of the trait by a character. S. Rimmon-Kenan advances that indirect presentation occurs through action, speech, external appearance, and environment.[60] Thus, readers learn about characters by observing how the character behaves, what the character says, what the character looks like, and what environment or

of a Gospel (Philadelphia: Fortress Press, 1982), p. 101.

56. E.M. Forster, *Aspects of the Novel* (New York: Harcourt, Brace & World, 1927), pp. 67-78.

57. Forster, *Aspects of the Novel*, p. 67.

58. See C.H. Holman, 'Characterization', in *idem, A Handbook to Literature* (Indianapolis: Bobbs-Merrill Educational Publishing, 4th edn, 1980), pp. 75-77; R. Scholes and R. Kellogg, *The Nature of Narrative* (London: Oxford University Press, 1966), p. 164.

59. On characterization by direct definition and indirect presentation, see Rimmon-Kenan, *Narrative Fiction*, pp. 59-67. These categories correspond to W.C. Booth's (*The Rhetoric of Fiction*, 2nd ed. [Chicago and London: University of Chicago Press, 1983], pp. 3-20) 'telling' and 'showing'.

60. Rimmon-Kenan, *Narrative Fiction*, pp. 61-67.

environments surround the character. A character's environment includes the character's physical surroundings, such as general geographical setting and specific place in a room. Environment includes human environment as well, such as a person's family lineage and social class, or the type of company the person keeps.[61] An example of a character trait assigned by indirect representation would be Jesus' 'concern' for the outcast in Luke's Gospel. This is a trait interpreters have inferred on the basis of repeated action on Jesus' part.

A character's point of view offers a second way to explain a character's roundness or flatness. B. Uspensky has shown that an author's point of view may be analyzed according to four 'planes' of point of view: the plane of ideology, the plane of phraseology, the spatial and temporal plane, and the psychological plane.[62] The plane of ideology describes an author's 'general system of viewing the world conceptually'.[63] The plane of phraseology refers to an author's linguistic means of expression, an author's speech characteristics. The spatial and temporal plane is the plane upon which action takes place. The psychological plane is the plane of thoughts, feelings, emotions, and motives.

Although Uspensky directs his attention to analysis of the point of view of a work's author, the planes Uspensky enunciates may serve as helpful tools in describing characterization. Characters may be described on at least one of these planes, and, I would contend, the more completely a character may be described on these planes, the more 'round' the character. The proof of this contention lies in how useful point of view actually is in explaining characters. M. Powell has successfully used Uspensky's 'plane of ideology' to provide insight into the Pharisees in Luke's Gospel.[64]

61. Rimmon-Kenan's categories for indirect presentation of character traits overlap B. Uspensky's (*A Poetics of Composition: The Structure of the Artistic Text and Typology of a Compositional Form* [trans. V. Zavarin and S. Wittig; Berkeley: University of California Press, 1973]) planes of point of view, which will be discussed below. This overlap is more significant at a theoretical level than at a practical level. Since this study is aimed toward the practical matter of interpretation, this overlap need not be considered here.

62. Uspensky, *Poetics of Composition*, pp. 6-63. Uspensky grants a certain arbitrariness to this division of planes. For the purposes of this study, however, this division provides an adequate heuristic measure of the relative roundness or flatness of a character.

63. Uspensky, *Poetics of Composition*, p. 8.

64. M.A. Powell, 'The Religious Leaders in Luke: A Literary Critical Study',

It should be kept in mind that no actual human being is ever so simple as the roundest of characters in a narrative. No narrative, not even modern narratives intended to be biography, can ever display the fullness of personality traits, the interweaving of relationships, the points of view, the predictability and unpredictability of actions, all of the enormous complexities that make up a human being. Characterization, then, is always fictive (and rhetorical). That is, characterization proceeds on the basis of how it serves the author's purposes. The author decides in one way or another how to present a character, whether the character will be one-, two-, or three-dimensional. Since no author can, or even desires, to describe everything about all persons, characterization is a fictive device. Persons in narrative are characterized to the degree the author needs to tell the author's story. In the Gospel of Luke, Jesus is the roundest of the characters. Yet Luke's presentation of Jesus is also fictive, because, despite all of the advantages of narrative over other forms of written and spoken discourse for presenting a person, Luke's presentation of Jesus is the product of Luke's creative choosing and organizing of narrative material.

Character traits and point of view suffice as heuristic categories for discussing characterization of the captive, the shattered, the blind, the deaf mute, the lame, lepers, the maimed, the dead, and the poor in Luke–Acts. Paradoxically, the more the critic can say about a character's traits and point of view, the less sufficient as descriptive tools these two categories become.[65] A truly complex character in narrative is more than the sum of traits and cannot be reduced to a point of view.[66] Truly complex characters are products of modern narrative, however, and are not found in ancient writing.[67]

Lukan interpreters today must recognize that characterization in ancient literature differs significantly from characterization in modern literature. Luke–Acts is ancient literature and conforms to ancient conventions of characterization. From our modern perspective, ancient

JBL 109 (1990), pp. 93-110. See also, *idem*, 'The Religious Leaders in Matthew: A Literary Critical Approach' (PhD dissertation, Union Theological Seminary in Virginia, 1988).

65. For further discussions of characterization in biblical narrative, see Alter, *The Art of Biblical Narrative*, esp. pp. 116-17, and Darr, *On Building Character*, pp. 37-59 (esp. pp. 42-47).

66. T.M. Leitch, *What Stories Are*, pp. 157-58.

67. Darr, *On Building Character*, p. 48.

characters lack profundity and realism compared to modern characters. If individuality and psychological depth are the standards by which literary characters are judged, ancient characters will inevitably be deemed wanting. For, as Scholes and Kellogg state, 'characters in primitive stories are invariably "flat", "static", and quite "opaque"'.[68] Modern characters, however, are products of our cultural paradigm, with its emphasis on individuality and psychological depth.

This pivotal difference between ancient and modern characterization is a difference of kind, however, and not one of quality. The difference has to do with the distinction between characterization that is representational and characterization that is illustrative, a distinction that is well known in literary circles. As Scholes and Kellogg explain,

> Illustration differs from representation in narrative art in that it does not seek to reproduce actuality but to present selected aspects of the actual, essences referable for their meaning not to historical, psychological, or sociological truth but to ethical and metaphysical truth.[69]

68. Scholes and Kellogg, *The Nature of Narrative*, p. 164. To illustrate this point, Scholes and Kellogg point to Homer's Achilles, who 'is presented to us almost exclusively in terms of one facet of life—the emotion of anger' (*The Nature of Narrative*, p. 161). In this section of their book, Scholes and Kellogg are arguing that Homer's narrative of Achilles' actions after the death of Achilles' companion, Patroclus, is mimetic in its own way. Though the hero Achilles is hardly an ordinary human being, the authors contend that important aspects of the scene in which Achilles bemoans the death of Patroclus and vows merciless, deadly vengeance upon the Trojans are mimetic: 'Death is common to all men' and 'The scene is mimetic in its "rightness"' (*The Nature of Narrative*, p. 163). Scholes and Kellogg explain that 'the blend of contempt and pity, of hostility and sympathy' expressed by Achilles 'is a very human blend, and Achilles' turn of thought. . . is a very human turn of thought, mimetic in the convincingness of its humanity' (*The Nature of Narrative*, p. 163). The authors' argument assumes that literary power adheres to mimesis, and consequently they feel constrained to display mimetic features of ancient literature to defend it. Scholes and Kellogg's larger point is that ancient characterization is merely different from modern characterization, not inferior to it. (See *The Nature of Narrative*, p. 161). Their point is well taken. See also F.W. Burnette, 'Characterization and Reader Construction of Characters in the Gospels', *Semeia* 63 (1993), pp. 3-28. For example, Burnette ('Characterization', p. 19) contends, 'Reading conventions for character construction in ancient literature (and drama) preferred indirect characterization, and personages were for the most part typical and flat.'

69. Scholes and Kellogg, *The Nature of Narrative*, p. 88. Quoted also by Tolbert, *Sowing the Gospel*, p. 76.

Ancient writers strove for truth in a manner that gave precedence to suprahistorical ethical and metaphysical truth. Correspondingly, in the words of Darr, in ancient literature

> narrative characters—even those in historical works—were largely illustrative, symbolic, and typed, rather than representational, mimetic, and heterodox as they tend to be in modern novels.[70]

It is precisely the difference between characterization in ancient narrative and characterization in modern narrative that requires that we not be totally content with Forster's designations of 'flat' and 'round' when these designations are applied to Luke–Acts. The shortcoming of Forster's designations is that they do not express the difference between illustrative characterization and representational characterization. Therefore, when Lukan characters are assessed along a continuum from relative roundness to relative flatness, it should be borne in mind that the continuum will naturally be narrower in Luke–Acts than it would be in modern writings, because of the nature of ancient characterization. With ancient characterization, there are varying degrees of flatness.

Yet even among ancient characters there are distinctions to be made. In Luke–Acts, the captive, the shattered, the blind, the deaf mute, the lame, lepers, the maimed, the dead, and the poor appear as types.[71] That is, they are not characters per se, not even flat or one-dimensional characters. They represent a literary class or kind of person in a stereotypical manner. Chapter 4 will draw attention to the fact that in Luke's Gospel these groups are assigned few character traits and display no point of view.

---

70. Darr, *On Building Character*, p. 48. See also Tolbert, *Sowing*, pp. 77-78. Theophrastus presents and discusses each of his characters on the basis of a single quality, such as 'arrogance' (ὑπερηφανία), 'cowardice' (δειλία), 'boorishness' (ἀγροικία), or 'pretentiousness' (ἀλαζονεία). Theophrastus, *The Characters* (ed. and trans. J.M. Edmonds; LCL; London: Heinemann; New York: Putnam's Sons, 1929).

71. Two generations ago, R. Bultmann (*Synoptic Tradition*, p. 67) called attention to types in apophthegms: 'For the most part those who figure in the stories are types, Scribes, Pharisees, disciples, publicans, inhabitants of Nazareth, etc. Dibelius is right when he speaks of collective treatment. But even individual persons who are indirectly characterized are in essence types.' See also *Synoptic Tradition*, p. 308. However, Bultmann did not pursue this literary observation.

Types are among the 'schematized aspects of the text'[72] that need to be filled out or 'concretized'[73] by the reader. One reason for the lack of consensus regarding the interpretation of the poor in Luke–Acts lies in the nature of the type as a schematicized aspect of the text.[74] The type invites concretization. The art of interpreting the type, however, is to concretize it without so loading it with connotations that it means everything, or so metaphorizing it that it has no link with its lexigraphical connotation. When directed to an intertext, readers fill out types by reading them through the lens of literary conventions established in the intertext. An audience-oriented, sequential interpretation asks how the use of this type, within conventional parameters, influences the reader's knowledge, sympathy, and judgment, that is, elicits convention-based cognitive and attitudinal responses.

Before turning to the Gospel of Luke, however, the literary competence of Luke's authorial audience from which our conventional types will be drawn must be established, and those types must be detailed. Chapter 4 addresses the former task. Chapter 5 addresses the latter.

72. This terminology is Iser's.

73. R. Ingarden, *The Cognition of the Literary Work of Art* (trans. R.A. Crowly and K.R. Olsen; Evanston: Northwestern University Press, 1973), p. 53. This work was originally published in Polish in 1937.

74. Hollenbach ('Defining Rich and Poor', pp. 59-60) is right when he cites several passages in the Gospel in which, he concludes, the meaning of the poor is ambiguous.

Chapter 4

THE SEPTUAGINT AS LUKAN INTERTEXT

I argued in Chapter 3 that a key activity of the reader in the reading process is the mental act of concretizing indeterminate aspects of the text. In other words, audiences fill in the 'gaps' in the text. Chapter 3 then suggested that the lack of intratextual description of the captive, the shattered, the blind, the deaf mute, the lame, lepers, the maimed, the dead, and the poor creates a gap. Audiences fill gaps, Chapter 3 asserted, by drawing on their extra-textual repertoire. An audience's extra-textual repertoire may include not only historical, geographical, and societal knowledge, but also familiarity with literature. Chapter 3 then argued for constructing Luke's authorial audience on the basis of the linguistic and literary competence the text assumes its hearer will possess. Chapter 3 went on to describe intertextuality and to raise the possibility that Luke expects his audience to concretize the captive, the blind, the poor, and so on by reference to an intertext, the LXX.

Chapter 4 now presents the argument that Luke's authorial audience should concretize the captive, the blind, the poor, and the others on the basis of the LXX. First, this chapter intends to establish that Luke assumes that his audience is familiar with the LXX. As a corollary, it will be argued that Hebrew terminology for the poor is irrelevant to interpretation of the poor when interpretation is oriented to Luke's authorial audience. Secondly, this chapter will argue that Luke prompts the authorial audience to invoke the LXX to understand the captive, the blind, the poor, and so on.

The Linguistic and Literary Competence
of Luke's Authorial Audience

An audience-oriented, sequential approach to Luke–Acts can bring together two tendencies of biblical scholarship: the lexigraphical move-ment to view New Testament words and phrases as ordinary Greek

words and phrases, led by Adolf Deissmann, and post-redaction critical efforts to treat Luke–Acts as a whole. With respect to the linguistic
competence of Luke–Acts's authorial audience, there is little to
dispute. Clearly, the authorial audience understands Greek, even if
hearers are illiterate. Beyond this, however, nothing in Luke–Acts
demands or even suggests that knowledge of any language other than
Greek is expected.[1]

This is not to deny that there are so-called Semitisms in Luke–Acts.[2]
These, however, are best thought of as 'Septuagintisms'. Students
investigating the translation techniques of the various LXX translators
will certainly be interested in what Hebrew word lies behind a
particular Greek word, just as they will be interested in how a Hebrew
syntactical construction was rendered into Greek. But the interpreter
of Luke–Acts must recognize when words and expressions in Luke–
Acts can be clarified by the LXX, and distinguish between this and true
Aramaisms or Hebraisms. For the audience-oriented critic constructing Luke's authorial audience, Hebrew or Aramaic words would
only be of interest if a Greek word in Luke's writing were a neolo-
gism, were simply a transliteration of Hebrew, or made absolutely no
sense as a Greek word in its context. In other words, one would look
for a Hebrew antecedent only where knowledge of Hebrew would be
required in order to make sense of the word. I know of no instance in
Luke–Acts where this is the case.

'Semitic' syntax raises a similar issue.[3] Any appeal to the need for

---

1. On what languages narratees know, see M.A. Piwowarczyk, 'The Narrative
and the Situation of Enunciation: A Reconsideration of Prince's Theory', *Genre* 9
(1976), pp. 161-77.

2. 'Semitism' is an imprecise term. On distinguishing between Hebraisms and
Aramaisms, see G.H.R. Horsley, *New Documents Illustrating Early Christianity*.
V. *Linguistic Essays* (NSW, Australia: Macquarrie University Press, 1989), p. 27.
For this study of Luke–Acts, such fine distinctions are immaterial because Luke–Acts
presumes familiarity with neither Hebrew nor Aramaic.

3. For example, καὶ ἐγένετο followed by an apodotic καὶ (Lk. 8.1). For
further examples of 'Semitic' syntax, see J.W. Voelz, 'The Language of the New
Testament', in H. Temporini and W. Haase (eds.), *Aufstieg und Niedergang der
Römischen Welt: Geschichte und Kultur Roms im Spiegel der Neueren Forschung*
(Berlin: de Gruyter, 1984), II.25.2, pp. 893-977 (959-64). Voelz distinguishes two
categories: 'frequent locutions which are possible in Greek but which correspond
closely to common Semitic constructions' (p. 959) and 'locutions which are poor
Greek and, therefore, almost certainly translations of Semitic constructions' (p. 962).

recourse to Hebrew or Aramaic for interpretation must first reckon with the LXX. To the LXX-competent audience, 'Semitic' syntax, if it is present in the LXX, makes sense as Greek, perhaps as idiosyncratic Greek, but nevertheless as Greek.

We are on the firmest ground when constructing an authorial audience when we hold to the strictest criterion for linguistic competence: the authorial audience possesses the reading competence the text requires. To move beyond what the text requires to competences deemed desirable (and desirable competences invariably approach the critic's competences) makes the critical endeavor more speculative and less precise.[4] Consequently, exegesis that adheres to the linguistic competence of Luke's authorial audience will not attempt to recover supposed Hebrew nuances to Luke's Greek words, phrases, and images.[5]

In large measure, this conclusion is a return to the lexigraphical stance put forward by Deissmann, who wrote, 'The meaning of a Septuagint word cannot be deduced from the original which it translates or replaces but only from other remains of the Greek language'.[6] Deissmann used the word ἱλαστήριον to illustrate that LXX words mean what they mean in Greek, not what the Hebrew words meant that they may have translated. Though ἱλαστήριον was used in place of the Hebrew word for 'lid of the ark of the covenant', ἱλαστήριον does not thereby mean 'lid of the ark of the covenant'; it still means 'object of expiation or propitiation'. 'In choosing the word ἱλαστήριον to denote the lid of the ark of the covenant the Septuagint has not translated the concept of 'lid', but has replaced it by another concept which brings out the sacred purpose of the ark.'[7] Students of lexicography

4.   Lack of conclusiveness about Lukan audiences has led recent scholarship to imply a general Hellenistic or Graeco-Roman reader with an ever broadening cultural and literary background. See, e.g., J. Darr, 'Glorified', p. 129; D.P. Moessner, *Lord of the Banquet: The Literary and Theological Significance of the Lukan Travel Narrative* (Minneapolis: Fortress Press, 1989), pp. 7-8, 83.

5.   With similar reasoning, J. Schneider (*Die Taufe im Neuen Testament* [Stuttgart: Kohlhammer, 1952], p. 37) questions appeals to a Hebraic understanding of οἶκος to support an argument for the baptism of little children in the New Testament. Schneider's reasoning is author oriented: would the writer Luke, being so Hellenistic, have grasped Hebrew connotations of a Greek term?

6.   G.A. Deissmann, *The Philology of the Greek Bible: Its Present and Future* (trans. L.R.M. Strachan; London: Hodder & Stoughton, 1908), p. 89.

7.   Deissmann, *Philology*, pp. 92-93.

are aware of this issue.[8] New Testament interpreters however, are only beginning to heed again Deissmann's insistence on reading Old Testament Greek as Greek.[9] Πτωχός in particular continues to be read by Lukan students in terms of proposed Hebrew vocabulary, particularly *ani* and *anaw*,[10] this despite the fact that the majority of interpreters would still contend that Luke's readers were gentiles.[11]

The compelling conclusion, then, is that the linguistic competence of Luke's authorial audience is limited to Greek. With the matter of linguistic competence now clarified, the next subject to be considered is literary competence. The task here is to demonstrate that Luke's authorial audience must know the LXX.

The strictest criterion for establishing the literary competence of the authorial audience is: 'What extra-textual literary competence does the text require?' The mere presence of citations from the Greek Bible is not enough to demonstrate that audience familiarity with the LXX is expected by the work. Even 'proof from prophecy' does not demonstrate LXX competence of the authorial audience.[12] 'Proof from prophecy' does provide a clue to the function of particular LXX quotes, for example, to heighten Jesus' authority in the narrative. But such a

8. J.A.L. Lee, *A Lexical Study of the Septuagint Version of the Pentateuch* (SBLSCS, 14; Chico, CA: Scholars Press, 1983), p.8: 'L[iddell] S[cott] J[ones] includes a large amount of LXX material, but as is mostly well known, is often in error. A particular fault is its tendency to equate the LXX word with the Hebrew it translates when there is no good reason to do so. In some instances, the meaning given seems to be adopted directly from one of the English versions of the Old Testament.'

9. See, e.g., S. Ringe, *Jesus, Liberation, and the Biblical Jubilee*, p. 34.

10. E.g. Seccombe, *Possessions*, esp. pp. 24-43; Hoyt, 'The Poor', pp. 49-51, 139 (cf. 16). So, O'Toole, *Unity*, p. 110: '[F]ew authorities deny that the Jewish notion of anawim forms the background for the narrative of the beatitudes'. See also O'Toole, *Unity*, p. 87, regarding analogous use of the Hebrew דבר. Other interpreters display ambivalence about applying Hebrew terminology to discussions of 'the poor' in Luke–Acts, e.g., Esler, *Community*, pp. 180-81.

11. For reviews of scholarly constructions of Luke's audience in terms of Jew and Gentile, see P. Meierding, 'Jews and Gentiles: A Narrative and Rhetorical Analysis of the Implied Audience in Acts' (ThD dissertation, Luther Northwestern Theological Seminary, 1992), pp. 15-31; M.A. Moscato, 'Current Theories Regarding the Audience of Luke–Acts', *CurTM* 3 (1976), pp. 355-61; and Powell, *What Are They Saying About Luke?*, pp. 51-59.

12. P. Schubert, 'The Structure and Significance of Luke 24', in W. Eltester (ed.), *Neutestamentliche Studien für Rudolf Bultmann* (BZNW, 21; Berlin: Töpelmann, 1954), pp. 165-86.

function would require only that the LXX be recognized by the authorial audience to be authoritative within the narrative world of Luke–Acts; it would not require that the authorial audience know the LXX.

Yet it is possible on other bases to demonstrate relatively quickly that the narrative does assume an LXX-competent audience, even when applying the strictest criterion. The argument may be made on several grounds: unclarified references to historic characters in the drama of Israel's story; unclarified references to particular biblical episodes; biblical quotations that require the audience to recognize the passage as biblical without help from the narrator; an implied warning against erroneous scriptural interpretation; and expressions that are explicable only to someone familiar with the LXX. The following paragraphs offer observations from Luke–Acts corresponding to these grounds.

Numerous passages contain unclarified references to historic characters in the drama of Israel's story. Consider, for example, Luke's matter-of-fact mention of the division of Abijah and daughters of Aaron (Lk. 1.5), Elijah (1.17), Gabriel (1.19), David (1.27, 32), Jacob (1.33), Abraham (1.55), David again (1.70), Asher (2.36), Abraham again (3.8), and Lot's wife (17.32). In 17.32, Jesus says simply, 'Remember Lot's wife'. These references to biblical persons would be a mystery to hearers unfamiliar with Israel's biblical story. Luke offers the audience no help in the narrative, but rather relies on his envisioned audience's knowledge of the LXX. Connections among Jacob, Abijah, Aaron, David, and others, and the cohesive wholeness that incorporates them, are made by the story in Israel's Scriptures. For Luke's writing to be coherent, especially but not exclusively the opening chapters, Luke's audience must make those connections and form the whole.

Luke 4.24-29 and 17.26-29 also presuppose recognition of biblical characters: Elijah and Elisha, and Noah and Lot respectively. In addition, these passages presuppose familiarity with particular biblical episodes involving these characters. Luke 4.24-29 implies that not only the synagogue-goers in Nazareth who are listening to Jesus, but also the readers of the narrative who observe the unfolding drama should recall the biblical stories of Elijah's visit to the widow Zarephath and Elisha's encounter with Naaman. Luke 17.26-29 relies on the audience's recollection of the sudden acts of punishment God meted out to the world in the days of Noah and to Sodom at the time of Lot.

In order for some scriptural quotations in the Gospel to be read as Scripture, the audience must be familiar with the LXX. Not all quotations from the LXX in Luke–Acts require LXX competence to be understood, though it may be argued that LXX competence is often presupposed in order to make the narrative fully understood or persuasive.[13] Yet the LXX is quoted in Lk. 23.34b and 23.46 such as to imply LXX competence. In neither of these cases is the LXX quotation preceded by an introductory formula, such as the common 'as it was written', or signaled by the context to be Scripture.[14] In Lk. 23.34b the narrator weaves Ps. 21.19 seamlessly into the action of the episode: 'and they cast lots to divide his garments'. In Lk. 23.46, Jesus' final words recite Ps. 30.6: 'into your hands I commend my spirit'. In both of these cases, the clauses as scriptural clauses underscore how thoroughly scripture-based the characterization of Jesus is in Luke's Gospel.

Luke 24.25-27 and 24.44-47, the classic 'proof from prophecy' texts, suggest still another way the narrative presupposes LXX competence. In these passages, the narrator summarizes the risen Jesus' teaching activity as scriptural interpretation: 'beginning with Moses and all the prophets, he interpreted to them the things concerning him in all the Scriptures' (24.27) and 'then he opened their minds to understand the Scriptures' (24.45). Within the narrative world of Luke–Acts, the narrator's comments establish that Jesus demonstrates to the two disciples on the road that the Scriptures guarantee that Jesus' death and resurrection are the will and plan of God.[15] To the Gospel's auditors, the narrator stresses the importance of correct interpretation of Scripture. We may see this stress not only in what the narrator says, but also in how the narrator says it. In 24.27, the narrator adds to Jesus' direct discourse and, in 24.45, actually interrupts Jesus' discourse to lift up as legitimate interpretation, interpretation that points to Jesus.[16] By implication, the narrator alerts the authorial audience to the prospect, not of lack of familiarity with Scripture, but of imperceptive interpretation of Scripture that does not recognize Jesus' messiahship foretold in Scripture.

13. For example, the scriptural proofs employed by Jesus and the devil in Lk. 4.4-12, Jesus' rebuke of the sellers in the Temple in Lk. 19.46, and the speeches in Acts. See Meierding, 'The Implied Audience in Acts', p. 155.

14. See also, Lk. 13.19b, 27, 35; 23.30.

15. Schubert, 'Luke 24', p. 176.

16. See also Lk. 24.32: 'Our hearts burned, did they not, as he walked with us and opened the Scriptures to us?'

The question of whether the presence of Septuagintal language in Luke–Acts implies that Luke's audience is expected to be familiar with the LXX raises the thorny issue of so-called 'Jewish Greek' or 'biblical Greek'. Despite the fact that Deissmann punctured the mystique of a supposedly special biblical language, debate over the issue continues.[17] The issue of 'Jewish Greek' is too complex to delve into in this study, and in-depth treatment of it would take me far afield. But mention of the issue is necessary for the purposes of this study. To summarize briefly, the issue has to do with the extent to which one can (or cannot) speak of a dialect or strain of Greek grammatically and philologically peculiar to the LXX, the New Testament, and other Jewish and Jewish–Christian literature.[18] Deissmann's lasting contribution to philological method has been the case he made for the correctness of looking first for the common, ordinary Greek meanings of biblical words and applying those meanings before resorting to idiosyncratic meanings drawn from Hebrew or Aramaic counterparts. But the question of how much Septuagintal Greek may have actually filtered into Greek language being used in the first century remains unanswered, and probably unanswerable. We can never know for certain whether expressions that to our knowledge are present only in the LXX prior to the writing of the New Testament are in fact absolutely unique to Scripture. This prevents us from drawing unequivocal conclusions about the audience competence assumed by the use of these expressions.

Nevertheless, Luke–Acts contains expressions that may be cautiously cited as evidence of a LXX-competent authorial audience.[19] For example, the phrase 'uncircumcised in hearts and ears' (Acts 7.51) comes from the LXX.[20] Uncircumcised hearts and ears are undesirable. Circumcised hearts and ears are what God desires. But without familiarity with the LXX, the reader would be baffled as to why God

17. A modern proponent of the theory that there existed a 'biblical Greek' dialect is N. Turner. See N. Turner, *Grammatical Insights into the New Testament* (Edinburgh: T. & T. Clark, 1965), esp. p. 183.

18. J.W. Voelz ('Language of the New Testament', pp. 894-930) provides an excellent summary of the debate. For discussions treating Luke–Acts specifically, see F.L. Horton, Jr, 'Reflections on the Semitisms of Luke–Acts', in C.H. Talbert (ed.), *Perspectives on Luke–Acts* (Danville, VA: Association of Baptist Professors of Religion, 1978), pp. 1-23; Fitzmyer, *Luke I–IX*, pp. 113-25.

19. No attempt is made here to provide a complete list. Such an attempt would be a major project in itself.

20. Lev. 26.41; Jer. 6.10; 9.25; Ezek. 44.7, 9.

would want 'mutilated' hearts and ears. To take a second example, much has been written about the idiom λαμβάνειν πρόσωπον (Lk. 20.21), which means 'to show partiality or favoritism'.[21] J. Fitzmyer rightly concludes that this phrase 'would have been unintelligible in classical or Hellenistic Greek writing'.[22] Understanding it requires LXX competence.

For an illustration of Septuagintal language evident in Lukan vocabulary, consider βάτος (βάδος). To read this as a unit of liquid (Lk. 16.6) and not as a fish or as a bush requires LXX competence (2 Esdr. 7.22). Since our interest is in constructing an authorial audience, it is worth noting how Luke and Josephus handle this word differently. Josephus also mentions this word as a unit of liquid, but in contrast to Luke, Josephus thenexplains it in terms of Roman measure.[23] Luke assumes his audience will understand βάτος without explanation. Josephus's handling of the word does not imply that he expects his audience to be familiar with the LXX. Luke's handling does.[24]

---

21. 'Πρόσωπον', BAGD, pp. 720-21. It is surprising that Horsley's otherwise exacting study (*Linguistic Essays*, p. 28) fails to mention the presence of this phrase in Luke's Gospel when Horsley discusses the relationship between this LXX phrase and New Testament words.

22. J. Fitzmyer, *The Gospel According to Luke X–XXIV* (AB, 28A; Garden City, NY: Doubleday, 1985), p. 1295.

23. *Ant*, 8.57.

24. In an extensive study of Lukan citations from Scripture, T. Holtz (*Untersuchungen über die alttestamentlichen Zitate bei Lukas* [TU, 104; Berlin: Akademie Verlag, 1968], pp. 169-70) concludes that Luke was certainly not familiar with legal portions of the Pentateuch, perhaps not familiar with the Pentateuch in general, and probably not familiar with historical portions of the Old Testament. If Holtz's conclusions were persuasive, they would have a bearing on assessments of Luke's authorial audience. But there are at least three flaws in Holtz's study, all of which stem from his methodological commitment to redaction criticism: (1) his dismissal of Luke chs. 1 and 2; (2) his failure to account for Luke's use of characters and episodes drawn from the LXX, such as Elijah and Elisha in Luke ch. 4; (3) his devaluation of material Luke shares with Matthew and Mark.

A growing number of scholars state or imply that Luke's intended readers had to be at least acquainted with the Old Testament: e.g., Darr, *On Building Character*, p. 28; J. Dupont, *Études sur les Actes des Apôtres* (LD, 45; Paris: Cerf, 1967), esp. pp. 245-82; Esler, *Community*, p. 25; and R.L. Maddox, *The Purpose of Luke–Acts*, p. 14. Also of interest in this regard is a comment by R. Bultmann (*Theology of the New Testament* [trans. K. Grobel; 2 vols.; New York: Charles Scribner's Sons, 1951, 1955], I, p.95) regarding other New Testament writings: 'The episto-

There appears to be, then, sufficient evidence from the Gospel material itself to conclude that the authorial audience of Luke–Acts is versed in the LXX.[25]

Steering the Audience to the Septuagint

The purpose of this section is to show that the rhetoric of the narrative itself prompts Luke's authorial audience to concretize the captive, the shattered, the blind, the deaf mute, the lame, lepers, the maimed, the dead, and the poor on the basis of the LXX. The goal is to demonstrate that by the time Luke introduces these character types into the narrative in Luke 4, the audience has been led to use the LXX to characterize them. The audience of Luke–Acts first encounters these character types at Lk. 4.18. This reference is pivotal, because it produces the formative characterization of the character types. Subsequent references to them are read against the background of the first reference. This section will not attempt to identify all of the textual signals that lead the audience to associate Luke's narrative with the LXX. Further study into other rhetorical devices used by the author of Luke–Acts to direct the audience to the LXX would confirm the thesis of this study.[26]

lary literature of the New Testament, with the exception of the Johannine epistles, shows that all the way through a certain familiarity with the Old Testament is assumed in the readers'. Note, too, Bultmann's (*Theology of the New Testament*, I, pp. 97-98) use of the LXX in his discussion of λαός.

25. After one determines that the LXX is the literary body to turn to, the question of what form of the LXX to use confronts the interpreter. The question of what Greek Old Testament was the Scripture of Luke's authorial audience is a problem both of the history of the LXX and of the text of Luke–Acts itself. There is great uncertainty about how the LXX developed, at what pace the LXX developed into a 'canon' of writings, and precisely what writings should be included in the LXX. Variations among the forms of the Greek Old Testament available do not affect this study because no text to be discussed is materially involved in textual disputes. Therefore, a discussion of LXX text types and history is not necessary. For discussions summarizing the issues involved and wrestling with reconstruction of the history and development of the LXX, see R.W. Klein, *Textual Criticism of the Old Testament: The Septuagint after Qumran* (Guides to Biblical Scholarship; Philadelphia: Fortress Press, 1974); R.A. Kraft, 'Septuagint: Earliest Greek versions', *IDBSup*, pp. 807-15; and the still valuable H.B. Swete, *An Introduction to the Old Testament in Greek* (rev. R.R. Ottley; Cambridge: Cambridge University Press, 1914; repr.; Peabody, MA: Hendrickson, 1989).

26. Avenues of further study include inquiry into the rhetorical effects and charac-

Luke's formal preface (1.1-4) has been likened to the prefaces in classical historical works of Herodotus, Thucydides, and Polybius, as well as to prefaces of other Hellenistic writing. It is widely noted that by opening his Gospel in this fashion, Luke deliberately places his work into the context of sophisticated Greek literature.[27] Moreover it is universally recognized that with Lk. 1.5, the writer abruptly changes his writing style.[28] The rhetorical effect of this feature should not be overlooked. The abrupt shift signals the presence of an intertext, and the specific style adopted at Lk. 1.5, that is, Septuagintal style, signals that the intertext is the LXX.[29] By his Septuagintal writing style and by the way he draws attention to that style as a style deliberately chosen, Luke indicates that the LXX is the background against which his account is to be read. That is, Luke's rhetoric invites his readers to look for patterns and conventions that arise out of the LXX.

If we want to read Luke–Acts as Luke intended them to be read, then we will look at opening episodes of the Gospel as the literary introduction to the narrative, for these episodes set the tone and direction for what follows.[30] Hellenistic writers laid the groundwork for

terization techniques of Luke's angelophanies, testimonies of Spirit-filled prophets and prophetesses, and poetry/hymns.

27. See, e.g., Danker, *Jesus and the New Age*, pp. 3-5, 23-26; and Fitzmyer, *Luke I–IX*, pp. 287-90.

28. See, e.g., W.K.L. Clarke, 'The Use of the Septuagint in Acts', in F.J.F. Jackson and K. Lake (gen eds.), *The Beginnings of Christianity, Part I, The Acts of the Apostles*. II. *Prolegomena II: Criticism* (London: Macmillan, 1920–33; repr.; Grand Rapids: Baker Book House, 1979), pp. 66-105 (105); Fitzmyer, *Luke I–IX*, pp. 308-309; Tannehill, *Narrative Unity*, I, pp. 15-19.

29. On 'biblical imitation' in Luke–Acts, see H.J. Cadbury, *The Making of Luke–Acts* (New York: Macmillan, 1927; repr.; London: SPCK, 1961), pp. 122-26.

30. Critical scholarship in the past tended to treat Luke 1–2 as something of an addendum to the whole work, Luke–Acts. These chapters were considered to be literarily discontinuous and theologically inconsistent with what follows. Hans Conzelmann's immensely influential interpretation of Luke, in *The Theology of St Luke*, is an outstanding example of an interpretation that sweepingly dismisses chs. 1 and 2. When Conzelmann does refer to these introductory chapters, it is usually to point to contrasts between them and what follows. (See Conzelmann, *The Theology of Luke*, esp. pp. 24, 118, 172, and 183 n. 2.) More recently, however, numerous studies have criticized isolating these first two chapters from the rest of the work and have persuasively emphasized the connectedness of Luke 1–2 to the rest of Luke–Acts. In one early study in this vein, Paul Minear ('Luke's Use of the Birth Stories', in Keck and Martyn [eds.], *Studies in Luke–Acts*, pp. 111-30 [esp. pp. 120-

The Blind, the Lame, and the Poor

their entire effort in their opening scenes, and at the outset had a
vision of the whole literary work in mind. The Septuagintal resonances in Luke 1-4 are not confined to syntax and vocabulary, though
these resonances are certainly present and significant. Episodes in
these chapters of the Gospel are narrated according to formal patterns
that are thoroughly Septuagintal, as can be seen by comparing the
episodes with literary conventions Robert Alter has identified in the
Old Testament.[31] A look at these episodes will show that Luke has so
permeated the first four chapters of the Gospel with Septuagintal
resonances that Luke's authorial audience is predisposed to interpret
the captive, the blind, the poor, and so on from the LXX.

According to Alter,

> The paradigmatic biblical story... starts with a few brief statements that
> name the principal character or characters, locate them geographically,
> identify significant family relationships, and in some instances provide a
> succinct moral, social, or physical characterization of the protagonist.[32]

Scene after scene in the first three chapters of the Gospel exhibits these
opening elements of 'the paradigmatic biblical story'. In Lk. 1.5-7,

---

25]) summarizes points of continuity. Minear's summary is too long to summarize
here, but let me mention a few key points. There is stylistic continuity, such as common use of the introductory phrase Ἐγένετο δὲ, e.g. Lk. 1.8; 2.1, 6; 3.21; 5.1; 6.1,
6, 12; Acts 4.5; 5.7; 8.1. Throughout Luke–Acts, 'Luke's thought gravitates toward
and is orientated around strategic speeches, citations, and hymns'. There is a 'reliance
upon epiphany and angels. The entire corpus gives many examples of complicated
and interrelated sets of visions (e.g. to Elizabeth [sic] and Mary, to Peter and
Cornelius, to Paul and Ananias).' There is 'the accent upon the fulfillment of God's
promise'. 'There is a typical Lukan syndrome descriptive of the true response to
God's redemption. It includes hearing, turning, repenting, praying, being forgiven,
rejoicing' (Minear, 'Luke's Use of the Birth Stories', pp. 115-18.) These common
qualities identified by Minear confirm the view that to treat Luke 1–2 as part of a
coherent whole is not to force an artificial consistency on the narrative. In addition,
literary considerations that imply a consistent authorial audience, such as the fact that
in the Gospel unclarified references to characters in the LXX extend beyond chs. 1
and 2, add weight to the argument for the integrity of the entire Gospel.

31. Alter, *The Art of Biblical Narrative*. Alter's work pertains to the Hebrew
Scriptures, but his insights which will be cited in this study are applicable to the LXX
as well. To avoid the potential confusion that using the terms 'Hebrew Scriptures' or
'Jewish Scriptures' may bring to this present discussion, this study will use the
designation 'Old Testament' as a convenience, without any intended prejudice.

32. Alter, *The Art of Biblical Narrative*, p. 80.

Zechariah, who is the principal character in the first scene, is identified along with his wife Elizabeth. They are located geographically in Judea, and temporally 'in the days of Herod' (1.5). Four other relevant biographical notations are provided. Zechariah is a priest; both Zechariah and Elizabeth are righteous; both are old; and Elizabeth is barren. Luke's introduction of Mary also fits the pattern of the paradigmatic biblical story, even though the information Luke gives about Mary is relatively sparse. Like Zechariah, she is located geographically—in the less pretentious region of Galilee, however—and her partner, Joseph, is named. The birth of Jesus is introduced in Lk. 2.1-5 according to the biblical paradigm. So, too, are the temple scenes (2.25; 2.36-37; and 2.41-42) and the introduction to John's ministry (3.1-3). Luke's account of Jesus' visit to the synagogue in Nazareth also opens in the form of this biblical convention (4.16), even though the form is abbreviated since Jesus has already been introduced in the narrative.

Alter has also identified 'the annunciation of the birth of the hero to his barren mother' as a biblical type-scene.[33] According to Alter, type-scenes are highly stylized narrative devices that display repeated features.

> There is a series of recurrent narrative episodes attached to the careers of biblical heroes that are analogous to Homeric type-scenes in that they are dependent on the manipulation of a fixed constellation of predetermined motifs.[34]

A type-scene is a fluid device, then, that revolves around certain motifs. Any given scene may depart from the type-scene at key points. Nevertheless, the stylized, 'fixed constellation of predetermined motifs' of the Old Testament annunciation type-scene consists of an announcement by God or God's messenger of the upcoming birth of a son to a barren woman plus a divine naming of the son and a statement of the child's future greatness.[35] These motifs are prominent in the

33. Alter, *The Art of Biblical Narrative*, p. 51.
34. Alter, *The Art of Biblical Narrative*, p. 51.
35. See the stories about births to Hagar (Gen. 16.7-14), Sarah (Gen. 17-18), Rebekah (Gen. 25.21-26), Rachel (Gen. 30.1-24), the wife of Manoah (Judg. 13.2-25), Hannah (1 Kgdms 1.9-18), Jedidah (3 Kgdms 13.1-3, cf. 4 Kgdms 22.1, 16-17), and the Shunamite woman (4 Kgdms 4.8-17). In a later publication, Alter suggests a simple tripartite schema for the annunciation type-scene: 'initial barrenness, divine promise, and the birth of a son': R. Alter, 'How Convention Helps Us Read:

annunciations to Zechariah and Mary.

The annunciation to Zechariah could be an archetypal example of the Old Testament annunciation type-scene. It contains all the expected motifs. Several of the standard motifs of the annunciation type-scene appear as well in the annunciation to Mary: God's messenger announces the upcoming birth of a son, names the child, and makes a statement about the child's future greatness. Yet the account of the annunciation to Mary incorporates a significant departure. Mary is not barren; she is a virgin. A literary reason for Luke's having constructed the two parallel episodes as he did appears to be that this construction enabled him to present a stereotypical, conventional annunciation scene first. Then, by holding up this first scene, Luke reinforces the LXX convention and makes certain that his hearers are aware of it as they move into the story about the angel and Mary. There is nothing cryptic about Luke's strategy here. The virginity of Mary has to be considered a major element of the story. The narrator refers to her as such twice in his initial introduction of her, and her virginity is the point where the story departs from the conventional type-scene. This variation functions rhetorically with respect to the focus of annunciation scenes: the sons. Mary's virginity highlights the uniqueness of Mary's child, the specialness of his relationship to God. Jesus is Son of God. For the purposes of this study, the point to be made is that even where the account of the annunciation to Mary departs from the conventional, Old Testament annunciation scene, the rhetorical effect of the account owes its poignancy to the Old Testament type-scene from which it departs.

In sum, the opening chapters of the Gospel immerse Zechariah, Mary, John, and Jesus in Old Testament forms in order to characterize them. Thus, the rhetoric of the Gospel characterizes these significant characters in such a way as to make them biblical characters. Moreover, this rhetoric assists Luke's audience to develop eyes to see other characters in the narrative as biblical characters as well.

The captive, the blind, the poor, and the others are introduced into the narrative at Lk. 4.18. Adding weight to the argument that the poor should be grouped with the captive, the blind, and so on is the fact that the first reference to these types is a reference to them as a group.[36]

The Case of the Bible's Annunciation Type-Scene', *Prooftexts* 3 (1983), pp. 115-30 (120).

36. Such a grouping is rare outside the LXX and New Testament. Cf. Plato, *Crito*, 14.53.

Moreover, the argument that these character types should be concretized on the basis of the LXX is strengthened further by the fact that this first reference to them occurs in a LXX quotation. This is the fourth instance of direct quotation from Scripture.[37] In Lk. 2.23, 24; 3.4; and four times in the temptation story in 4.4-12, the narrative explicitly states that Scripture is being quoted. In the first instance, 2.23, 24, the narrator cites the scriptural law regarding temple sacrifice following the birth of the first born. The application of this Scripture to the Lukan context is obvious. Jesus is the first born of Mary, and Jesus' pious family abides by the law.

In the second instance, 3.4b-6, again the narrator introduces the scriptural passage. In 3.3-4a, Luke writes,

> And he (John) came into the whole region around the Jordan preaching a baptism of repentance for the forgiveness of sins, as it was written in the book of the words of the prophet Isaiah. . .

The Isaiah passage is to be read as a direct reference to John.

As the devil and Jesus match wits and will in 4.1-13, Jesus quotes Scripture three times and the devil quotes it once. In this instance, Scripture forms part of each disputant's discourse. Here one finds not prophecy and fulfillment, but simply the direct authoritative or, in the case of the devil, pseudo-authoritative comment by characters on the event as it is occurring in the narrative.

Since reading is sequential, prior moments in the experience of the reader shape the reader's experience in the present moment. Therefore, Luke's audience comes to the story of Jesus' return to Nazareth (Lk. 4.16-30) having heard Scripture quoted in prior episodes. By learning from the experience of these prior uses of Scripture, the audience develops the habit of immediately dissolving hermeneutical distance between the scriptural quote and the narrative situation. The Scripture illumines directly the action taking place. It does so as clarification (2.23, 24), as validation (3.4), and as argument (4.1-12). Therefore, when Scripture is quoted in 4.18-19, the LXX becomes the interpretive context for the character types listed in the LXX reading, and the LXX reading becomes the context for interpreting the entire episode in the Nazareth synagogue. Luke 4.18-19 reads,

---

37. For the sake of simplicity, the two citations in 2.23, 24 are regarded as one instance and likewise the scattered quotes within the temptation scene (4.1-13).

> The Spirit of the Lord is upon me, because he anointed me to announce
> good news to the poor. He sent me to proclaim release to the captives and
> recovery of sight to the blind, to send the shattered into release, and to
> proclaim the acceptable year of the Lord.

I shall investigate this text in detail in a later chapter.

The purpose of this chapter has been to argue that Luke's discourse
in the first four chapters of the Gospel predisposes the authorial audience of Luke–Acts to look to the LXX to concretize the captive, the
shattered, the blind, the deaf mute, the lame, lepers, the maimed, the
dead, and the poor. It has been argued that beginning with Lk. 1.5, the
author has thoroughly integrated the LXX into his rhetoric of characterization. Moreover, when in Lk. 4.18 the poor, the captive, the
blind, and so on enter the narrative within a quotation from the LXX,
the LXX is all the more forcefully implicated in their characterization.

The impact of the LXX on the characterization of the poor in Luke–
Acts has been vastly underestimated, indeed ignored. Chapter 5 sets
out to fill this gap by surveying πτωχός in the LXX and Old Testament
pseudepigrapha. This survey is a prelude to concretizing πτωχός in
Luke's Gospel on the basis of the LXX. Consistent with the conclusion
that other character types from Luke's Gospel grouped with the poor
need to be treated along with the poor, Chapter 5 will also survey
αἰχμάλωτος, θραύειν, τυφλός, κωφός, χωλός, λεπρός, ἀνάπηρος,
and νεκρός in the LXX and Old Testament pseudepigrapha, again with
the intent ultimately to concretize them in Luke–Acts on the basis of
this Greek-language Jewish religious literature.

Chapter 5

CONSTRUCTING CHARACTER TYPES FROM THE SEPTUAGINT

Preliminary Comments

Chapter 4 of this study argued that the rhetoric of Luke's Gospel assumes that the authorial audience is familiar with the LXX and directs the audience to concretize the captive, the shattered, the blind, the deaf mute, the lame, lepers, the maimed, the dead, and the poor on the basis of the LXX. Implicit in the method of reader-response interpretation sketched in Chapters 3 and 4 is the interpreter's desire to join Luke's authorial audience. For those who are far removed from Luke in time and space, this is an act of the imagination. None of us can transcend our language and culture. It is possible, however, to broaden our hermeneutical horizon and inform our imagination by engaging the ancient LXX writings, since these are presumed by Luke–Acts to be within the repertoire of its readers. The hoped-for result is engagement with Luke–Acts on its own terms, as much as engaging Luke–Acts on its own terms is possible for persons living at near the turn of the twenty-first century. To this end, I turn to the LXX.[1]

Since the interest of this study is the captive, the shattered, the blind, the deaf mute, the lame, lepers, the maimed, the dead, and the poor as character types in Luke–Acts, the words αἰχμάλωτος, θραύειν, τυφλός, κωφός, χωλός, λεπρός, ἀνάπηρος, νεκρός and πτωχός comprise the vocabulary that will be surveyed in this chapter. The vocabulary is scattered throughout most of the LXX, and is broadly represented in Exodus, Leviticus, Deuteronomy, 2 Kingdoms, and Isaiah. These books will be referred to repeatedly. As Table 1 in Appendix B shows,

---

1.   A number of other interpreters have argued for the importance of the LXX in interpretation of Luke–Acts, though they differ in the manner in which they shape their arguments. See, e.g., Esler, *Community*, p. 25; Hoyt, 'The Poor', pp. 6-7; Maddox, *The Purpose of Luke–Acts*, pp. 14, 15; and Tiede, *Luke*, pp. 21, 26-27.

however, this vocabulary of character types is absent from a number of LXX writings; in fact, it is strikingly absent from several of the minor prophets where social concerns and issues of justice are paramount. The words αἰχμάλωτος, θραύειν, τυφλόν, κωφός, χωλός, λεπρός, ἀνάπηρος, νεκρός, πτωχός do not appear in fifteen of the fifty-two books of the LXX:[2] Joshua, 1 Chronicles, 1 and 2 Esdras, Canticles, Hosea, Micah, Joel, Obadiah, Jonah, Haggai, Zechariah, Susanna, Daniel, and Bel and the Dragon. In another seven, νεκρός is the sole representative: Genesis, Judges, 3 Kingdoms, 4 Maccabees, Ecclesiastes, Baruch, and Lamentations.

Of note as well is the distribution of each term individually. The most broadly occurring term is νεκρός mentioned in twenty-four of the LXX writings, followed by πτωχός, which appears in twenty. Λεπρός disappears after 2 Chronicles. Ἀνάπηρος is rare altogether. Table 1 in Appendix B shows which LXX writings contain the terms under discussion.

The conclusion suggested by a simple statistical overview is that the LXX provides ample material from which to construct character types corresponding to this vocabulary. On the other hand, LXX themes or motifs keyed to these terms can be understood best by keeping a sense of proportion in mind. The LXX-competent audience has a large and diverse store of LXX images, themes, and stories in its repertoire. When Luke wants his audience to draw on particular elements of this store, he will signal those elements to his audience. Luke will direct his audience to the LXX images he wants it to recall.

Throughout this discussion, I will look at connotative as well as denotative images of these terms that emerge from the literature. Secondly, I will give special attention to instances where several of these terms are grouped together.

I will occasionally translate LXX references in full.[3] The LXX often differs from the MT, and from general English language translations of the Bible, which work from the MT where it is available. The

---

2.	Numbered in the LXX of this study are the works contained in A. Rahlfs (ed.), *Septuaginta* (Stuttgart: Deutsche Bibelgesellschaft, 1935, 1979), with the exception of the Odes appended to the Psalms. The Odes are canticles extracted from a variety of biblical and extrabiblical sources, even from the Gospel of Luke.

3.	All LXX references are cited according to Rahlfs' *Septuaginta*. I consulted the published Göttingen editions for text-critical matters, but found nothing to preclude referring to Rahlfs' edition.

Brenton[4] and Thompson[5] translations of the LXX, though readily available, are not widely used. Moreover, my reading of a given passage often differs from the readings provided by Brenton and Thompson.

As this study surveys the captive, the shattered, the blind, the deaf mute, the lame, lepers, the maimed, the dead, and the poor in Jewish religious literature, it will not distinguish between 'early' and 'late' writings, nor will it distinguish between redactional strata of individual writings such as First Isaiah and Second Isaiah. These are modern distinctions drawn for purposes of historical reconstruction. They would not have been meaningful to Luke's authorial audience.

The Captive

Αἰχμάλωτος and related words αἰχμαλωτεύειν, αἰχμαλωτίζειν, and especially αἰχμαλωσία, appear frequently in the LXX: αἰχμάλωτος 23 times, the verb forms 45 and 23 times respectively, and αἰχμαλωσία 124 times. Αἰχμαλωσία is captivity that results from losing a war. Αἰχμαλωτεύειν means to take war captives, human or animal, as does αἰχμαλωτίζειν.[6] An αἰχμάλωτος is a war captive.[7]

The appearances of αἰχμάλωτος and related forms of the word are associated with a variety of themes and settings in the LXX. Yet the Lord's role as sovereign and savior is a consistent thread throughout references to captives and captivity. As these references are surveyed, note as well the helplessness of the captives.

The Lord possesses the capacity to lead individuals and peoples into captivity. A typical expression of this image appears in Job 12.13-25. Here the biblical writer emphasizes God's power, specifically God's power to establish and reverse the fortunes of human beings. Kings and priests are subject to God's sovereign power. In this passage, spoken by Job in reply to Sophar, the writer contends that among God's actions

4.   C.L.C. Brenton, *The Septuagint with Apocrypha: Greek and English* (London: Samuel Bagster, 1851; repr.; Peabody, MA: Hendrickson, 1986).

5.   C. Thompson, *The Septuagint Bible: The Oldest Version of the Old Testament* (ed., rev., and enlarged C.A. Muses; Indian Hills, CO: Falcon Wing's Press, 1954).

6.   E.g. Gen. 34.29; Num. 24.22; Judg. 5.12; 1 Kgdms 30.2, 3, 5; 3 Kgdms 8.50; 4 Kgdms 6.22; 1 Chron. 5.21; 2 Chron. 6.36, 38; 28.5, 8, 11, 17; 1 Esd. 6.16; Est. 1.1; 2.6; Jdt. 5.18; Tob. 1.2; 14.15; Job 1.15, 17; Amos 1.5, 6; Isa. 14.2; Ezek. 6.9; 39.23; Jer. 27.33; 1 Macc. 1.32; 5.13; 8.10; 9.72.

7.   E.g. Exod. 22.14; Num. 21.29; Tob. 2.2; Est. 2.6; Amos 6.7; 7.11, 17.

of casting some people down and setting up others, the Lord makes leaders captives (Job 12.17, 19). In the same breath (12.21), Job notes that the Lord pours dishonor on rulers (ἄρχοντας) and heals the lowly (ταπεινούς).

In another setting, the Lord establishes laws regarding appropriate interaction between Israelites and their captives. If, for example, an Israelite man marries a woman from among Israel's captives, he shall take away her clothes of captivity and treat her as a wife rather than as a slave (Deut. 21.13).

Being captive is associated with being persecuted and humiliated (Ps. 105). The rhetoric of Exodus expresses the totality of inhabitants of Egypt as a continuum from pharaoh to captive (Exod. 12.29), in other words, from the most exalted and powerful to the least exalted and least powerful. The rhetoric of Job illustrates the emotive force of the image of captivity: the serpent (40.25) is so powerful that he rules over the lowest part of the deep as if it were his captive (41.24). Captors oppress (Jer. 27.33). Captives weep (Ps. 136). The captivity of one's people is a cause for grieving (Mic. 1.16).

God's people may fall into captivity.[8] Israel's captivity may indeed be God's doing.[9] Israel may be threatened with captivity if she does not obey the Lord (Deut. 28.41). Moreover, captivity may be divine punishment or wrath for sin.[10] But Israel may also enjoy taking captives as spoils of war,[11] or hope that the Lord will make Israel's enemies suffer captivity.[12]

Captivity is often linked with sin, that is, sin is the antecedent condition (see, for example, Ps. 84). Correspondingly, the Lord's forgiveness accompanies the Lord's action to end captivity.[13] It should be pointed out that being taken captive is not always the consequence of one's own sin. This is apparent in the case of the Israelite girl taken captive by Naaman (4 Kgdms 5.2), and in the case of Ezekiel when the Lord tells the prophet to prepare himself for captivity because he dwells in the midst of injustices (Ezek. 12.1-6). One may, then, become

---

8.　　Num. 21.1; 2 Chron. 6.36, 37, 38; Pss. 13.7; 52.7; Ezek. 6.9; 39.23; 4 Kgdms 5.2.

9.　　Ps. 77.61; Bar. 4.10.

10.　　Num. 31.12, 19, 26; Judg. 5.12.

11.　　2 Chron. 28.5-17; 1 Esd. 8.77; 2 Esd. 9.7; Amos 9.4; Jer. 15.2; 38.19.

12.　　2 Esd. 13.36.

13.　　Ps. 84.1-2; 2 Chron. 6.36-39.

a captive because those around you have abandoned the Lord. Moral failure causes captivity which is political, social, and economic. That there may be a moral failure leading to the captives' circumstance does not redefine 'captive' to mean 'captive in spirit' or 'spiritually captive'.[14]

Whereas αἰχμαλωσία is a generic term for war captivity, it also appears as a technical term for the Babylonian Captivity.[15] Isaiah's Song of the Vineyard (5.1-7) bespeaks Israel's fate allegorically. It is followed by a series of woes, which dominate the rest of the chapter (vv. 8-23). Especially significant for this study is the cluster of images in vv. 13-17. Specifically, the text clusters together images of captivity, lifelessness, hunger, and thirst. This clustering makes the images cohere, even if the reader has to draw the connections between the images. Because of striking differences between the MT and the LXX, it is necessary to pay careful attention to the LXX. The translation given here is a deliberately wooden, literal translation in order to be transparent to the underlying Greek.

> So my people became a captive, because they did not know the Lord. And a large number became dead ones from hunger and thirst for water. And Hades enlarged its being and opened its mouth ceaselessly. Her [presumably Jerusalem's] glorious and great and wealthy and pestilent go down. And the person will be brought down and the man disgraced, and uplifted eyes brought down. And the Lord of hosts will be exalted in judgment, the holy God glorified in righteousness. And the spoiled will be fed like bulls, and lambs will eat the wilderness of those taken away.[16]

The passage moves from a description of the present to a prediction of the future. God's people suffer from captivity, hunger, and thirst in the present. The glorious, the wealthy, and the irritating people are singled out for a future fall. In v. 15, 'to be brought down' (ταπεινωθήσεται) and 'to be disgraced' (ἀτιμασθήσεται) are synony-

---

14. I came across one figurative use of αἰχμαλωτίζειν in the LXX. Jdt. 16.9 reads, 'Her sandal snatched his eye and her beauty captured his soul'.

15. 4 Kgdms 24.14; 1 Esd. 2.15; 5.7, 56, 67; 6.5, 8, 16 [-οτευειν], 28; 7.6, 10, 11, 12, 13; 8.65, 77; 9.3, 4, 15; 2 Esd. 2.1; 3.8; 5.5; 8.35; 9.7; 11.2, 3; 17.6; 18.17; Est. 1.1; Isa. 45.13; Jer. 20.6; Ezek. 1.1, 2; 3.11, 15; 11.15, 24, 25; 12.3, 4, 7, 11; 25.3; 33.21; 40.1 (elsewhere in Ezekiel we read that the Lord will turn back the captivity of Egyptians [29.14]—but Egyptian young men will fall by the sword and women go into captivity [30.17; 32.9]); Dan. 2.25; 1 Esd. 6.16.

16. Isa. 5.13-17.

mous, the former term emphasized by repetition (ταπεινωθήσεται and ταπεινωθήσονται). Finally, the passage establishes a contrast between those people who will be brought down, and God, who will be exalted and glorified. The passage concludes with figurative language of lambs and bulls, rich in pleonasm and memorable imagery.

Isaiah 46.1-2 appears to fill out the Septuagintal image of the captive and to begin a transition in this discussion from the woefulness of captivity to the hopefulness of captives. Here again it is necessary to pay attention to the LXX because it departs from the MT.

> Bel fell, Dagon was broken down; their carved images have become wild animals and domesticated animals. Take these things [i.e. the carved images] packaged like cargo to the weary and hungry and discouraged— not, meanwhile, to the strong—[to the weary and hungry and discouraged] who will be unable to be rescued from war; rather, they will be led away captives.[17]

The MT lacks mention of the weary person, the hungry person, and the discouraged person. The sentence 'Take these things to the weary and the hungry and the discouraged' is ironic. It mocks the impotence of these idols that must be carted around. By inference, real divine power is manifested in the preservation of those who are weak. It is no feat to save the strong from captivity. Real power is displayed when the weary and hungry are preserved from being made captives. On this score, Bel and Dagon are found wanting.

Rescue from captivity comes from the Lord. When the Lord has mercy on Jacob and restores Israel to its land, the tables will be turned: 'Those who took them captive will be captives; those who ruled over them will be ruled over' (Isa. 14.2).[18] The Lord will bring similar reversal of fortunes when Barak and Deborah triumph: Barak will take captivity captive (Judg. 5.12). Tobit's prayer for rejoicing (ch. 13) speaks of God who afflicts and then shows mercy (13.2). This motif of twofold action surfaces repeatedly in Tobit's prayer and provides justification for happiness on the part of captives: 'Praise the Lord worthily and bless the king of the ages in order that his tent may be erected again for you with joy, both to gladden the captives among you and to love the distressed among you for all generations forever'

---

17. Isa. 46.1-2.
18. Note the recurring formula, 'In that day there will be. . . ', of Isa. 14.3; 17.9; 19.24.

(13.11-12). Hope resides in the promise that the Lord will deliver captives.[19]

In sum, the captive has no personality. The captive is not an actor, but is one who is acted upon. When the psalmist says that captives weep, the psalmist is expressing a reaction to suppression. The captive is powerless, at the mercy of the captor. Captives are not predisposed to faith. The image of the captive is of a faceless, nameless, powerless type. Moreover, the captive attracts the sympathy of the reader. This is true whether captivity involves the innocent or is the result of sin. On the hopeful side, the captive's release comes from God. The LXX provides Luke's audience with a clear precedent for divine rescue from captivity and even for a future reversal of fortunes as a result of God's intervention on behalf of the captive.

Where the αἰχμάλωτος is Israel, captive Israel has sinned, and in captivity is helplessly dependent on the Lord for salvation.[20] Captive Israel, though not nameless, takes on the connotations of weakness associated with the captive in general. Once captive, Israel ceases to be in control of its destiny. Rather than displacing the general LXX image of the captive, references to captive Israel gain emotive force from the general image.

The Shattered

Θραύειν means 'to shatter'. It appears 22 times in the LXX.[21] In the participial form quoted in Lk. 4.18, it appears three times: speaking of the potential fate of the Israelites (Deut. 28.33), of those to be treated favorably by the house of Jacob (Isa. 58.6), and of Antiochus (2 Macc. 9.11). Though not as common a word in the LXX as forms of αἰχμάλωτος, θραύειν is, nevertheless, readily understandable. The

19. Num. 21.1-3; 2 Chron. 6.36-38; Pss. 13.4-7; 52.7; 84.1; 125.1, 4; Hos. 6.11; Amos 9.14; Joel 4.1-2; Zeph. 2.7; 3.20; Isa. 1.27; Jer. 25.19; 26.27; 37.18; 38.23; Bar. 4.23-24; Ezek. 39.25.

20. Where the captive in the LXX is specifically captive Israel, this is clearly signaled by the context, as in Isa. 5.15.

21. Exod. 15.6; Num. 17.11; 24.17; Deut. 20.3; 28.33; 1 Kgdms 20.34; 2 Kgdms 12.15; 2 Chron. 6.24; 20.37; Jdt. 9.10; 13.14; Isa. 2.10, 19, 21; 42.4; 58.6; Jer. 28.30; Ezek. 21.7, 15; 2 Macc. 9.11; 15.16; *3 Macc.* 6.5. In addition, θραῦσμα appears once (Jdt. 13.5), θραυσμὸς once (Nah. 2.11), and θραῦσις 12 times (Num. 17.12, 13, 14, 15; 2 Kgdms 17.9; 18.7; 24.15, 21, 25; Ps. 105.23, 30; Wis. 18.20).

Lord shatters enemies (Exod. 15.6) and is to be feared as the shatterer (Isa. 2.10, 19, 21; 10.19). The Lord's wrath may even shatter God's people (Num. 17.11). An Israelite will rise up who will shatter the princes of Moab (Num. 24.17). A psalmist calls upon the Lord to raise up a king, the son of David, who will shatter unrighteous rulers (*Pss. Sol.* 17.22) On the other hand, Solomon prays that if the people of Israel are shattered before their enemy, the Lord may be merciful and restore them (2 Chron. 6.24). These are military images. A shatterer is one who effects violent destruction.

Θραύειν also admits to broader use than the strictly military. The Lord shatters the child of David and Bathsheba, that is, brings about the child's death (2 Kgdms 12.15). Jonathan is shattered, that is, he is distressed, by his father Saul's plans to do in David (1 Kgdms 20.34). A similar use to this last one occurs in the book of Ezekiel: Ezekiel is to prophesy against the land of Israel and every heart will be shattered (Ezek. 21.12).[22] These are figurative uses. On the other hand, Antiochus is more than broken in spirit (2 Macc. 9.11). A violent fall from his chariot has torn up every part of his body. Worms swarm his body. His flesh is rotting (2 Macc. 9.7-10). In the instances where θραύειν is figurative, the context clearly indicates this.

In passages that may be especially significant for this study, Isaiah employs θραύειν in the battlefield sense. The Servant will not be shattered (Isa. 42.4). Later, the people are commanded to send the shattered into freedom (Isa. 58.6).[23] In this latter passage, the shattered are not named or identified in any specific way. Moreover, the reader is not given information about a specific shattering. Yet the reader's sympathies are expected to lie with the shattered if for no other reason than that the Lord wants the shattered released, and the reader of the LXX is assumed to want to adopt the Lord's point of view.

In Isa. 58.6-7, the shattered appear within a clustering of character types. Isaiah adds to this command from the Lord to free the shattered commands to tear up unjust contracts, break bread for the hungry, bring the poor (πτωχός) into their house, and clothe the naked. In this

---

22. The sole figurative use in the LXX of a related form is clearly signaled by the text: καρδίας θραυσμὸς (Nah. 2.11).

23. There is a curious shift from plural to singular in the Lord's address from Isa. 58.3-5 to 58.6-14. But the addressee remains God's people, the house of Jacob (58.1).

context, the shattered are numbered among those whom genuinely righteous people aid.

To summarize, the shattered are not presented as characters per se in the LXX, not even as flat characters, except in Isa. 58.6. The participial form is used in two of its three appearances to be descriptive of specific antecedents. In Isa. 58.6, the shattered are a nameless and faceless type. Nevertheless, a typical image of what it means more broadly in the LXX to be shattered does emerge from the LXX. The image has much in common with that evoked by αἰχμάλωτος. Being shattered is predominantly a warfare image. A shattered one has lost the capacity to be an actor, but rather is a figure acted upon. The shattered have suffered defeat and destruction. The shattered are helpless, at the mercy of others, human and divine. Though the Lord is to be feared as a shatterer, feared by both God's people and their enemies, the Lord is also the hope for those who are shattered.

The Blind

Τυφλός appears 24 times in the LXX and means 'blind person'. It refers overwhelmingly in the LXX to physical blindness, usually of people, but also of animals.[24] The majority of references fall into two categories: first, commands to be courteous to the blind or statements of ethical conduct toward the blind;[25] and secondly, references to healing or the promise of healing.[26]

Paradoxically, the LXX presents blindness as an unacceptable blemish in the presence of God. Blindness disqualifies the would-be priest (Lev. 21.18) and potential sacrificial animals (Lev. 22.21-22; Deut. 15.21; Mal. 1.8). Yet the Lord's salvific action promises to include future blessings to the blind.

The word rarely refers to figurative blindness.[27] The only explicitly figurative use of blindness in the LXX occurs in Wis. 2.21-22. There,

---

24.   Exod. 4.11; Lev. 19.14; 21.18; Deut. 15.21 (of oxen and sheep); 27.18; 28.29; 2 Kgdms 5.6,8; Job 29.15; Ps. 145.8; Zeph. 1.17; Mal. 1.8; Isa. 29.18; 35.5; 42.7, 16 (perhaps); 59.10; Ep. Jer. 36; Tob. 7.6.

25.   Lev. 19.14; Deut. 27.14-26; Job 29.12-17.

26.   Isa. 29.18; 35.5; 42.7, 16, 18; Ep. Jer. 36.

27.   Isa. 42.16 (perhaps), 18 (probably), 19; 43.8 (perhaps, but the meaning is obscure); Wis. 2.21-22.

the writer contends that the evil of the impious blinded them to the mysteries of God.[28]

One of the more dramatic instances where character types in this study including the blind are brought together is Job's speech in ch. 29:

> For I rescued the poor one from the hand of the mighty one and I helped the orphan for whom there was no helper. . . The mouth of the widows blessed me. I clothed myself with righteousness; I put on justice like a double cloak. I was the eye of the blind and the foot of the lame. I was father to the powerless and sought out justice which I did not know. I shattered the molars of the unrighteous and pulled the booty from between their teeth.[29]

Here Job claims to have exhibited exemplary behavior in his actions. Job appeals to an expansive catalog of beneficiaries. Commendable conduct self-evidently includes beneficent action toward the poor, the orphan, the widow, the blind, the lame, and the powerless.

Another expansive grouping of character types including the blind appears in Psalm 145. This time the character acting upon them is the Lord.

> [The Lord is] producing justice for those being treated unjustly, giving nourishment to those who are hungry. The Lord sets loose those who were shackled. The Lord restores the broken down. The Lord makes the blind wise. The Lord loves the righteous. The Lord guards the sojourner. He will take to himself the orphan and widow, but he will wipe out the way of sinners.[30]

Certain motifs of divine action appear in this Psalm that coincide with material in Luke's Gospel: nourishment to the hungry (Lk. 1.53), freedom to the shackled, and restoration to those broken down (Lk. 4.18, from Isaiah 61). Curiously, the blind receive wisdom, not sight. One may wonder whether in this Psalm blindness is some sort of moral or spiritual blindness that wisdom will correct. But two observations raise persuasive objections to such an interpretation. First, the companion maladies are clearly physical and concrete. The text speaks of the unjustly treated, the hungry, the shackled, the broken down, the sojourner, the widow, and the orphan. Secondly, the Lord is not correcting

28. Tangentially related to this study is the grouping of the righteous needy (πένητα δίκαιον), the widow, and the elderly in Wis. 2.10. Included in the false reasoning of the impious is the decision to oppress these groups.
29. Job 29.12-17.
30. Ps. 145.7-9.

people's hearts in this Psalm. On the contrary, sinners are eliminated, not reformed. It is noteworthy, and will receive future comment, that those receiving the Lord's favor are those being treated unjustly, those who are hungry, those who were shackled, the broken down, the blind, the orphan, and the widow, along with the righteous. Set apart, clearly distinct from these groups, are sinners.[31]

Isaiah ranks the blind among those to receive future divine beneficence. In the passages below, note the characters mentioned together with the blind. In the first passage, note as well the character types mentioned in contrast to them.

> In that day the deaf mute will hear the words [read from] a book, and the eyes of the blind will see in darkness and fog. And the poor will rejoice with gladness because of the Lord and those without hope among people will be filled with gladness. The wicked one died and the arrogant one perished.[32]
>
> Be strong, do not fear. Behold our God returns judgment and will repay. He will come and save us. Then the eyes of the blind will be opened and the ears of the deaf mute will hear. Then the lame one will leap like a deer and the tongue of the dumb will be clear.[33]
>
> I the Lord God called you in righteousness and will take over your hand and strengthen you. I granted that you be a covenant clan, a light to the nations, to open the eyes of the blind, to lead those bound out of bonds, and those sitting in darkness from the guard house.[34]

In the first two of these three passages, the Lord himself is the hoped for savior of the blind. In the third of the three, the Lord's chosen people act with the Lord's strength to fulfill his purposes, including giving the blind sight.

Echoes of Isaiah are heard in the Letter of Jeremiah. Recall, in addition to the passages immediately above, how Isaiah (46.1-2) mocked Bel and Dagon as powerless carved images. According to the Letter of Jeremiah, the powerlessness of idols is shown by their inability to punish or reward (vv. 33-34), to save a person from death, to rescue the weak from the strong (v. 35), to bring the blind one into seeing, to rescue someone in physical anguish (v. 36), to have mercy on the widow, or to do good for the orphan (v. 37).

---

31. See below, pp. 117-20, the discussion of 'sinners' in the Psalms.
32. Isa. 29.18-20.
33. Isa. 35.4b-6.
34. Isa. 42.6-7.

The blind are paired with the lame in 2 Kgdms 5.6-10. The treatment given them in this passage is as startling as it is brutal. In terms
of the LXX depiction of the blind and the lame as character types, this
passage is the exception that proves the rule. It is an odd account of
how the blind and the lame were brought by the Jebusites to stand up
to David. David, however, orders the blind and the lame to be slain
and prohibits future entry into the Lord's house by any blind and
lame. The assumption by the Jebusites that David would show deference to the blind and lame implies a convention. Part of the impact of
this narrative derives from David's departure from conventional,
God-fearing treatment of the blind and lame.[35]

Like captivity, blindness can be divine punishment for sin. It may
come on the day of the Lord (Zeph. 1.17), or earlier, as when Moses
in his farewell speech makes blindness one of the afflictions with
which the Lord threatens the people if they do not heed his commandments (Deut. 28.29). The consequences of blindness emphasize
the helplessness of that state.[36]

The blind stand out as a type in the LXX. The characteristics of the
type may be summarized in three points. First, the blind are divinely
appointed targets of human magnanimity. This magnanimity is a
corollary to the impression that the blind are extraordinarily vulnerable to being treated unjustly. Secondly, the blind may be healed by
God or God's agent. Indeed, being able to give sight to the blind is
proof of the powerfulness of God or God's agent. Thirdly, the blind
are fated for eschatological wholeness. A distinguishing mark of the
day of the Lord is that it will be the occasion when the blind will
receive sight.

The Deaf Mute

Κωφός appears 12 times in the LXX. Often it is paired with τυφλός or
mentioned in context with several character types.[37] Κωφός may mean
someone who is strictly deaf. In Ps. 37.14, for example, κωφός denotes
a person who cannot hear; ἄλαλος denotes a person who cannot

---

35.   On departure from convention as a rhetorical tool in the Hebrew Scriptures,
see Alter, *The Art of Biblical Narrative*, p. 52.
36.   See also Isa. 59.10.
37.   With τυφλός Exod. 4.11; Lev. 19.14; Isa. 42.18, 19; 43.8. With several
other character types: Isa. 29.18; 35.5.

speak.[38] Yet κωφός may also mean mute or deaf mute, as it does in reference to people in Wis. 10.21 and in reference to idols in Hab. 2.18. In the case where the sense of κωφός is figurative (Isa. 42.19), the context signals that clearly.[39]

Leviticus 19.14 calls for deference toward the deaf mute as it does toward the blind. Moses commands, 'You shall not speak ill of the deaf mute and not put up a stumbling block in front of the blind'.

In contrast to the lawless person and the arrogant person who will perish in the day of the Lord (Isa. 29.20), the deaf mute will hear (Isa. 29.18). Among those, reeled off in rapid succession, who will share in joy and the Lord's future benefactions with the deaf mute are the blind, the poor, and the hopeless (Isa. 29.18-20). Isaiah 35.4b-6 recites the same for the blind, the deaf, the lame, and the dumb.[40]

The Lame

Χωλός appears 11 times in the LXX. Of those, two are merely passing references that Memphibosthe, the son of Jonathan, was lame in both legs (2 Kgdms 9.13; 19.27). The remaining ten betray the same paradox as appears with respect to the blind.[41] In addition, the LXX routinely mentions the lame along with companion groups. The only exceptions are the two references in 2 Kingdoms mentioned above and Isa. 33.23, to be mentioned below. Typically, the lame are paired with the blind or fill out a listing of character types.[42]

Leviticus 21.18 declares that no priest shall be lame, blind, or disfigured in any of a number of ways. Deuteronomy 15.21 states proscriptions against lame and blind sacrificial oxen and sheep.[43] So, on the one hand, lameness is an imperfection and the lame (persons and animals) are excluded from divine service. On the other hand, as with the blind, commendable conduct includes beneficent action toward the

38. See also Isa. 29.18; 35.5; 42.18.

39. Another exception to literal deafness may occur in Isa. 44.11. In this passage, κωφός is an obscure reference either to shameful people who make idols or to the unhearing and unspeaking idols themselves. The Greek text is simply puzzling.

40. See above, p. 104, the translations of Isa. 29.18-20 and 35.4b-6.

41. Lev. 21.18; Deut. 15.21; 2 Kgdms 5.6, 8 (twice); Job 29.15; Mal. 1.8, 13; Isa. 33.23; 35.6.

42. Lev. 21.18; Deut. 15.21; 2 Kgdms 5.6, 8; Job 29.15; Isa. 35.6; Mal. 1.8, 13.

43. See also Mal. 1.8, 13.

lame (Job 29.15), and the lame may look forward to God's return when God will restore their legs (Isa. 35.6).

The lame are weak and at the mercy of others. Isaiah 33.23 plays off this stereotypical weakness when the writer looks forward to the time when the impious will be so weakened by the Lord that even many lame persons will plunder them. The image of being plundered by the lame is an exaggerated image of the ultimate in helplessness.

Lepers

There is a certain consistency with respect to the captive, the shattered, the blind, the deaf mute, and the lame in the LXX. They are at the mercy of others, at God's behest to be afforded generosity by God's people, to be accorded sympathy, and destined for God's favor. Lepers are a somewhat different sort of character in the LXX.

Λεπρός appears 14 times in the LXX.[44] These references are concentrated largely in the books of Leviticus, 4 Kingdoms, and 2 Chronicles. Leviticus 13 and 14 have to do with the determination of leprosy in a person, confirmation of the end of leprosy, the disposition of a leper's clothing, and the ritual obligations of the cleansed leper. These 116 verses make provisions for reintegration of former lepers back into the community upon being declared clean by the priest. But lepers as lepers are to be set apart from the people. One finds no command that healthy Israelites have a responsibility to see to the wellbeing of lepers.

Lepers are not stereotypically poor. Lev. 14.21-22 provides a poverty clause in case the cleansed leper is poor (ἐὰν δὲ πένητα) and cannot afford the regular sin offering and whole burnt offering. The presence of a poverty clause shows that the leper as portrayed by Leviticus is not assumed to be poor.[45] Naaman is not poor (4 Kgdms 5.1-23).

God could effect leprosy as punishment. The Lord touched king Azarias (Azariah) of Judah with leprosy, apparently because he left pagan shrines standing, though he otherwise did well in the Lord's

---

44.   Lev. 13.44, 45; 14.2, 3; 22.4; Num. 5.2; 2 Kgdms 3.29; 4 Kgdms 5.11; 7.3, 8; 2 Chron. 26.20, 21 (twice), 23.

45.   See also Lev. 14.30-32. The same point can be made from 2 Kgdms 3.29 where one reads that among the tragedies David wishes on the house of Joab are leprosy and to have little to eat.

eyes (4 Kgdms 15.5). The Lord punished Miriam with temporary leprosy (Num. 12.10).[46] God's agent, Elisha, sentenced Gehazi to permanent leprosy (4 Kgdms 5.27).

Leprosy was a serious business. On the one hand, leprosy was a dreaded disease for which persons were quarantined, not treated. On the other hand, a person's leprosy also branded that person as ritually impure and, therefore, as dishonored. Through leprosy, the Lord rebuked and disgraced Uzziah. Uzziah's leprosy stayed with him the rest of his life and cost him his throne (2 Chron. 26.21).

But the Lord can also heal leprosy. Moses cried to the Lord for the Lord to heal Miriam. This God did after seven days of exile for Miriam (Num. 12.10). Add to that the well-known story of the healing of Naaman through the Lord's prophet (4 Kgdms 5.11) and one sees that the might of the Lord's saving power is exhibited by the Lord's authority over leprosy.

The image constructed by drawing together the disparate references to lepers is of the leper as a character ejected from the town. The leper may or may not deserve this affliction, that is, may or may not be responsible because of sin. But clearly healing must come from God, or through God's agent, if it is to come at all. In this respect, lepers are like the blind, the deaf mute, and the lame.

The Maimed

Ἀνάπειρος (ἀνάπηρος) appears only twice in the LXX (2 Macc. 8.24; Tob. 14.2).[47] A corresponding verb form, ἀναπείρεσθαι, appears once (2 Macc. 12.22).[48]

2 Maccabees 8.24 reports that in a battle with Nicanor's army, the Maccabean fighters, with the help of God, killed 9000 and left the greater part of the enemy forces wounded and maimed. The reference in Tobit is less brutal. Near the middle of his long life, Tobit became blind (ἀνάπειρος τοῖς ὀφθαλμοῖς) and subsequently regained his sight.

---

46. This is recalled by Deut. 24.9.

47. In Tob. 14.2, ἀνάπειρος appears in Codex Sinaiticus, and not in Codices Vaticanus and Alexandrinus.

48. In flight from Judas Maccabeus's forces, the army of Timothy, the Ammonite military leader, became so disorganized that they maimed themselves with their weapons.

The maimed are not established as a character type as such in the
LXX. They take on that function in association with other character
types in the Gospel of Luke. Being maimed, however, presumes no
piety, and like the other terms I have looked at, is not a desired self-
designation in the LXX.

The Dead

Νεκρός appears 81 times in the LXX.[49] The term may be used as a
noun or as an adjective. It may refer to the deceased[50] or to a corpse,[51]
though often either of the two denotations makes equally good sense.

As the LXX portrays the dead, they are in a pitiable state. The dead
know nothing.[52] The dead do not praise the Lord.[53] The dead may
have experienced the Lord's anger.[54] The dead are weary and without
strength.[55] The abode of the dead is Hades.[56] They are not to be con-
jured up.[57] Corpses are food for birds and beasts.[58] 'Positive' references to the dead are hardly positive at all. Consider these words from
Sirach:

---

49.   This study will make no attempt to treat the theme of death in the LXX. My
interest is in 'the dead' as a literary figure. On the theme of death in the Hebrew
Bible, along with bibliographical references, see L.R. Baily, *Biblical Perspectives
on Death* (Overtures to Biblical Theology, 5; Philadelphia: Fortress Press, 1979);
M. Krieg, *Todesbilder im Alten Testament* (ATANT, 73; Zürich: Theologischer
Verlag, 1988); L. Wächter, *Der Tod im Alten Testament* (Arbeiten zur Theologie,
2.8; Stuttgart: Calwer Verlag, 1967). The latter two are detailed and comprehensive.
Krieg is interested in contemporary applications of images of death. Wächter's work
is more purely *religionsgeschichtlich*.

50.   E.g. Deut. 18.11; Ps. 113.25; Isa. 8.19; 2 Macc. 12.44.

51.   E.g. Gen. 23.3-15; Num. 19.16; Deut. 28.26; Isa. 14.19; Jer. 7.33; 9.21;
19.7; 40.5; Ep. Jer. 70.

52.   Eccl. 9.5.

53.   Ps. 113.25; Sir. 17.28.

54.   E.g. Isa. 26.14; 34.13; Jer. 7.33; 19.7; Ezek. 9.7; 11.6, 7. This is a
common motif in the LXX.

55.   Deut. 18.11; this may also be the sense of Isa. 8.19.

56.   Job 3.17; Ps. 88.4.

57.   Hades is mentioned 97 times in the LXX: in Genesis, Numbers, Deutero-
nomy, 1 Kingdoms, 3 Kingdoms, Tobit, Esther, Job, Psalms, Proverbs, Ecclesiastes,
Canticles, Wisdom of Solomon, Sirach, Hosea, Amos, Jonah, Habacuc, Isaiah,
Jeremiah, Baruch, Ezekiel, *2 Maccabees* and *3 Maccabees*.

58.   Deut. 28.26; Jer. 7.33; 19.7.

> Weep for the dead one, for light has abandoned him. And weep for the fool, for understanding has abandoned him. Weep less for the dead because he has rested. The life of the fool is a greater evil than death.[59]

> Being dead is unfortunate, but being a fool is more unfortunate.[60]

The Preacher, however, claims that even the worst of situations in life is better than being dead: 'Better to be a living dog than a dead lion' (Eccl. 9.4). In short, the dead are non-entity entities.

Idols or false gods may be spoken of as 'the dead'.[61] The point in speaking of them as 'the dead' is to emphasize that idols can do nothing for the people. The dead are useless. It is foolish and futile to appeal to them. On the other hand, the Lord is living, capable of action, and deserves to be honored.

The power to bring the dead back to life is God's and God's alone. Sirach makes this clear when he praises Elijah as the one 'who raised the dead one from death and from Hades by the word of the Most High' (Sir. 48.5).

Two instances where νεκρός is mentioned along with other terms focused on in this study stand out. In a general exhortation that includes admonitions to assist the poor, the weeping, and the sick, Sirach exhorts his reader to be kind to the dead (Sir. 7.33). The dead, then, take their place among other characters on whom godly persons bestow kindness. In Psalm 87, the psalmist mixes several images corresponding to types under consideration. Praying for salvation, the psalmist considers himself as good as dead (vv. 4-5). He is in great distress, his eyes weakened by poverty (v. 10). He calls himself poor, having been abased and reduced to despair (v. 16). In making his case before God, the psalmist draws on the store of conventional imagery at his disposal designed to gain Lord's favor: the imagery of the dead, the blind (in so many words), and the poor.

Whereas in Psalm 87 the psalmist uses connotations associated with the dead to gain the Lord's sympathy for the psalmist, Isaiah uses connotations associated with the dead to highlight expressly the greatness of the Lord and the day of the Lord. In that day when the Lord restores Judah, brings salvation, and abases the lofty, some unfortunate ones will not be there to enjoy it, says Isaiah.[62] 'The dead will not see life,

59. Sir. 22.11.
60. Sir. 23.11-12.
61. Wis. 13.10, 18; 15.5, 17.
62. Isa. 26.1-19.

nor will physicians raise them up' (Isa. 26.14). Or will the dead be
excluded in the day of the Lord? No, Isaiah goes on to say, 'The dead
will rise up, and those in tombs will get up, and they will celebrate on
the earth' (Isa. 26.19). In contrast, the land of the ungodly will fall
(Isa. 26.19). In his own rhetorical way, Isaiah heightens the magnificence of 'that day' by first reiterating the hopeless condition of the
dead and then announcing the Lord's joyful restoration of the dead to
life.

'The dead' as a typical term carries much the same connotative force
in the LXX as do the captive, the shattered, the blind, the deaf mute, and
the lame. The dead have no personality. The dead possess no capacity
to change their lot. They are acted upon, not actors themselves. Godly
people are expected to pity the dead and to exhibit an etiquette of
generosity toward them. Finally, the prophet Isaiah holds out hope for
the dead as beneficiaries of the Lord's salvation.

The Poor

The amount of commentary about 'the poor' in the Hebrew Bible and
early Judaism, especially commentary built upon analyses of *ani* and
anaw, is immense.[63] Also, πτωχός occurs in the LXX more frequently
than do the other terms under scrutiny. Consequently, it is necessary
to provide a discussion of πτωχός that will be considerably longer than
the surveys of the other words considered.

One need not look far to find πτωχός grouped with other character
types in the LXX: for example, with stranger, orphan, and widow
(Deut. 24.19); with orphan, widow, blind, lame, and powerless (Job
29.12); with orphan and lowly (Psalm 9); with orphan, widow, and
shackled (Psalm 67) and with shackled (Psalm 68).

From the opposite perspective, the poor are frequently set apart from

---

63. The classic study is A. Rahlfs, *Ani und Anaw in den Psalmen* (Göttingen:
Dieterichsche Verlagsbuchhandlung, 1892). See also, Bammel, 'Πτωχός'; Dibelius,
James, pp. 39-45; F.C. Grant, *Economic Background*, p. 120; Keck, 'The Poor
among the Saints', pp. 54-78; A. Kuschke, 'Arm und Reich im Alten Testament mit
besonderer Berücksichtigung der nachexilischen Zeit', *ZAW* 57 (1939), pp. 44-57;
C. Osiek, *Rich and Poor in the Shepherd of Hermas: An Exegetical-Social
Investigation* (CBQMS, 15; Washington DC: The Catholic Biblical Association of
America, 1983), pp. 15-20; J. van der Ploeg, 'Les Pauvres d'Israel et leur Piete',
Old Testament Studies 7 (1950), pp. 242-70. Hoyt ('The Poor', pp. 13-96) devotes
a large section of his dissertation to this course of study.

other character types by clear contrasts: for example, mighty (Lev. 19.15); haughty (2 Kgdms 22.28); leaders, mighty and strong, artisans, and smiths (4 Kgdms 24.14); sinners, heathen, and impious (Psalm 9); wealthy (Psalm 9); strong (Psalm 34); wealthy sinners (Psalm 36); sinner (Psalm 81).

Πτωχός appears 123 times in the LXX. More than a quarter of these are in the Psalms alone. In addition, πτωχεία (or πτωχία) is used 20 times. LXX references to 'the poor' divide themselves into two broad categories: standards of human etiquette toward the poor and proclamations that the Lord is the salvation of the poor. As a matter of shorthand, I will refer to passages in the former category as etiquette passages and to passages in the latter category as salvation passages. Exceptions to these broad categories will be noted.

Exodus, Leviticus, and Deuteronomy
Exodus 23.11; Lev. 19.10; 23.22; and Deut. 24.19 are similar passages belonging to the etiquette motif.[64] All four passages command that harvesting be left incomplete so that the poor may gather something. The poor are joined by wild animals in Exod. 23.11 and by the stranger or sojourner in Lev. 19.10 and 23.22. In Deuteronomy 24, the poor, the stranger, the orphan, and the widow are to receive crops left in the field.

Leviticus 19.15 is an interesting verse for several reasons. For the purpose of establishing the poor as a LXX type character, it is sufficient to point out that the poor (singular) parallel the mighty (singular) and to explain the imagery of the poor and the mighty.

οὐ λήμψῃ πρόσωπον πτωχοῦ
οὐδὲ θαυμάσεις πρόσωπον δυνάστου

Thackeray does an excellent job of translating the verse. He takes the latter expression, θαυμάσεις πρόσωπον, to be a generally accepted manner of expressing 'to accept the person (to favor or be partial to anyone)' in the LXX.[65] To support this reading, he cites Gen. 19.21;

64.   Deut. 24.19 is so similar to Lev. 19.10 and 23.22 that its present shape may be the result of harmonization with those passages. The text is uncertain and πτωχός is not mentioned among the orphan, the widow, and the stranger in surrounding passages Deut. 24.17, 21.

65.   H.StJ. Thackeray, *A Grammar of the Old Testament in Greek According to the Septuagint*. I. *Introduction, Orthography and Accidence* (Cambridge: Cambridge University Press, 1909), p. 43.

Deut 10.17; 28.50; 4 Kgdms 5.1; Prov. 18.5; Job 13.10; and Isa. 9.15. The former clause, λήμψη πρόσωπον, is then parallel to the latter. While λήμψη πρόσωπον is a more literal rendering of the Hebrew expression behind the latter clause, θαυμάσεις πρόσωπον, the translator apparently chose θαυμάσεις πρόσωπον to avoid word-for-word repetition. Thus, the sense of the verse would be 'show favoritism neither toward the poor nor the mighty'.[66] The poor and the mighty, then, represent extreme ends of the spectrum of humanity.

4 Kingdoms
From 4 Kingdoms, those whose position, abilities, or talents could threaten the Babylonians are deported. By contrast, the poor are left to remain (4 Kgdms 24.14; 25.12).

Tobit and Esther
Tobit serves as a model for proper behavior toward the poor. He expresses his desire to share his abundance with the poor or needy person (Tob. 2.2, 3).[67] He instructs his son not to turn his face from the poor lest God turn God's face from him.[68] Similarly, it is taken for granted in Est. 9.22 that sending a portion of the feast to the poor is a generous and worthy act. These are passages that display the etiquette motif.

Job
The book of Job groups the poor with parallel character types and uses πτωχός and πένης synonymously. Job, recounting his praiseworthy deeds, includes saving the poor from the hand of the mighty and aiding the orphan (29.12). So esteemed was he, says Job, that both perishing ones (ἀπολλυμένοι) and widows blessed him (29.13). He was the eye of the blind, the foot of the lame, and the father of the powerless (29.15, 16). Correspondingly, Job's unfriendly friend Elihu chastens Job with the assurance that the Lord listens to the cry of the poor (34.28).[69]

It is difficult to tell whether πτωχός is literal or metaphorical in Job

66. Thackeray, *Grammar*, p. 44.
67. Πτωχός in Codex Sinaiticus, ἐνδεής in Codices A and B.
68. Πτωχός in Codices A and B.
69. The 'cry of the πτωχῶν' is synonymous with the 'cry of the πένητος' in Job 34.28.

36.6. It is paired with the ἄκακον of v. 5, but later in v. 8 reference is made to the cords of poverty.

Psalms
The Psalms play a vital role in shaping the LXX-competent reader's image of 'the poor' because, as was noted above, fully one quarter of the occurrences of πτωχός in the LXX are in the Psalms. Moreover, the psalms were liturgy and song. One may speculate that psalms may have become firmly ingrained in the minds of those who used the LXX in the first century CE, not unlike the way the lyrics of hymns are ingrained in the minds of many Christians today who may not be able to recite the Decalogue but can recall with ease the words of 'Amazing Grace'.

L.J. Hoppe has recently said of the Psalms,

> Here the poor are idealized. Here poverty takes on an aura of sanctity as if
> it possessed a religious character. In the psalms, the poor are meek,
> lowly, humble, faithful, righteous, dependent, hopeful.[70]

This observation from Hoppe captures as well the spirit of the influential views of A. Gelin[71] and M. Dibelius[72] and may be considered the consensus view.[73] Both Gelin and Dibelius sketch socio-religious models of historical development toward a time when 'the poor' equaled 'the pious' in Jewish religious communities and both rely on the Psalms to support their respective models.

When interpreters such as Gelin and Dibelius say or imply that 'the poor' and 'the pious' are synonymous concepts in the Psalms, it is important to look more closely at the nature of the relationship to which they point. The interpretation may actually be proposing analogy or metaphor, as when it is said that piety is the stance of being poor before God. Or the interpretation may actually be simply appealing to a common denominator, as when it is said that the poor are humble

---

70.   L.J. Hoppe, *Being Poor: A Biblical Study* (Good News Studies, 20; Wilmington: Michael Glazier, 1987), p. 114.
71.   A. Gelin, *The Poor of Yahweh* (trans. K. Sullivan; Collegeville: The Liturgical Press, 1964), esp. pp. 36-37.
72.   Dibelius, *James*, p. 39.
73.   Hoppe (*Being Poor*, p. 118) qualifies his assent to the consensus with comments such as 'there is no hint of idealizing the state of the poor', and 'if there is a spiritualization of the poor in these psalms, it is the result of a secondary development'.

before God and the pious are humble before God. From there it is a short leap in logic to suppose that one may be called 'the poor' in the Psalms because one is humble. This study intends to show that it is necessary to revise this view of 'the poor' as equivalent to 'the pious' in the Psalms when we look specifically at the LXX and πτωχός.

Psalmists routinely appeal to God for deliverance from their enemies, from persecutors, from the ungodly, from Gentiles, and from sinners.[74] Psalmists call upon God to destroy their enemies and sinners.[75] They ask for relief from afflictions.[76] They ask for direction in life.[77] They plead for forgiveness from sins.[78] As the discussion below will show, whether pleading for God's help or affirming God's benevolence, psalmists treat as self-evident that God is surely the salvation of the poor.

The term πτωχός occurs in 23 of the 151 psalms. In eight of these, 'the poor' is one of the psalmist's self-designations: Psalms 24, 33, 39, 68, 69, 85, 87, and 108. In another four psalms, the psalm appears to imply that the writer is a πτωχός: Psalms 21, 34 (perhaps), 101, and 139. Finally, eleven psalms refer to the poor without identifying the poor with the psalmist: Psalms 9, 11, 13, 36, 40, 67, 71, 73, 81, 112, and 131.

I will look first at psalms that refer to the poor without identifying the poor with the psalmist. In Psalm 9, the πτωχός and the πένης are destined to receive the Lord's benefits (v. 19; see also v. 10), in contrast to sinners (v. 18) and in contrast to the nation or the heathen (vv. 18, 20, 21).[79] Further synonymous use of πτωχός and πένης in this psalm appears in vv. 29, 30, 31, 33, 35, and 38.[80] In v. 23, πτωχός

---

74.   Pss. 3.8; 7.2-3; 9.18; 12.1-5; 16.13; 17.44-49; 26.12; 30.1-9; 42.1-3; 58.2-3; 68.2-5, 14-19; 70.1-13; 139.2-6; 141.7-8; 142.7-9.

75.   Pss. 5.9-11; 6.11; 9.26; 16.13-14; 27.4; 30.19; 36.15; 54.13-16; 58.12-16; 108.6-15; 142.12.

76.   Pss. 6.3-5; 9.14, 22; 19.2-3; 21.12; 24.22; 30.10-13; 33.7; 43.24-25; 59.13; 114.1-4; 117.5; 141.2-4.

77.   Pss. 16.5; 24.4-5; 26.11; 118.33-40, 133–135, 144; 142.10.

78.   Pss. 24.7, 11, 18; 38.9; 50.3-14.

79.   Psalm 9 (MT Psalms 9 and 10) draws attention from Gelin as the psalm that most clearly reflects *anawim* piety. See Gelin, *Poor of Yahweh*, p. 54.

80.   Synonymous and parallel use of πτωχός and πένης abounds. In other words, the two terms are interchangeable. A conservative list of such use includes Pss. 9.19, 29, 30, 31, 33, 35, 38; 11.6; 34.10; 36.14; 39.18; 69.6; 71.13; 81.4; 85.1; 108.16; 112.7; and 139.13. Synonymous and/or parallel use of πτωχός and

is set over against ἀσεβής. But in v. 29, πένης is contrasted with πλούσιος. In v. 35, πτωχός is matched with the orphan; and in vv. 38-39, πένης is matched with the orphan and the abased (ταπεινός).

Rhetoric that includes orphans with the poor and the needy appears again in Psalm 81. The psalmist contrasts providing justice for the unjust and flattering sinners (Ps. 81.2) with providing justice for the orphan and the poor one, justifying the lowly one and the needy one (v. 3). The psalmist pleads: 'Rescue the needy one and deliver the poor one from the hand of the sinner' (v. 4).

Similarly, the inclusion of another character in context with the poor points away from spiritualizing the poor in Ps. 112.5-9:

> Who is like the Lord our God, who dwells in the highest and gazes on the lowly things in heaven and earth, who raises the poor one from the earth and lifts the needy one up out of the dungheap to set him with rulers, with rulers of his people, who settles the barren one in a house to be a rejoicing mother of children?

Here the reference to the barren woman, a character with a specific plight that God addresses, suggests that beneficence to the poor and needy is a particular action of God that expresses God's nature. 'The poor' are not metaphorical, but 'raising the poor' is illustrative. The Lord displays his glory (v. 4) by aiding the poor and needy. Yet this is not a complete reversal of fortunes. The needy are raised to the level of rulers in an act of divine equalization. Rulers are not simultaneously cast down.

The poor are mentioned only briefly in Psalms 11, 13, and 67. These cameo appearances, by their very brevity, provide solid insight into the stereotypical nature of the poor. The poor, along with the needy, are destined for the Lord's salvation (σωτηρία) (Ps. 11.6). The Lord is the hope of the poor (Ps. 13.6). God provides for the poor (Ps. 67.11).

πένης cuts across all three categories of psalms distinguished above. The combination 'πτωχός καὶ πένης' appears 13 times in the LXX, exclusively in the Psalms and Ezekiel: Ps. 34.10; 36.14; 39.18 (ἐγὼ δὲ πτωχός εἰμι καὶ πένης); 40.2; 69.6; 71.13; 73.21; 85.1; 108.16 (πένητα καὶ πτωχὸν), 22; Ezek. 16.49; 18.12; 22.29. However, see also Amos 4.1 (αἱ καταδυναστεύουσαι πτωχοὺς καὶ καταπατοῦσαι πένητας). Cf. Ps. 68.30 (πτωχὸς καὶ ἀλγῶν); 81.3 (ὀρφανὸν καὶ πτωχόν and ταπεινὸν καὶ πένητα); Deut. 15.11 (τῷ πένητι καὶ τῷ ἐπιδεομένῳ); 24.14 (πένητος καὶ ἐνδεοῦς); Isa. 41.17 (οἱ πτωχοὶ καὶ οἱ ἐνδεεῖς).

Just how a single, brief reference to the poor informs the reader's image of the poor may be illustrated by a further look at Psalm 67. This psalm appears to have no single coherent theme. Rather, it strings together diverse laudatory verses.[81] Within this choppy collection, however, are depictions of circumstances in which God's saving action takes concrete form. God is 'the father of orphans and the adjudicator of widows' (Ps. 67.6). God leads out those who are bound (πεπεδημένους) (Ps. 67.7), an action which is a constituent element of 'taking captivity captive' (Ps. 67.19). God likewise leads out 'those dwelling in tombs' (Ps. 67.7). The phrase 'those dwelling in tombs' may be in apposition to the phrase 'those rebelling'. Or the psalmist may be listing two beneficiaries of God's liberation.[82] In any case, this psalm hails God as liberator, also for the poor, and, in words faintly echoed in Luke 4, the Lord provides the content of the good news being announced (εὐαγγελιζομένοις) in the process (Ps. 67.12).

Wealth and ungodliness overlap in a number of the Psalms. In Psalm 36, there is a corresponding overlapping of poverty and righteousness.[83] Sinners, who have much wealth (v. 16), attack the poor and needy and slay the upright in heart (v. 10). Yet despite the ostensible success of sinners, the salvation of the righteous is coming (vv. 23-40).

Because sinners crop up so regularly in opposition to the poor in the Psalms and because discourse about sinners creates an important narrative dynamic in Luke's Gospel, a few explanatory comments about the term ἁμαρτωλός in the Psalms are in order. Everything said in the Psalms about sinners is negative. Sinners afflict and oppress several groups not deserving such treatment: the poor and needy, orphans, widows, the righteous, and sojourners.[84] Psalms contrast the attitudes and actions of the sinner with the attitudes and actions of the

81.   Psalms are occasionally inconsistent as well. In Psalm 118, the psalmist admits to not keeping the Lord's law (Ps. 118.136), yet claims to have kept the Lord's commandments (Ps. 118.87, 141, 168).

82.   In this case, are 'those dwelling in tombs' deceased persons, or deranged persons, as in Luke's Gospel? This ambiguity adds to the rhetorical flair of the psalm, while preserving the direction of its lauds.

83.   See Dibelius, *James*, p. 40 n. 137.

84.   Pss. 9.29-32 (where sinners team up with the wealthy); 36.12-17; 54.4; 81.4; 93.6; 108.16; 118.53, 61, 95, 110.

righteous person.[85] Psalm 57.4-5 is typical of scathing descriptions of sinners:

> Sinners are estranged [from God] from the moment they left their mothers; they went astray right from the womb. They lie. Rage makes them snake-like, like the deaf asp with stopped up ears who will not hear.

As a result of their manifest evil and arrogance, sinners are condemned by their own works and by God.[86] The Lord punishes sinners.[87] The rhetoric against sinners is as gruesome as it is vitriolic: 'The righteous one will be glad when he sees the condemnation of the impious ones; he will wash his hands in the blood of the sinner' (Ps. 57.11); 'The righteous Lord broke the necks of sinners into pieces' (Ps. 128.4). Psalmists have no qualms about petitioning God for violence against sinners.[88] In Ps. 108.9-10, the psalmist hopes that the sinner's children become homeless orphans and that his wife becomes a widow, and more, that the sinner's children be utterly destroyed. The writer of Psalm 100 extols as a virtue that he has killed all the sinners of the land (Ps. 100.8).

Psalms censure fraternization with sinners.[89] By contrast, Psalm 1 proclaims that those who avoid sinners will prosper (Ps. 1.1-3).

There is a distinct rhetorical difference in the Psalms between being one who sins and being a sinner. Psalmists acknowledge their sinfulness and the sinfulness of God's people,[90] but no psalmist is ever called a 'sinner' (ἀμαρτωλός) and not once are God's people called 'sinners'. Those enjoying the Lord's mercy may be 'those who sin' (ἀμαρτάνοντας) (Ps. 24.8), but not sinners (ἀμαρτωλούς). It is not as though psalmists did not have the opportunity to attach this label to Israel. Yet in Deuteronomistic-like Psalm 77, for example, in which Israel's history of sinfulness is vividly recounted, the people of Israel are never in these 72 verses named 'sinners'.[91] Sinning, of itself, does

---

85. Pss. 7.9-10; 10.2-3; 74.11. Ps. 9.24-25 is similar.
86. Pss. 9.17-19; 36.12-17, 20, 32; 91.8; 118.155; 144.20; 145.9; 146.6.
87. Pss. 3.8; 128.4.
88. Pss. 9.36; 103.35; 108.9-10.
89. Pss. 1.5; 83.11.
90. See Psalms 24, 31, 77, 102, and 105.
91. The same is true of Deuteronomistic-like Psalm 102. The lone exception to the rule may be Psalm 105. Psalm 105 is also a Deuteronomistic-like recounting of Israel's history: Israel sins repeatedly, yet God, who punishes, is ultimately merciful. Ps. 105.16-18 says that at one point in the wilderness 'our fathers' (v. 7) angered

not brand one a sinner. The title 'sinner' implies unremitting recalci-trance, and permanent opposition to God and to God's people.

The distinction between one who sins and the sinner helps explain the apparently contradictory language of Psalm 31. Sins may be forgiven, the psalmist asserts (Ps. 31.1-2). Indeed, the psalmist, being fortified by forgiveness, confesses having sinned (Ps. 31.5). Yet the psalm concludes with bad news for the sinner:

> Many are the floggings of the sinner; but (δε) mercy will surround the one who hopes in the Lord. Rejoice in the Lord and be glad, you righteous; and boast, all you upright in heart (Ps. 31.10-11).

It may be that this conclusion envisions a sinner who hopes in the Lord, thereby gains mercy, and is subsequently deemed righteous. More likely, though, the psalmist concludes with traditional termi-nology that contrasts the sinner, who is prima facie unrepentant, with the person who hopes in the Lord, who may then be exhorted in the plural as the righteous and upright in heart.

In short, sinners alienate themselves from God. They are wholly responsible for God's inevitable condemnation. Righteous persons are more than justified in avoiding interaction with sinners; righteous persons are divinely directed to shun them.

This study's conclusions about the poor in the Psalms can be antici-pated by observing the nature of the contrast between sinners and the poor. Whether the poor in a given psalm are merely powerless or are also pious, they are destined for good fortune. God is their rescue, their salvation. Sinners, whether they are wealthy and oppress indirectly, or violent and afflict directly, or simply impious, are destined for God's wrath. Thus, with respect to their ultimate fate, sinners are the antithesis of the poor.

Incidentally, Ps. 93.5 reads 'Lord, they [sinners] abased your people, they mistreated your heritage'. If v. 6 went on to speak of sinners killing the poor, commentators who gravitate toward the focus of a figurative interpretation of 'the poor' would likely claim on the basis of parallelism that juxtaposition of 'your people' and 'the poor' signals

---

Moses and Aaron, and 'the earth opened and swallowed Dathan and closed upon the assembly of Abiron, and fire was kindled in their assembly and flames consumed the sinners'. Rather than being an exception, though, this passage looks to be rhetorical theodicy: those destroyed—only a portion of the people in the wilderness—were sinners and therefore deserving of destruction.

that 'the poor' has become a designation for Israel or for pious people of God in general.[92] But v. 6 places the widow, sojourner, and orphan parallel to 'your people' of v. 5: 'They [that is, sinners] killed the widow and the sojourner, and murdered the orphan'. The psalmist is multiplying charges against sinners. The psalmist employs shotgun prosecution to evoke the Lord's vengeance. Clearly, the terms 'the widow', 'the sojourner', and 'the orphan' are not synonymous with 'your people'. The implication for interpretation of the poor in the Psalms is obvious. When similar juxtaposing involving 'the poor' occurs, the example of Ps. 93.5-6 should caution against facile identification of 'the poor' with 'the Lord's people' or 'the righteous', as the case may be.[93]

With respect to their ultimate fate, sinners are the antithesis of the poor. With respect to their actions, however, sinners are the antithesis, not of the poor, but of God and God's king. Sinners persecute the poor; God and God's king rescue the poor. There are several references to the poor in Psalm 71, all of which portray the ideal king's responsibility to be benevolent toward the poor. Six verses will be translated here. For the sake of simplicity, πτωχός in the singular will be translated 'poor one', in the plural, 'poor'.

> O God, give your discernment (κρίμα) to the king and your righteousness to the king's son, to judge your people with righteousness and your poor with discrimination (κρίσει). (vv. 1-2)
> He [David or Solomon] will judge (κρινεῖ) the poor of the people and will save the sons of the needy and will abase (ταπεινώσει) the extorter. (v. 4)
> . . . because he has delivered the poor one from the hand of the powerful one and the needy one who had no helper. He will spare the poor one and needy one and save the lives of the needy. He will redeem their lives from interest [on money] and injustice, and their name is dear to him (vv. 12-14).

Note that while 'your people' and 'your poor' clearly parallel each other in v. 2, v. 4 refers to 'the poor of the people', implying that 'your poor' and 'your people' are not synonyms even if poetically parallel. Other nations will honor the king's son because he is the guardian and deliverer of those with no means or power.[94]

92. See above, ch. 2.
93. See the discussion of Psalm 71 below.
94. Contra Seccombe (*Possessions*, pp. 95-96) the poor are not ciphers for

Psalm 131 is particularly illuminating when we look carefully at the Greek terminology. It underscores the ideal king's character-revealing treatment of the poor and confirms the typical cast of πτωχός. David has meekness or humility (πραΰτης, v. 1), but not poverty. The psalm lists four provisions accompanying election by the Lord: blessed hunting, bread for the poor (v. 15), priests clothed with salvation, and joyful holy ones (v. 16). Provision made for the poor is a standard element of God's beneficent activity.

I now turn to those psalms in which the psalm appears to imply that the writer is a poor one. These psalms confirm the impressions of the poor given by psalms that do not identify the poor with the psalmist.

The word πτωχός appears in the title of Psalm 101, which calls this 'a prayer for the poor one when he may be weary and pour out his supplication before the Lord'. Πτωχός does not occur in the body of the psalm.[95] Yet the psalm is instructive because it paints a portrait capable of being invoked by the term πτωχός. The image is of one blighted, whose heart has dried up, and whose bone clings to his flesh from groaning. Does the psalmist have sufficient food and simply forget to eat it because of his distress? Or is the writer so poor as to eat ashes as if they were bread and have nothing but tears to drink? The psalm does not spell this out. But the overall image conveyed is that of a pathetic character.

Two established patterns in the Psalms—that πτωχός is synonymous with πένης and that the Lord delivers the poor—continue in Ps. 34.10:

> All my bones will say: Lord, who is like you—you who delivers the poor from the hand of one stronger than he, the poor and needy from the one plundering him?

Psalm 139 strikes themes similar to Psalm 36. The evil person (πονη-ροῦ, v. 2), the unjust person (ἀδίκου, vv. 2, 5), the sinner (ἁμαρτω-λοῦ, v. 5), and the arrogant (ὑπερήφανοι, v. 6) are overlapping designations. The psalmist does not directly call himself poor. But this psalm is a supplication (v. 7), and the psalmist is confident that the

---

Israel here. The nations will not honor the king's son because he is Israel's champion. They will honor him because he has proven himself to be outstandingly chivalrous with respect to the poor. This is not to say that the poor and needy might not be ciphers for Israel in Psalm 73.

95. Variant readings in Ps. 101.18 of πτωχων and πενητων in place of ταπεινῶν appear to be harmonizations with the title.

Lord 'will exercise judgment for the poor and justice for the needy' (v. 13). The righteous (δίκαιοι) and upright (εὐθεῖς, v. 14) are, like the poor and needy, on God's side, in contrast to sinners and others. But it is not so clear that the poor and needy are to be equated with the righteous and upright.

I now take up those psalms in which 'poor one' is one of the psalmist's self-designations.[96] In a plea for forgiveness, the writer of Psalm 24 asks the Lord to look upon him and have mercy on him because he is an only child and poor (v. 16). In Psalm 33, the psalmist refers to himself as 'this poor one' (v. 7).[97] Psalm 39 points out the relationship with the Lord to which the self-described poor psalmist lays claim. The psalmist calls himself poor and needy, and calls God his helper and protector (v. 18). The psalmist looks for the Lord's compassion, mercy, and truth (v. 12); he expects the Lord to deliver him and help him.

Much the same is seen in Psalm 68. The psalmist calls himself poor and suffering (v. 30), admits to being foolish and guilty of transgressions (v. 6), asks to be saved (v. 15), and asks that enemies receive God's wrath (vv. 23-29). The poor in general ought to see and rejoice (v. 33) because the Lord listens to the needy and does not treat the shackled[98] with contempt (v. 34).

Psalm 69 is strongly reminiscent of Psalm 39. The writer calls himself poor and needy (v. 6), and calls on God as helper and deliverer. Psalm 85 is likewise reminiscent of Psalm 39. The psalmist asks the Lord to listen to him because he is poor and needy (v. 1). The psalm is a plea for guidance (v. 11), mercy, strength, and rescue (v. 16). Physical need overlaps with spiritual disposition in Psalm 85; in sentence structure parallel to v. 1, the psalmist refers to himself also as holy and calls himself God's servant (v. 2).[99]

Several images merge in Psalm 87. The psalmist likens himself to the dead (vv. 4-7; 11-12). He lists among his tribulations that his eyes

96. Ps. 24.16; 39.18; 68.30; 69.6; 85.1; 87.16; 108.22.

97. Psalm 33 offers an example of the rich as ungodly, and eventual negative consequences for the rich for their ungodliness. In contrast to those who seek the Lord diligently, the rich have become poor (ἐπτώχευσαν) and hungry (ἐπείνασαν) (33.11).

98. Cf. Ps. 67.7.

99. Ps. 85.1-2a: Κλῖνον, κύριε, τὸ οὖς σου καὶ ἐπάκουσόν μου, ὅτι πτωχὸς καὶ πένης εἰμὶ ἐγώ. φύλαξον τὴν ψυχήν μου, ὅτι ὅσιός εἰμι.

have been weakened by poverty (πτωχείας, v. 10). Later, he calls himself poor, and claims to have been abased (ἐταπεινώθην) and become despondent (v.16).

A fresh look at the Psalms suggests that the psalmists do not say in effect, 'I am poor because I bend the knee to the Lord'. Rather, the psalmists say, 'I am poor because my enemies afflict me'. The coincidence in many psalms of piety and affliction that adheres to 'the poor', in particular in those psalms that identify the psalmist as poor, does not make poverty and piety synonymous. All of the psalms are products of piety. Some of the psalms are laments by individuals and communities afflicted, persecuted, or oppressed.

When psalmists call themselves 'poor', they do so to express their affliction. Calling themselves poor functions rhetorically to emphasize the desperate nature of their plight vis a vis enemies. In every case, the context of this self-designation is a plea for rescue.

Scattered comments in the Psalms weigh further against a simple identification of 'the poor' and 'the pious'. Ps. 111.1-3 points out that the righteous person, who fears the Lord, enjoys glory and wealth. According to Ps. 20.2-8, the king who trusts in the Lord has glory and blessings and joy. Psalm 71 holds that if God should grant to the king power to adjudicate justly and God's righteousness, one of the benefits to the king will be gold from Arabia. Psalmists thank the Lord for blessings, which include abundant crops, the reverse of poverty.[100]

The point is not to try to suggest that the Psalms promote wealth as a product of piety, but to point out that godly psalmists do not expect poverty to accompany piety. On the contrary, they are baffled when righteous persons are afflicted in this way, and equally baffled when sinners are materially rewarded. These phenomena are inconsistent with a world ruled by the God who loves righteousness.

In psalms where the poor are not identified with the psalmist, the poor are purely passive except for cries to the Lord, which express their distress. In psalms where the poor are identified with the psalmist, the poor may possess the capacity to be righteous or have possessed that capacity prior to their current state. But in every case, the poor are typically characters who have no control over their destiny. They are utterly vulnerable to persecution and oppression. They cannot force justice. They do not have the resources to show mercy. This places the

---

100. Psalms 22, 66, 102, and 106.

poor on a different plane from sinners, who have options and resources and have chosen to misuse them.[101] The poor may be looked after by pious and righteous persons, but rescue or a reversal of fortunes comes from God or God's agent, the king. The poor are indeed idealized in the Psalms, if being idealized means that the poor are romanticized as that group self-evidently destined for God's salvation, that is, as a group that God will surely deliver from its plight.

Proverbs

In Proverbs, the poor are consistently contrasted with the wealthy, despite the fact that the Lord made them both (22.2). Wealth holds the rich man's soul for ransom, but does not threaten the poor (13.8). The rich have many friends; the poor are hated (14.20; 19.1). Yet, it is better to be poor righteous than wealthy false (19.22; see also 28.6).[102]

In Proverbs, etiquette toward the poor is paramount. Dishonoring the needy is a sin; those showing mercy to the poor are blessed (14.21; 22.9, 22). Treatment of the poor and needy is explicitly tied to the reaction of the deity: exhorting or oppressing the needy provokes God, while having mercy on the poor honors God (14.31). Prov. 17.5 is similar in language to 14.31: ridiculing the poor provokes the creator. Again, showing mercy to a poor one is lending to God, who will repay accordingly (19.17). Ironically, those who are generous to the poor will not be in need themselves, while those who overlook the poor will be in great distress (28.27; a similar thought is expressed in 28.8). When a king judges the poor truthfully, his throne is secure (29.7). A person's character is betrayed by his or her treatment of the poor: one of the characteristics of the noble woman is that she opens her hand to the needy one and reaches out fruit to the poor one (31.20).

The poor person's destiny is always in someone else's hands. The question then presents itself, who should determine the destiny of the poor? Proverbs 29.7 declares that the righteous one is capable of judging the poor (πενιχροῖς), but the impious are unfit for ruling the

---

101. In his discussion of 'rich' and 'poor' in the eastern Mediterranean in New Testament times, Malina ('Wealth and Poverty', p. 355) reaches a strikingly similar-sounding conclusion from the perspective of cultural anthropology: '[T]he words are not opposites and really refer to two qualitatively different spheres'.

102. Wealth is not universally condemned. Prov. 22.4 speaks of wisdom, wealth, glory, and life stemming from fear of the Lord.

poor one (πτωχῷ). Note that in this proverb, the righteous are not poor and the poor are neither righteous nor impious.

Amos and Habakkuk

Proper etiquette toward the poor is central also to the prophet Amos's message. His accusations against Israel pound away at mistreatment of those whose fate is in another's hands, be they the righteous, the needy, the poor, the lowly, or the servant girl (Amos 2.6-8; 5.11-12; 8.6). The case against 'the heifers of Basan' is that they exploit the poor and trample on the needy (4.1). The prophet promises destruction upon those who destroy the needy and exploit the poor (8.4).

How are the mighty (δυναστῶν) punished? The prophet Habakkuk states that the Lord reverses their situation and makes the mighty like the poor one (Hab. 3.14).

Isaiah

In Isaiah, πτωχός occurs 11 times.[103] Like Amos, Isaiah charges Israel and its rulers with mistreatment of the poor. They have plundered the goods of the poor (3.14), shamed them (3.15), and denied them justice (10.2).

In Isa. 3.14-15, the Lord makes his accusations against the leaders of the people in the form of an interrogation. The structure of vv. 14-15 is a-b-a'-b':

> v. 14 a: Ὑμεῖς δὲ τί ἐνεπυρίσατε τὸν ἀμπελῶνά μου
>   b: καὶ ἡ ἁρπαγὴ τοῦ πτωχοῦ ἐν τοῖς οἴκοις ὑμῶν
> v. 15 a´: τί ὑμεῖς ἀδικεῖτε τὸν λαόν μου
>   b´: καὶ τὸ πρόσωπον τῶν πτωχῶν καταισχύνετε

Setting the vineyard on fire (a) is parallel to treating my people unjustly (a'). Plundering the poor (b) is parallel to shaming the poor (b'). The Lord goes on in ch. 3 to lodge other charges: the daughters of Zion are haughty and vain. These subsequent charges are more prosaic in style than the more poetic ones in vv. 14-15 and are directed against a new subject.

Returning to Isa. 3.14-15, do these verses refer to one inclusive wronged population or to a general population and a subset of that population? If 'the poor' is equivalent to 'my people', then one population is referred to, and 'the poor' is a technical term for 'the people'.

---

103. Isa. 3.14, 15; 10.2; 14.30 (twice); 24.6; 25.3; 29.19; 41.17; 58.7; 61.1.

If 'the poor' carries its normal denotative sense, then 'the people' is a general category and 'the poor' is a specific subset of that category. The immediate context does not offer a conclusive answer.

If Isa. 10.1-2 informs the interpretation of Isa. 3.14-15, the poor are a portion of the people. The conventional pairings of the poor and needy, and the widow and orphan occur in ch. 10:

> v. 1 Woe to those writing evil [verdicts]. For when they
> v. 2 write, they write evil [verdicts], shunning justice for the poor, snatching the legal decision away from the needy of my people, so that the widow becomes their plunder (ἁρπαγὴν) and the orphan their booty.

The needy are specified as the needy of my people (πενήτων τοῦ λαοῦ μου). The widow and orphan appear to be examples of the poor and needy. Interestingly, ἁρπαγή occurs in Isaiah only in these two places: 3.14 and 10.2.

The context of Isa. 14.30 is a rebuke of all foreigners. But who the poor are who will be fed and refreshed in peace is unclear. Nor is it clear if these poor are to be identified with 'the lowly of the people' (10.32).

In Isaiah 24, the prophet speaks of the desolation to come. Everyone will be leveled: the people will be like the priest, the servant like the master, the maid like the mistress, the buyer like the seller, the lender like the borrower, the one owing like the one to whom it is owed (v. 2). All inhabitants of the earth will be poor (v. 6). After the devastation, the poor people (ὁ λαὸς ὁ πτωχός)—who else is there?—will bless the Lord and the cities of the people wronged (ἀνθρώπων ἀδικουμένων) will bless the Lord (25.3).

Isaiah 29 returns to the theme of devastation: 'in that day the deaf will hear... and the eyes of the blind will see (29.18), and the poor will be glad because of the Lord' (29.19). By contrast, the lawless and proud are destroyed (29.20), along with those who make people sin (29.21).

The context of Isaiah 41 is the Lord's soothing words to Israel. Israel is chosen and loved (41.8), the Lord's servant (or child, παῖς) (41.9). Israel's adversaries will be confounded and destroyed (41.11). The poor and impoverished (οἱ ἐνδεεῖς) will be glad, because when they seek water for their parched tongues the Lord will open rivers and fountains (41.17-18). Even if 'poor' and 'impoverished' are references to the nation Israel, the connotative force of the words is not diffused because the context is Israel in distress.

Isaiah further asserts that the unrighteous and impious will not have rest or joy (57.20-21). What are the righteous to do? Not fast, says the prophet, but loose unjust bonds, untie knots of forced agreements, send the oppressed into freedom, cancel every unjust account, break their bread with the hungry, lead the unsheltered poor into their house, clothe the naked, and not overlook family members in their household (58.6-7).

In the end, the Lord has anointed the prophet to proclaim good news to the poor, heal the broken hearted, preach freedom for captives and sight for the blind, declare the acceptable year of the Lord and the day of recompense, and comfort and give glory to those who mourn (61.1-3). This is a memorable Scripture. The passage waxes poetically and displays numerous rhetorical devices: an *inclusio* formed by the spirit of the Lord and the spirit of heaviness, *paromoiosis* achieved by beginning clauses with an infinitive verb and matching elements within clauses, the pleonasm of 'the acceptable year of the Lord and the day of recompense', a figure of speech in 'the oil of gladness', and repetition of 'the mourners'. Surely one could find more. The interpretive tendency to spiritualize this section receives impetus from the end of 61.3, which foretells that those who have mourned in Zion will be called generations of righteousness.[104] But rather than collapsing distinctions between the poor, the broken-hearted, the captive, and the blind into a general spiritual state, these individual examples are illustrations of the multifaceted salvation of God. Here, God's prophet is sent to effect God's salvation.

Jeremiah

Jeremiah's only use of πτωχός is a rather disparaging comment. At second glance, however, it fits the stereotype emerging from the LXX as a whole: the poor cannot be held morally responsible. Jeremiah is looking for someone in Jerusalem practicing justice and seeking faithfulness. The first ones he looks at are obdurate. Jeremiah ventures the opinion that maybe they are to be excused because they are poor.

> Perhaps they are [the] poor, and for that reason unable (ἐδυνάσθησαν), since they do not know the way of [the] Lord and the justice of God (5.4).

---

104. Perhaps the subject of κληθήσονται (Isa. 61.3b) is all of the types mentioned in 61.1-3a, but this is unlikely.

So Jeremiah goes to the well bred (ἁδροὺς, 5.5). They have the wherewithal, yet they disappoint Jeremiah as well.

Epistle of Jeremiah
The sole reference to πτωχός in the Epistle of Jeremiah complements this picture. The poor and powerless (ἀδυνάτῳ, v. 27) are contrasted with priests and their wives (v. 28).

Ezekiel
With Ezekiel there is a return to an emphasis on etiquette toward the poor. Sodom's sin was arrogance or pride (ὑπερηφανία). Sodom lived with fullness of bread and with abundance, but did not help the hand of the poor and needy (16.49).

Ezekiel 18 provides a thumbnail description of a righteous person, that is, the person practicing justice and righteousness.[105] Along with avoiding idolatry and adultery, the righteous person does not oppress anyone, gives bread to the hungry, and clothes the naked (18.6, 7).[106] By contrast, the sinner has, among other things, practised idolatry, committed adultery, and oppressed the poor and needy (18.11, 12). Mistreatment of the poor is not the sin, but it ranks with others as cause for divine recompense. Likewise, in Ezek. 22.29 oppression of the poor and needy one is among the numerous sins of Israel.

Sirach
The proverbial wisdom of Sirach also admonishes justice and generosity toward the poor. The poor are often mentioned along with other groups that ought to be shown patience and care.

> Son, do not defraud the livelihood of a poor person and do not shut off the expectations of the needy. Do not vex the soul of those who are hungry and do not provoke a man who is anxious. Do not trouble further the heart of someone provoked and do not shut off a donation for someone who needs it. Do not reject the supplicant who is in distress and do not turn your face away from a poor person... Incline your ear to the poor person and answer him peaceably, with meekness (πραΰτητι) (4.1-4, 8).

---

105. ὁ ποιῶν κρίμα καὶ δικαιοσύνην Ezek. 18.5; cf. Jer. 5.1: ποιῶν κρίμα.

106. The full list in Ezek. 18.6-8 also includes no intercourse with a menstruating woman, repayment of debts, no plundering, no charging interest on debts, and the rejection of injustice.

> Stretch out your hand to the poor person, that your blessing may be complete. [Exhibit] free goodwill before all the living, and do not withhold good will from the dead (7.32-33).

The issue in the following passage is that fear of the Lord should be the sole criterion for praising people. External circumstances are irrelevant.

> The stranger's and the foreigner's and the poor one's right to boast is fear of the Lord. It is not right to dishonor an intelligent poor person and it is not fitting to praise a sinful man (10.22-23).

Of added interest in the following passage is that πτωχός and ταπεινός are equivalent and denote material circumstances.

> A poor person is praised because of his knowledge and a wealthy person is praised because of his wealth. How much more would the one praised in poverty be praised in wealth. And how much more would the one jeered in wealth be jeered in poverty. The wisdom of the lowly person (ταπεινοῦ) lifts up his head and seats him in the middle of those who are great (10.30–11.1).

The following verse is a sarcastic statement about the state of affairs.

> The wealthy person did wrong and nevertheless he snorted threateningly; the poor person was wronged and nevertheless he had to beg (13.3).

In 13.18-23, πτωχός, πένης, and ταπεινός are synonymous and all contrasted with πλούσιος.

> What peace is there between the hyena and the dog? What peace is there between the rich and the needy? Just as lions prey on the donkey in the wild, so the rich feed on the poor. Just as the arrogant abhor lowliness, so the rich person abhors the poor person. The rich person in trouble is supported by friends; the lowly person in trouble is rejected by friends. When the rich person trips up, many fawn over him; when he has spoken nonsense, they make excuses for him. When the lowly person has tripped up, they tell him to pipe down; when he has spoken intelligently, he is ignored. The rich person spoke and everyone was quiet and lauded his speech to the clouds. The poor person speaks and they say 'Who is this?'; let him stumble and they will push him further (13.18-23).

Sirach concludes this section in sarcasm worthy of Juvenal or Lucian by stating that, according to the impious, wealth is a good that can do no wrong, whereas evil resides in poverty (13.24).

Remaining references to πτωχός in Sirach continue in the same vein. Sirach advises the reader not to become poor by feasting on borrowed

money (18.33). Sirach hates the pride and deceitfulness of the rich
and arrogant, and advises that the poor, who have no grounds for
arrogance, will get a hearing from God (21.5; 25.2). Sirach offers
more folk wisdom in the saying that it is better to live poor on your
own than to live it up dependent on someone else (29.22); it is better
to be poor and healthy than wealthy and physically emaciated (30.14);
it is wrong to victimize the poor and needy (31.25); God listens to the
prayers of the poor, the mistreated, the orphan, and the widow and
cannot be bribed (32.16-17). Sirach observes that, whereas the rich
person labors and then rests surrounded by delicacies, the poor person
labors and is still needy when quitting time comes (34.4).[107]

Psalms of Solomon

E. Bammel singles out for comment the use of πτωχός in the Psalms
of Solomon:

> Materially πτωχός is here identical with δίκαιος and ὅσιος and denotes
> more of an inner quality, especially when used in confrontation with
> adversaries. Where used, πτωχός is always the chief term and it thus
> represents an essential aspect in the self-understanding of the community
> which expresses itself in the Psalms.[108]

Bammel's assertion can be divided into two related claims: first, the
claim that πτωχός is materially identical with δίκαιος and ὅσιος and
denotes an inner quality; secondly, the claim that πτωχός expresses the
self-understanding of a community. The latter claim is inferred on the
basis of the methodological assumption that the Psalms of Solomon are
community generated and may be made transparent to that community
by identifying the community with persons or groups favored in the
psalms.[109] The former claim rests on slim evidence. Though the identification of πτωχός with δίκαιος and ὅσιος is not demonstrated by
Bammel in the article, the flow of his discussion suggests that his
methodological assumptions again play a decisive role in his conclusion. If those favored by God in the Psalms of Solomon represent a
community, and if this divinely favored community may be designated
'the righteous', 'the holy', and 'the poor' respectively, then 'the right-

107. A final reference to the poor in Sir. 38.19 seems to equate the poor with the
dead. Sir. 38.16-23 provides instructions for proper lament for and treatment of the
dead, but the meaning of 38.19 is not clear.
108. Bammel, 'Πτωχός', p. 896.
109. See the discussion of form criticism, pp. 29-31 above.

eous', 'the holy', and 'the poor' are materially identical.

The immediate purpose of passages in the Psalms of Solomon containing πτωχός, however, is to say something about God: 'God is the refuge of the poor one' (Pss. Sol. 5.2). If this verse may be said to reflect as well the hopes of a community that looks to God for refuge, Pss. Sol. 5.11 does not lend itself to such expansion of πτωχός: 'God nourishes the kings and rulers and the people (λαούς), and is the hope of the poor one and the needy one'. In this verse, the poor one is part of a whole social order dependent upon God. What calls for comment is that the rhetoric of this psalm distinguishes the poor and the needy from kings, rulers, and the people. God nourishes those who have options and resources, and is the hope of those without options that result from resources. Such a distinction is consistent with a typological image of the poor as those without the capacity to direct their destiny.

Later, the psalmist also says, 'God will have mercy on the poor, to the joy of Israel' (Pss. Sol. 10.6). In context, this perhaps contains the notion that 'the poor' are 'those who truly love the Lord' (10.3). But more likely it expresses one of God's particular benefactions that will elicit joy from the wider company of God's people. In the two remaining references, Pss. Sol. 15.1 and 18.2, the poor one(s) may be appealing to God, but πτωχός expresses the desperation of their plight rather than the degree of their piety.

Concluding Comments

Before leaving this discussion of the poor in the LXX, let me mention again the importance of attention to the Greek terminology in the Jewish Scriptures of the first century. A. Gelin speaks of Zephaniah as a 'turning point in history'.[110] According to Gelin, Zephaniah introduces a metaphorical sense to 'the poor'. Being 'poor' means abandoning oneself to God. Following Gelin's lead, Hoppe summarizes Zephaniah's message to be that 'since God is the protector of the poor, Judah must act like the poor to enjoy that protection'.[111] So 'poor' becomes, in Hoppe's words, a metaphor for 'the ideal relationship of human beings to God'.[112]

---

110. Gelin, *Poor of Yahweh*, p. 31. So also, with reservations, Hoppe, *Being Poor*, p. 77.
111. Hoppe, *Being Poor*, p. 77.
112. Hoppe, *Being Poor*, p. 77.

In the LXX, however, πτωχός is not used in the Greek Zephaniah. Neither is πένης. The vocabulary of key passages for Gelin and Hoppe is ταπεινός and πραΰς. In translation, the passages read as follows:

> Seek the Lord, all lowly of the earth. Practice justice and seek righteousness. Be answerable to them so that you might be hidden in the day of the Lord's wrath (Zeph. 2.3).
> And I will take up among you the pious and lowly people (Zeph. 3.12).

Zephaniah is demanding a spiritual stance on the part of the people. But the text does not use πτωχός to express it. Luke's authorial audience would not read πτωχός into πραΰς and ταπεινός here.

Two diagrams may help to clarify what this study is presenting as the typal image of the poor constructed by and displayed in the LXX. Diagram 1 summarizes the traditional interpretation of the poor in the Hebrew Bible based on socio-religious historical reconstruction and word studies of *ani* and *anaw*. Traditional interpretation holds that the denotative and connotative senses of 'the poor' evolved roughly along a time line stretching from pre-exilic Israel through post-exilic early Judaism. What began as an expression of material poverty became increasingly associated with spiritual piety. Though most interpreters want to retain some sense of the original link to material poverty in later references to the poor, the standard interpretive model is that as time went on, the designation 'the poor' became relatively less a matter of means and relatively more a symbol of spirituality. This model presents the interpreter with an image of the poor roughly equivalent to the pious in New Testament times.

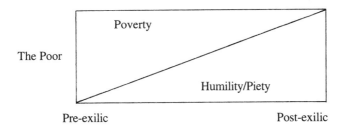

Diagram 1

By contrast, the LXX portrait of the poor, sketched here with an eye toward the authorial audience of Luke–Acts, looks more like Diagram 2. The frame of reference is not a time line, but a montage.

Several images coalesce in the term πτωχός to create a recognizable and consistent character type. The psalms in which the psalmists call themselves poor notwithstanding, the poor are not so much faithful as they are powerless and a-responsible, that is, depicted as behaving neither responsibly nor, for that matter, irresponsibly. They are acted upon, not actors. They have neither the resources to be generous or merciful nor the capacity to oppress or even influence others. Most importantly, God is the source of salvation for the poor, and God's magnificence is displayed by divine rescue of the poor.

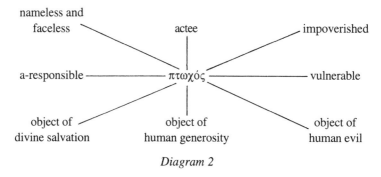

Diagram 2

Old Testament Pseudepigrapha

Extant Greek-language literature of Judaism of the first century CE consists of the LXX and an assortment of religious writings, as well as the works of Philo and Josephus. The assortment includes literature of various categories: testament, psalm, novel, apocalypse, and wisdom. These categories are not pure genre designations, but illustrate a breadth of literary form and subject matter. This assortment has been loosely called 'intertestamental literature', 'Old Testament pseudepigrapha', and 'the apocryphal Old Testament'. None of these designations is totally satisfactory as an all-encompassing label.[113] 'Intertestamental' is imprecise. Moreover, if attempts at dating undated

---

113. For discussions about how to label this assortment of writings, see J.H. Charlesworth, 'Introduction for the General Reader' in *Old Testament Pseudepigrapha*, pp. xxiii-xxv; G.W.E. Nickelsburg, *Jewish Literature between the Bible and the Mishnah: A Historical and Literary Introduction* (Philadelphia: Fortress Press, 1981), pp. 1-6; H.F.D. Sparks, 'Preface' in *Apocryphal Old Testament*, p. xvii.

ancient material are at all accurate, much of this literature antedates the Wisdom of Solomon, which is in the LXX. Not all of this literature is, strictly speaking, pseudepigraphic, for example, *Joseph and Aseneth* and the *Life of Adam and Eve*. On the other hand, some works within the LXX are pseudepigraphic, such as the Wisdom of Solomon and the Letter of Jeremiah. The *Psalms of Solomon* may be included in the LXX or in 'the Old Testament Pseudepigrapha', or both.[114] Likewise, *3 Maccabees* and *4 Maccabees* fall into both collections.[115] Finally, 'apocrypha' has become a prejudicial term; what is apocryphal and what is not depends on one's canon. In this study, the term 'Old Testament pseudepigrapha' will be used for convenience.[116]

I am not suggesting that Luke's authorial audience necessarily knows the Old Testament pseudepigrapha.[117] Nor is it necessary to establish from the Old Testament pseudepigrapha images of the captive, the blind, the poor, and the others to direct our interpretation of Luke's use of these images. Rather, observations from Greek-language Old Testament pseudepigraphic material, material which also implies LXX

---

114. The *Psalms of Solomon* and the *Odes*, with the exception of the *Prayer of Manasseh*, are the only writings included in Rahlf's LXX not treated in *Harper's Bible Commentary*. The inside front cover of *Harper's Bible Dictionary* lists the *Psalms of Solomon* among 'Poetic and Prophetic Books' of the LXX. But in the list of abbreviations in both the commentary and the dictionary, the Psalms of Solomon are categorized not with 'Books of the Bible (with Apocrypha)' but with 'Pseudepigrapha and Early Patristic Books'. P.J. Achtemeier (gen. ed.), *Harper's Bible Dictionary* (San Francisco: Harper & Row, 1985); J.L. Mays (gen. ed.), *Harper's Bible Commentary* (San Francisco: Harper & Row, 1988).

115. Rahlf's LXX includes *3 Maccabees* and *4 Maccabees*; they are translated in Charlesworth's collection *Old Testament Pseudepigrapha*, and *Harper's Bible Commentary* interprets them.

116. For the purposes of this study, the *Psalms of Solomon* are included in the LXX and not in the Old Testament pseudepigrapha. Conclusions drawn about the Old Testament pseudepigraphic material are drawn without reference to the *Psalms of Solomon*. Setting these parameters for discussion is particularly noteworthy with respect to πτωχός, as will become evident below.

117. Various scholars have pointed out similarities between Luke–Acts and writings of the Old Testament pseudepigrapha. G.W.E. Nickelsburg ('Riches, the Rich, and God's Judgment', pp. 324-44) lists comparable motifs and formal elements; D. Reeves ('Studies in the Ethics of Luke' [PhD dissertation, Harvard University, 1971], p. 51) contends that Luke 21 resembles *4 Ezra* and *2 Baruch*. These studies treat themes and motifs, however, not audience competence.

competence of its authorial audience, may confirm the literary quality of the terms for the captive, the blind, the poor, and the others being considered. This, in turn, makes a literary interpretation of these character types in Luke–Acts more plausible.

The vocabulary I am concentrating on in this study is present in 16 of the approximately 80 works covered by A.-M. Denis's invaluable *Concordance Grecque des Pseudepigraphes d'Ancien Testament*.[118] This vocabulary clearly does not dominate the Old Testament pseudepigrapha. Nevertheless, the reader does get a clear sense of the import of each term. Several observations may be mentioned briefly.

As Table 2 in Appendix B shows, νεκρός appears in eight of these writings, followed by αἰχμάλωτος in seven, τυφλός in six, and πτωχός in five. These will be discussed in turn. By contrast, θραύειν appears only in *Joseph and Aseneth*, and there only once (27.11): Aseneth recalls that the Lord shattered the swords of Dan, Gad, Naphtali, and Asher when they sought to kill her; their swords were miraculously reduced to ashes. Likewise, λεπρός appears only in the *Lives of the Prophets*, and there only once (22.16): when Elisha cursed his servant Gehazi for secretly going to Naaman, Gehazi became a leper. *Lives of the Prophets* 22.16 is a midrashic paraphrase of 4 Kgdms 5.27.[119] Ἀνάπηρος also occurs only once. A tribute to Abraham's hospitality asserts that he received everyone: 'rich and needy, both kings and rulers, the maimed and the weak (ἀδυνάτους), both friends and strangers, both neighbors and travelers' (*T. Abr.* 1.2). Whereas the maimed are not established as a type character in the LXX, the potential for such is there. Ἀνάπηρος in *T. Abr.* 1.2 taps this potential.

Αἰχμάλωτος retains its normal sense of war captive in the Old Testament pseudepigrapha. The context determines the precise referent in each case. In whatever circumstance, the captive epitomizes defeat and loss of volition. Captives are the spoils of battle, taken by the Assyrian king Sennacherib (Demetrius the Chronographer in Clem. Alex. *Strom.* 1.142), taken by Abraham (Pseudo-Eupolemus in Eus. *PrEV* 9.17.5), and taken by Jacob's sons (Theodotus in Eus.

---

118. A.-M. Denis, *et al.*, *Concordance Grecque des Pseudepigraphes d'Ancien Testament* (Louvain-la-Neuve: Université Catholique de Louvain, Institut Orientaliste, 1987).

119. On Midrash as paraphrase, see J. Neusner, *What is Midrash?* (Guides to Biblical Scholarship; Philadelphia: Fortress Press, 1987), pp. 1-12, 23-30. Neusner does not discuss the Old Testament pseudepigrapha, though his thesis applies here.

PrEV 9.22.11). Levi predicts, tragically, that his sinful descendants
will be scattered as captives among the Gentiles (*T. Levi* 10.4; 15.1).
Aristeas bargains for the release of Jewish war captives (*Ep. Arist.*
33.3; 35.5; 37.1). In rehearsing the story of his slavery, Joseph quotes
a Memphian woman who refers to him as an αἰχμάλωτος, though
strictly speaking he is not a war captive (*T. Jos.* 14.3). Just how
stripped of self-determination the αἰχμάλωτος is comes through in
Joseph and Aseneth: Aseneth is offended that she would be given in
marriage to Joseph and likens the prospect to being treated as a captive, that is, forced into sexual relations with someone base or vulgar
(*Jos. Asen.* 4.9 [12]).

As a substantive, τυφλός refers to a person who lacks eyesight.[120]
The blind appear twice as typical objects of hospitality and generosity,
and in both instances the blind are mentioned together with other
nobly-assisted groups. Pseudo-Phocylides includes them in a series of
admonitions:

> Give to the poor man (πτωχός) at once, and do not tell him to come
> tomorrow. . . Give alms to the needy (χρήζοντι). Receive the homeless
> in [your] house, and lead the blind man (καί τυόν ὁδηγεῖ). Pity the ship-
> wrecked, for navigation is unsure. Extend your hand to him who falls,
> and save the helpless one (ἀπερίστατον ἄνδρα).[121]

At his death, Job is eulogized by the needy, orphans, and all the weak
(ἀδυνατοις) as having been 'the strength of the weak, the light of the
blind, the father of the orphan, receiver of strangers, [and] the clothing
of the widow' (*T. Job* 53.1-3). In addition, earlier in the Testament
the devil, disguised as the king of Persia, accuses Job of squandering
his goods by sharing them with the needy (ἐπιδεομένοις), the blind,
and the lame (17.3). By means of the devil's accusations, the writer
cleverly establishes Job's virtue by means of criticism by an enemy
whose point of view is the opposite of God's.

Ten of the 11 occurrences of χωλός in the Old Testament pseudepigrapha are found in the allegorical story of the lame man and the
blind man in the *Apocryphon of Ezekiel*. It is an amusing story that

---

120. *T. Reub.* 2.9; *T. Job* 17.3; 53.3; *Sib. Or.* 5.350; *Apocryphon of Ezekiel*;
Ps.-Phoc. 24. Yet the *Testaments of the Twelve Patriarchs* speak freely of being
blinded in one's mind, heart, or soul by deceit or by the ruler of deceit: *T. Sim.* 2.7;
T. Jud. 11.1; 18.3, 6; 19.4; *T. Dan* 2.4; *T. Gad* 3.3.

121. Ps.-Phoc. 22-26. The translation is from P.W. Van der Horst, 'Pseudo-
Phocylides', in Charlesworth (ed.), *Old Testament Pseudepigrapha*, II, pp. 574-75.

plays off the convention of the helplessness of the lame and the blind. In this story, the lame man and the blind man, helpless apart, team up for crime in a way that each compensates for the other's malady. Their alibi rests on the assumption that the lame and the blind are incapable of committing the crime. The eleventh occurrence of χωλός is in the devil's ironic accusation in *T. Job* 17.3, discussed in the previous paragraph.

Κωφός is used in reference to idols, not to persons, in the Old Testament pseudepigrapha. The term makes a pejorative point of the inability of idols to act: idols are dead and deaf mute (*Jos. Asen.* 8.5; 11.8; 12.5; 13.11), deaf mute and toothless (*Sib. Or.* 4.9), deaf mute shrines of stone (*Sib. Or.* 4.28), lifeless and deaf mute (*Sib. Or.* 5.84).

Of the vocabulary being surveyed νεκρός is the most frequently met of the vocabulary in the Old Testament pseudepigrapha. In the singular or the plural, the dead are usually spoken of as simply no longer living, though according to *1 Enoch* the dead reside in an interim world until the day of judgment.[122] As in the LXX, idols are said to be dead,[123] the point being that they are useless. God, by contrast, brings the dead to life.[124] Or, God's prophet may raise the dead.[125]

The Testament of Judah 25.4 speaks of an eschatological reversal of fortunes for those who have experienced poverty and those who have experienced death for the Lord's sake. The specific terms πτωχός and νεκρός are lacking from this passage. Moreover, unlike other passages I have cited, this one refers explicitly to those who suffered in these ways as a consequence of faith: οἱ ἐν πτωχεία διὰ κύριον is correctly translated 'those impoverished for the Lord's sake'.[126] A subsequent reference in the same verse to οἱ διὰ κύριον ἀποθανόντες establishes the accuracy of this translation.[127] Judah foretells that

122. *1 En.* 22.3, 5, 9; 103.5.
123. *Jos. Asen.* 8.5; 11.8; 12.5; 13.11.
124. *Jos. Asen.* 20.7; *Par. Jer.* 7.14-18; *Liv. Proph.* 21.5.
125. *Liv. Proph.* 10.5; 22.12; 22.20 (Elisha's bones).
126. Both H.C. Kee ('Testaments of the Twelve Patriarchs', in Charlesworth (ed.), *Old Testament Pseudepigrapha*, I, p. 802) and M. de Jong ('The Testaments of the Twelve Patriarchs', in Sparks [ed.], *The Apocryphal Old Testament*, p. 550) adopt this translation of διὰ κύριον.
127. On this use of διὰ with the accusative, see C.F.D. Moule, *An Idiom Book of New Testament Greek* (Cambridge: Cambridge University Press, 2nd edn, 1959), pp. 54-55.

Those having come to an end in grief will rise in joy. And those in poverty for the Lord's sake will be enriched. And those in need (ἐν πενία) will be satisfied. And those in weakness will be strengthened. And those having died for the Lord's sake will be awakened in life.

Despite the difference in terminology from other passages this study has drawn attention to, this passage resonates with those that predict salvation for the poor, albeit *T. Jud.* 25.4 presents salvation only for those in poverty and in death through faith.

Turning to the word πτωχός, while it appears in five of the writings of the Old Testament pseudepigrapha, it is employed extensively only in the *Testament of Job*.[128] In all instances, the term denotes someone who occupies the opposite end of the human spectrum from kings[129] and receives donated food and goods.[130] Πτωχός is synonymous with πένης.[131] Giving to the poor is a pious, virtuous act.[132] The poor are stereotypically flat, impersonal characters. The poor are at the mercy of generous, God-fearing persons for subsistence, and persons demonstrate their God-pleasing character by being generous to the poor. Surprisingly lacking from the Old Testament pseudepigrapha, as the works are extant in Greek, are passages promising an eschatological reversal of fortunes for the πτωχός and passages extolling God's protection of the poor.[133]

We came to the Old Testament pseudepigrapha looking for evidence of a typical literary quality to the vocabulary of this study. Old Testament pseudepigraphic writings do not echo all of the LXX motifs involving the captive, the blind, the poor, and the others, particularly the motif of future salvation secured for them by God. Yet Old Testament pseudepigraphic writings provide examples of αἰχμάλωτος, τυφλός, κωφός, χωλός, λεπρός, ἀνάπηρος, νεκρός, and πτωχός as conventional images. Moreover, these images, not surprisingly, are consistent with the images identified in the LXX.

---

128. Of the 25 instances of πτωχός, 15 occur in the *Testament of Job*.

129. *T. Jud.* 15.5-6.

130. *T. Ash.* 2.6; *Jos. Asen.* 10.11-12; *T. Job* 11.3, 5, 9, 11; 12.1; 32.2.

131. *T. Iss.* 7.5; *Jos. Asen.* 10.11; *T. Job* 10.7; 12.1; 15.5; 32.7; 44.4; Ps.-Phoc. 22.

132. *T. Iss.* 7.5; *Jos. Asen.* 10.12; *T. Job* 10.7; 11.9-11; 12.1; 15.5; 30.5; 32.7; 44.4; 45.2; Ps.-Phoc. 22; *Anon. Frag.* 1. 217. 2, 4; 1. 218. 1.

133. Cf. *T. Jud.* 25.4 discussed above.

Summary

To a great extent, the captive, the shattered, the blind, the deaf mute, the lame, the dead, and the poor share distinct characteristics that mark them as comparable types in the LXX. In the LXX, the captive, the shattered, the blind, the deaf mute, the lame, lepers, the maimed, the dead, and the poor are not 'the neglected mass of humanity'. Rather, they are, with some exceptions, types of a different sort. They have no personality. They are anonymous. They do not act upon others; rather, they are acted upon in the course of human events. Correspondingly, they are at the mercy of others. Importantly, however, these types routinely attract the sympathy of the LXX reader. In fact, the ancient biblical authors relied on sympathy for these types to create a rhetorical effect, as can be seen especially with reference to the poor in the Psalms.

R. Alter has shown that type-scenes in biblical narrative communicate by manipulating a fixed constellation of motifs.[134] While the constellation is fixed, Alter points out that it is only relatively fixed. Not every scene will contain every element of the constellation. Moreover, not simply the presence of the constellation, but how the constellation is manipulated guides the effect of the narrative. Something analogous to the effect of a repeatedly employed constellation of motifs takes place in the LXX with a repeatedly employed constellation of stereotypical characters.

In the LXX, the captive, the shattered, the blind, the deaf mute, the lame, and the poor are among the characters that constitute such a constellation of stereotypical characters. The broader contours of the constellation take shape when these characters are clustered together in specific texts: the shattered, the hungry, the poor, and the naked (Isa. 58.6-7); the poor, orphans, widows, the blind, the lame, and the weak or powerless (Job 29.12-17); the shackled, the broken down, the blind, the righteous, the sojourner, the orphan, and the widow (Ps. 145.7-9); the deaf mute, the blind, the poor, and those without hope (Isa. 29.18-20); the blind, the deaf mute, the lame, the dumb (Isa. 35.4-6); the blind, those bound, and those imprisoned (Isa. 42.6-7); and those weaker, the blind, the physically anguished, the widow, and the orphan (Ep. Jer. 35-37).

---

134. Alter, *The Art of Biblical Narrative*, pp. 47-62.

The constellation is, then, a fluid device that offers a writer a selection of established characters. Though fluid, it is a stylized feature of the LXX, that is, a convention. The rhetorical effect of clustering these stereotypical characters is to heighten the magnificence of God's saving action, or in the case of human generosity to exaggerate the giver's virtuous character or to magnify the evil of the sinner, who routinely acts against them.

The repertoire of the LXX-competent audience includes this constellation of characters and the conventional images evoked by the individual types. Out of this repertoire, the audience concretizes the terms αἰχμάλωτος, τυφλός, κωφός, χωλός, λεπρός, ἀνάπηρος, νεκρός, and πτωχός. In Chapter 6, I shall show how the function of these character types in the narrative of Luke–Acts is related to the way Luke's authorial audience concretizes them on the basis of the LXX.

The captive, the shattered, the blind, the deaf mute, the lame, the dead, and the poor elicit the sympathy of the reader of the LXX. But they are not to be envied. All of these fates are unfortunate fates, with the occasional exception of death, and God-fearing people grieve when such a fate befalls a friend or kinsperson. Moreover, God-fearing people demonstrate their piety and righteousness in kindness and generosity toward these groups. But those so afflicted are in some way also the promised beneficiaries of God's protection, God's saving action, or God's intrusion into human affairs to reverse this fate. This is to be a cause of joy for all God's people. Lepers, too, are dependent upon divine intervention for healing. The benefits of almsgiving pale in comparison, though almsgiving is regularly commended. In the end, the LXX presents these characters as character types who are standard, conventional recipients of God's favor. Often they are almost romanticized, because their future is ultimately secured by God, and indeed, by God alone.

Chapter 6

APPLYING SEPTUAGINT INSIGHTS TO INTERPRETATION
OF THE CHARACTER TYPES IN LUKE'S GOSPEL

Preliminary Comments

The Structure of the Argument

This study opened with the observation that so-called outcast characters such as the blind, lepers, the poor, and the deaf are prominent in
the Gospel of Luke and all but absent in the Acts of the Apostles. I
then proceeded to argue several points. First, this discontinuity between
the Gospel and Acts with respect to how frequently the blind, the poor,
and so on are mentioned needs to be explained, since on numerous
grounds Luke–Acts forms a unified, two-volume whole. The need for
explanation is particularly heightened if 'concern for the poor' is
thought to be a major Lukan theme. However, interpretations of the
poor in Luke–Acts have not provided an adequate explanation.

Secondly, a literary critical explanation for this discontinuity has
not been explored and literary qualities of the Lukan blind, poor, and
others have been overlooked. Nevertheless, a literary approach to this
question is especially appropriate because, on the one hand, the captive,
the shattered, the blind, the deaf mute, the lame, lepers, the maimed,
the dead, and the poor are presented in Luke's narrative in such a way
that they lack intratextual definition and, on the other hand, the potential
for an intertextual resource to provide that definition is great.

Thirdly, Chapter 4 argued that the rhetoric of Luke's narrative
directs his authorial audience to concretize the captive, the shattered,
the blind, the deaf mute, the lame, lepers, the maimed, the dead, and
the poor by reference to the LXX. Chapter 5 then surveyed the occurrences of the captive, the shattered, the blind, the deaf mute, the lame,
lepers, the maimed, the dead, and the poor in the LXX and concluded
that in the LXX they fit together as a constellation of character types
with clearly evident stereotypical features. These character types are

typically anonymous, powerless, vulnerable, and a-responsible. Most importantly, however, these character types are standard, conventional recipients of God's saving action. If the Lukan captive, poor, blind, and so on do indeed lack intratextual description, as this study has suggested and will continue to argue, then it is this conventional LXX image of these character types that Luke expects his authorial audience to invoke to concretize this indeterminacy.

Lukan Characters
Chapter 3 discussed the nature of characterization in narrative and pointed out that in ancient narrative characters are illustrative, in contrast to the tendency in modern narrative for characters to be representational. Thus, characters in ancient narratives align themselves along a continuum of relative flatness. Nevertheless, Chapter 3 argued that even in ancient literature some characters are more developed than other characters. A character may display numerous and varied character traits, and may exhibit a distinctive point of view. On the other hand, a character may lack character traits and betray no point of view.

This chapter will draw attention to the degree to which characters in Luke's narrative display character traits and points of view. Such judgments are crucial to interpretive conclusions regarding the captive, the shattered, the blind, the deaf mute, the lame, lepers, the maimed, the dead, and the poor in Luke–Acts. A goal of this study is to reach interpretive conclusions regarding these character types that are consistent with the canons of ancient characterization.

Ancient characterization is rooted in the view put forward in Aristotle's *Poetics* that character is subordinate to plot,[1] plot being the orderly arrangement of actions.[2] Action creates the poetic work, according to Aristotle, and characters are significant to the narrative as vehicles for action that can be readily understood by the audience.[3]

---

1.   Aristotle, *Poetics*, 1450a. See also Leitch, *What Stories Are*, p. 149; and Tolbert, *Sowing*, pp. 76-77.
2.   Aristotle, *Poetics*, 1449b-50a.
3.   Ancient Greek characterization displays a degree of variety. In his fine synopsis of characterization in Greek drama, Leitch (*What Stories Are*, pp. 149-53) concludes that in the plays of Euripides and Sophocles there are tendencies toward 'character', for particular characters act as individuals. According to Leitch (*What Stories Are*, p. 153), 'Here is a formula for the historical emergence of character:

Characters act in stylized, conventional ways.[4] In this manner, they reveal to the reader their moral fortitude or lack of moral fortitude by their actions. The ability to act, or to refrain from acting, lies at the heart of ancient characterization. For 'character in ancient literature was revealed by choices: what one wills to do or avoids doing'.[5]

In Luke's narrative, a character's response in a situation may be monolithic and thereby express only one character trait. For example, Simeon's and Anna's praises to God express piety. Or a character may fulfill one simple plot function, as, for example, Pilate does as he functions as civil judge or Judas does as he functions as betrayer. Yet such simple or flat characters are characters nonetheless, in the sense of the term drawn from Aristotle, because they wilfully act. The categories of 'character traits' and 'point of view', which were introduced in Chapter 3, serve as heuristic devices for determining the relative capacity of a character to illustrate character through wilful action. At times during the course of this chapter's exegesis, I will say that the blind, the poor, the lame, and so on are not really characters. The point to be made by saying that they are not really characters is that in their narrative context these character types lack the basic building block of Greek characters: the capacity to illustrate character through free action. Moreover, stating that the blind, the poor, the lame, and so on are not really characters in a given episode emphasizes the rhetorical significance of the fact that the blind, poor, or lame 'character' has no personality, or authority, or virtue as the case may be in that episode.

Lukan Narrative Levels
Audience-oriented analysis of the texts involving the blind, the lame, the poor, and so on in Luke–Acts leads us to discriminate among

When the bonds joining the individual to the larger communities and ideals of worship, religious belief, and kinship have become tenuous enough to make piety a matter of choice rather than a requisite of personal identity, then it becomes possible to speak of character as a distinctive trope for human identity.' Yet Leitch's observation that characters in the works of Euripides and Sophocles show movement in the direction of individualization does not contradict the fundamental point that ancient characters are essentially vehicles for action and not characters presented with psychological complexity. It is noteworthy in this regard that Leitch entitled this section in which he discusses characterization in fifth-century Greek works, 'Before Character'.

	4.	See Aune, *The New Testament in its Literary Environment*, pp. 32-34, and Darr, *On Building Character*, p. 48.

	5.	Tolbert, *Sowing the Gospel*, p. 224. See also Aristotle, *Poetics* 1450b.

rhetorical effects occurring at hierarchically-related narrative levels.[6] S.S. Lanser's model of narrative discourse in prose fiction is a helpful starting point. Lanser's model identifies communication processes taking place on several levels respectively.[7] The narrative levels on which these acts of communication are taking place in any given work are distinguished by the voice that is conveying a message to an audience.[8] At the top of the hierarchy, on the most encompassing level, the flesh-and-blood author tells a story to a flesh-and-blood audience. Immediately below the level of the real reader and real audience sits the level of the implied author, namely, the authorial presence the reader encounters when reading the text. As this authorial presence, the implied author is responsible for what is told and how it is told. The implied author establishes the narrative world, controls characterization, and organizes the plot of the narrative. Unlike the flesh-and-blood author, who is subject to the inconsistencies and paradoxes of human nature, the implied author comes across as a stable and consistent guiding hand. The implied author tells the story to the text's authorial audience.[9] Occupying the next level below that of the implied author and authorial audience are the narrator and narratee. The narrator is the voice in the text that tells the story. An easy way to grasp the distinction between implied author and narrator is to recall a drama—any drama—that conveys an authorial presence but has no narrator. As an illustration of the different reading dynamics possible on the implied author-authorial audience level and narrator-narratee level respectively, consider that the implied author and authorial audience of G. Orwell's *Animal Farm* know that pigs cannot speak, while the narrator and narratee believe that they can. Of course, the range of possible types of narrators is vast. For example, the narrator may be omniscient or naive, reliable or unreliable. In addition, a narrator may or may not be a character within the story.

Within the world of the narrative itself, characters interact with other characters. This character-to-character discourse constitutes another

---

6.   Lanser, *The Narrative Act*, pp. 118-34; See also M.A. Powell, *What is Narrative Criticism?* (Guides to Biblical Scholarship; Minneapolis: Augsburg–Fortress, 1990), pp. 19-20, 25-27; Rimmon-Kenan, *Narrative Fiction*, pp. 86-94; and Tolbert, *Sowing*, pp. 92-98.

7.   Lanser, *The Narrative Act*, p. 118.

8.   Lanser, *The Narrative Act*, p. 118.

9.   For an extended discussion of authorial audience, see Chapter 3 above.

narrative level. The number of narrative levels present in a work is potentially limitless. To quote S. Rimmon-Kenan,

> A character whose actions are the object of narration can himself in turn engage in narrating a story. Within his story there may, of course, be yet another character who narrates another story, and so on in infinite regress. Such narratives within narratives create a stratification of levels whereby each inner narrative is subordinate to the narrative within which it is embedded.[10]

In short, the hierarchically-related narrative levels, identified in Lanser's model and confirmed by the work of other literary theorists, arrange themselves as follows, beginning with the primary level of communication.

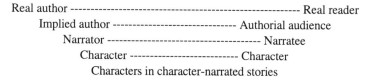

Real author --- Real reader
Implied author ----------------------------- Authorial audience
Narrator ------------------------------------- Narratee
Character -------------------------- Character
Characters in character-narrated stories

Turning to the New Testament, it must be recognized immediately that anything having to do with the biography or personality of the anonymous and long-deceased author of Luke–Acts is unavailable to modern scholars and known only through the authorial presence provided by the text. Setting aside speculation about the real author and hypothetical real readers of the Gospel of Luke, we may nevertheless benefit from the insights of Lanser and others. M.A. Tolbert has simplified Lanser's model of narrative levels to apply it to literary-historical study the Gospel of Mark.[11] She points out that 'in the case of the [Markan] Gospel, the levels of implied author–implied reader and narrator–narratee coalesce into one, the first degree narrative'.[12] It is true as well for Luke–Acts that there is no practical benefit in trying to distinguish between the implied author and the narrator, for the Lukan narrator is 'reliable', and 'omniscient'.[13] That is, the narrator's voice leads the narratee unerringly to appropriate judgments

10.   Rimmon-Kenan, *Narrative Fiction*, p. 91.
11.   Tolbert, *Sowing*, pp. 92-93.
12.   Tolbert, *Sowing*, p. 93. *Pace* W.C. Booth, *Rhetoric of Fiction* (Chicago and London: University of Chicago Press, 2nd edn, 1983), p. 73.
13.   Darr (*On Building Character*, p. 51) uses the phrase 'omniscient, omnipresent, retrospective, and fully reliable' to describe the narrator of Luke–Acts.

about events and characters;[14] and there are no boundaries to the narrator's knowledge.[15] The narrator knows what is in Mary's heart (Lk. 1.51). He is present in the sanctuary of the Temple with Zechariah (Lk. 1.9-20) and in Jesus' solitude on the Mount of Olives (Lk. 22.41-45). The narrator is with Peter as he denies knowing Jesus (Lk. 22.54-62); at the same time, the narrator is with Jesus in another location as Jesus is beaten and mocked (Lk. 22.63-65).

14.   'Reliable narrator' is a designation that people tend to understand almost intuitively. Literary critics' conversations about reliable narration focus on varying aspects of the narrator's reliability. W. Booth appeals to the norms of the work to define 'reliable narrator'. Says Booth (*Rhetoric of Fiction*, pp. 158-59), 'For lack of better terms, I have called a narrator *reliable* when he speaks for or acts in accordance with the norms of the work (which is to say, the implied author's norms), *unreliable* when he does not'. S. Rimmon-Kenan, on the other hand, reminds us that a narrator's reliability may be defined in terms of the reader's expected response. Says Rimmon-Kenan (*Narrative Fiction*, p. 100), 'A reliable narrator is one whose rendering of the story and commentary on it the reader is supposed to take as an authoritative account of the fictional truth.' Both of these critical angles enlighten Lukan study. Booth's definition helps to explain the reliability of the Lukan narrator in terms of the fusion of the Lukan implied author and narrator into one voice. Rimmon-Kenan's definition alerts us to the persuasive effect of a reliable narrator's comments. Thus, when the narrator of Luke–Acts says that 'all were amazed' (Lk. 1.63; 2.18, 47; 4.22, 36; 5.9; 9.43), readers are expected to accept that observation without question because the narrator is reliable.

J. Dawsey (*The Lukan Voice: Confusion and Irony in the Gospel of Luke* [Macon, GA: Mercer University Press, 1986]) attempts to demonstrate that the Lukan narrator is unreliable, but is unsuccessful. An example of the methodological weaknesses that plague Dawsey's study is the problem that his study does not adequately account for the fact that an unreliable prologue, which the logic of Dawsey's argument requires Lk. 1.1-4 to be, would be totally out of keeping with the ancient reading and writing environment of Luke–Acts.

15.   Rimmon-Kenan (*Narrative Fiction*, p. 95) summarizes the characteristics literary critics usually associate with the designation 'omniscient narrator': 'familiarity, in principle, with the characters' innermost thoughts and feeling; knowledge of past, present, and future; presence in locations where characters are supposed to be unaccompanied (e.g. on a lonely stroll or during a love-scene in a locked room); and knowledge of what happens in several places at the same time'. The Lukan narrator displays all four of these characteristics. Tannehill (*Narrative Unity*, II, p. 264 n. 5) and W.S. Kurz (*Reading Luke–Acts: Dynamics of Biblical Narrative* [Louisville: Westminster/John Knox, 1993], pp. 113-14) note that the first person narrator of the 'we' sections of Acts is not omniscient. For the purpose of this discussion, however, it is not necessary to be sidetracked by a discussion of the 'we' passages.

Since the reliable and omniscient narrator of Luke's work is for all practical purposes indistinguishable from the work's implied author, this study will refer to the level of discourse occupied by the implied author–narrator and authorial audience–narratee in Tolbert's terms as 'first-degree narrative'.[16] References to 'Luke' are to be understood as references to the implied author–narrator of Luke–Acts.

Moving one step down the hierarchy, I will speak of character-to-character interaction, such as Jesus' conversation with two disciples on the road to Emmaus in Luke 24, as 'second-degree narrative'. Accordingly, 'third-degree narrative' occurs when a character narrates another story with its own characters and action. The most prominent examples of 'third-degree narrative' in Luke–Acts are the parables narrated by Jesus, though Peter's account of his dream (Acts 11.5-10) and Paul's accounts of his experience on the road to Damascus (Acts 22.4-16; 26.9-18) also introduce third-degree narrative.[17]

Several references to the character types in this study occur in parables: Lk. 6.39-40; 14.12-24; 15.24, 32; 16.19-31. The parable has long captured the imagination of New Testament interpreters, in the words of C.H. Dodd, 'arresting the hearer by its vividness or strangeness, and leaving the mind in sufficient doubt about its precise application to tease it into active thought'.[18] Thus, parables are attractive because they charm the New Testament reader into pursuit of interpretation. The guiding hand of the implied author seems to disappear as the parables appear to take on a life of their own.[19] The ostensible

16.   Tolbert, *Sowing the Gospel*, p. 93.

17.   The terminology of 'first degree narrative', etc. is not standardized in the field of literature. For example, Rimmon-Kenan (*Narrative Fiction*, p. 91) refers to stories told by characters as second degree narrative.

18.   C.H. Dodd, *The Parables of the Kingdom* (New York: Charles Scribner's Sons, rev. edn, 1961), p. 5.

19.   Modern research is dominated by the tendency to carry the process of distancing the Lukan parables from the hand of the implied author by severing them from their Gospel context in order to interpret them in other contexts as parables of the historical Jesus. See J.D. Crossan, *In Parables: The Challenge of the Historical Jesus* (New York: Harper & Row, 1973); Dodd, *Parables*; J. Jeremias, *The Parables of Jesus* (trans. S. H. Hooke; New York: Charles Scribner's Sons, 2nd rev. edn, 1972); N. Perrin, *Jesus and the Language of the Kingdom* (Philadelphia: Fortress Press, 1976), esp. pp. 89-205; D.O. Via, *The Parables: Their Literary and Existential Dimension* (Philadelphia: Fortress Press, 1967); and A. Wilder, *Early Christian Rhetoric: The Language of the Gospel* (Cambridge, MA: Harvard

disappearance of the guiding hand of Luke when Jesus tells a parable is not due solely to the creative substance of the parable itself. Third-degree narrative, as third-degree narrative, produces the rhetorical illusion that the implied author has departed. In fact, however, the implied author uses parables to show the authorial audience how to assess second-degree narrative characters and situations.[20] I will return to this feature of parables in Luke's Gospel when I look at specific passages.

The question of the rhetorical effect of a given action in Luke–Acts is actually, therefore, at least two questions. Consider, for example, the angelic announcement to shepherds of Jesus' birth (Lk. 2.8-15). To ask about the effect that this announcement has on Luke's authorial audience is to ask a question that pertains to first-degree narrative. To inquire about the effect this announcement had on the shepherds is to ask a question that pertains to second-degree narrative. The two effects are distinctly different and should not be confused. The shepherds are afraid and subsequently curious about the newborn (Lk. 2.9-15). Luke's authorial audience, however, is not afraid, and it has been informed of the child's magnitude as God's Son (Lk. 1.32-33). Neither the angelophany itself nor the content of the angel's message would be particularly striking to Luke's authorial audience by this point in the narrative, because the authorial audience has witnessed the angel's appearances to Zechariah and Mary (1.11-20; 26-38). Rather, the scene's new and freshly intriguing aspect, which would attract the attention of the authorial audience, is the fact that this is an angelophany *to shepherds*.

The authorial audience's superior knowledge regarding the action taking place in the story makes irony possible. For example, the irony of Jesus' crucifixion is that the crucifixion is not what it appears to

University Press, 1971). On interpreting the parables as parables of Jesus in contrast to interpreting them as parables *of the Gospel*, see M.A. Tolbert, *Perspectives on the Parables: An Approach to Multiple Interpretations* (Philadelphia: Fortress Press, 1979), pp. 19-23. The interest of this study is in the parables as parables of the Gospel.

20.   On the mimetic authority of parables, i.e. their persuasiveness accomplished through showing actions to the New Testament reader, over against the diegetic authority of second-degree narrative, i.e. persuasiveness accomplished by the narrator and reliable characters *telling* information to the New Testament reader, see Tolbert, *Sowing*, p. 106.

Jesus' contemporaries to be.[21] Jesus' disciples and detractors believe Jesus' death to be his defeat. Yet the authorial audience knows it to be the divinely ordered culmination of God's salvific plan. Thus, by controlling what his authorial audience knows and what the characters know, Luke is able to create irony.

A conventional effect of irony is to draw the point of view of the authorial audience to the point of view of the implied author. Through irony, Luke and his intended audience become confidants, equally superior to the characters in the narrative because they share knowledge that is hidden from the characters. Thus, irony has a rhetorical effect on the authorial audience akin to the bonding effect sharing secrets has on two friends.

Wherever Luke offers his audience insight into the words or actions of an episode beyond the insight available to characters in the episode, Luke is doing more than simply conveying information. Luke is manipulating the authorial audience's attitude toward the narrative action and toward the characters in the episode. In a word, Luke rhetorically aligns his authorial audience with his perspective in order to mold its beliefs.[22]

The Task, Purpose, and Scope of this Chapter
The task of this chapter is to carry out an audience-oriented, sequential reading of texts in Luke's Gospel involving the captive, the shattered, the blind, the deaf mute, the lame, lepers, the maimed, the dead, and the poor. In performing such a reading, this chapter seeks to show convincingly that in Luke's Gospel the captive, the shattered, the blind, the deaf mute, the lame, lepers, the maimed, the dead, and the poor are character types and lack intratextual definition. This chapter also seeks to analyze the role these character types play in the narrative rhetoric of the passages in which they appear. In other words, it seeks to uncover the immediate effect the character types have in shaping the audience's attitudes and sympathies during the reading process.

The purpose of this chapter is to establish that these character types function christologically in Luke's narrative. When Jesus brings salvation to the blind, the poor, and the others, these acts display Jesus'

21. See D. Juel, *Luke–Acts: The Promise of History* (Atlanta: John Knox, 1983), pp. 50-52.
22. The terminology of 'molding beliefs' is W. Booth's. See Booth, *Rhetoric of Fiction*, pp. 172-95, 264-66.

LXX-based messianic credentials. That is, Jesus' beneficent deeds toward these character types serve to confirm Jesus' status as God's eschatological agent of salvation.

Every text in Luke's Gospel that uses the vocabulary αἰχμάλωτος, θραύειν, τυφλός, κωφός, χωλός, λεπρός, ἀνάπηρος, νεκρός, and πτωχός is discussed in this chapter. Exegesis typically includes a translation of the pertinent verse or verses, a sketch of literary and rhetorical features including the significance of the placement of each passage in the Gospel narrative, observations on characterization, and an assessment of the function of the character type or types present in the text on interpretation of the passage. The length and fullness of the discussion of a text is dictated primarily by how significant the types are to the episode and secondarily by the complexity of the rhetorical structure of the passage. Occasionally, translated phrases are deliberately wooden or awkward in English where this is necessary to show in English verbal repetition or other patterns that are present in the Greek.

Since the scope of this chapter is limited to the rhetorical significance of the blind, the poor, and so on, the extent to which each of the pertinent texts is discussed varies considerably. I will not attempt to discuss every exegetical aspect of these passages. I will limit myself to matters having to do specifically with the character types under discussion. Consequently, where the character type or types play a significant role in the authorial audience's response to a passage, my discussion is extensive. On the other hand, where the role of the character type or types may be appraised quickly, I will do so.

Exegesis

Luke 1.22: Zechariah Rendered Deaf and Dumb

> When he came out [of the Temple], he was not able to speak to them, and they realized that he had seen a vision in the Temple. And he kept nodding to them and remained deaf mute.

'Deaf mute' is the preferable translation of κωφός in Lk. 1.22. That Zechariah is unable to hear as well as unable to speak is appropriately less of a surprise to the English-language reader in 1.62 if κωφός is recognized as 'deaf mute' in 1.22. Explicitly said in 1.22 to be unable to speak, Zechariah makes signs (διανεύων) to the people at the Temple. In Lk. 1.62, Zechariah and Elizabeth's neighbors and relatives make signs (ἐνένευον) to Zechariah because he is unable to hear.

Κωφός labels Zechariah's new affliction. The LXX associations Zechariah's new malady trigger are those of divine punishment for faithlessness.[23] Zechariah is a rather developed character, who is assigned or shown to have several character traits: he is a priest (Lk. 1.5), an Israelite with specific lineage (1.5), respectably married (1.5), righteous (1.6), aged (1.7), capable of fear (1.12), and not inclined to take even an angel's word at face value (1.18). Because Zechariah's character is fleshed out, this passage does not suggest the type character κωφός, although the passage does assume LXX knowledge to explain Zechariah's affliction. The intrigue of the episode (1.8-23) is built on Zechariah's enigmatic relationship with God. Zechariah's and God's points of view overlap and diverge. The unfolding of God's pleasure and displeasure with Zechariah is vital to the plot. Consequently, the import of his being made deaf mute is governed by the dynamics of the larger plot and incorporated into the overall process of Zechariah's characterization.

Luke 4.16-30: Jesus in Nazareth

> And he came to Nazareth, where he had been brought up, and as was his custom on the Sabbath day he went into the synagogue and stood up to read. And the book of the prophet Isaiah was handed to him, and opening the book he found the place where it was written: 'The Spirit of the Lord is upon me, because he anointed me to announce good news to the poor. He sent me to proclaim release to the captives and recovery of sight to the blind, to send the shattered into release, and to proclaim the acceptable year of the Lord.' And closing the book, giving it back to the attendant, he sat down. And the eyes of everyone in the synagogue were fixed on him. He began, then, to say to them, 'Today this Scripture was fulfilled in your hearing.' And everyone affirmed him and admired the gracious words that came from his mouth and said, 'This is Joseph's son, isn't it?' And Jesus said to them, 'Surely you will tell me this parable, "Physician, cure yourself. Do here in your hometown the things we heard were done in Capernaum."' But he said, 'Amen, I tell you: no prophet is acceptable in his hometown. In truth I tell you. There were many widows in Israel in the days of Elijah when heaven was shut for three years and six months,

---

23. For example, captivity as divine punishment for sin (Num. 31.12, 19, 26; Judg. 5.12); the Lord's threat to blind God's people if they do not heed the divine commandments (Deut. 28.29); and leprosy as punishment on King Azarias (4 Kgdms 15.5), Miriam (Num. 12.10), and Gehazi (4 Kgdms 5.27).

during which time there was a severe famine over the entire land. And Elijah was sent to none of these, except, into Zarephath in Sidon, to a widow. And there were many lepers in Israel during the time of Elisha the prophet, and none of them was cleansed except Naaman the Syrian. And they in the synagogue were all filled with fury when they heard this, and getting up, they threw him out of the town and led him to the brow of the hill on which their town was built, in order to hurl him down. But passing right through the middle of them, he left.

Literary and Rhetorical Features. A general summary of Jesus' ministry in Galilee (Lk. 4.14-15) introduces the subsequent unit, 4.16-43. This unit consists of two episodes, the first set in Nazareth (4.16-30),[24] the second set in Capernaum (4.31-43). Pairing these scenes sets

24.   The Nazareth pericope is universally labeled 'programmatic'. The more prominent studies consulted for this study include: R. Albertz, 'Die "Antrittspredigt" Jesu im Lukasevangelium auf ihrem altestamentlichen Hintergrund', *ZNW* 74 (1983), pp. 182-206; H.-W. Bartsch, *Wachet aber zu jeder Zeit! Entwurf einer Auslegung des Lukasevangeliums* (Hamburg: Herbert Reich Evangelischer Verlag, 1963), pp. 59-63; R.L. Brawley, *Luke–Acts and the Jews: Conflict, Apology, and Conciliation* (SBLMS, 33; Atlanta: Scholars, 1987), pp. 6-27; U. Busse, *Das Nazareth-Manifest Jesu: Eine Einführung in das lukanische Jesusbild nach Lk 4,16-30* (SBS, 91; Stuttgart: Katholisches Bibelwerk, 1977); H.J.B. Combrink, 'The Structure and Significance of Lk 4:16-30', *Neotestamentica* 7 (1973), pp. 27-47; W. Eltester, 'Israel im lukanischen Werk und die Nazarethperikope', in W. Eltester (ed.), *Jesus in Nazareth* (BZNW, 40; Berlin: de Gruyter, 1972), pp. 76-147; C.A. Evans, 'Luke's Use of the Elijah/Elisha Narratives and the Ethic of Election', *JBL* 106 (1987), pp. 75-83; D. Hill, 'The Rejection of Jesus at Nazareth (Luke iv 16-30)', *NovT* 13 (1971), pp. 161-80; J.L. Nolland, 'Impressed Unbelievers as Witnesses to Christ (Luke 4.22a)', *JBL* 98 (1979), pp. 219-29; J.L. Nolland, 'Words of Grace (Luke 4,22)', *Bib* 65 (1984), pp. 44-60; B. Reicke, 'Jesus in Nazareth—Lk 4, 14-30', in H. Balz und S. Schulz (eds.), *Das Wort und die Wörter* (Festschrift G. Friedrich; Stuttgart: Kohlhammer, 1973), pp. 47-55; J.A. Sanders, 'From Isaiah 61 to Luke 4', in J. Neusner (ed.), *Christianity, Judaism, and Other Greco-Roman Cults* (Leiden: Brill, 1975), I, pp. 75-106; A. Strobel, 'Die Ausrufung des Jobeljahrs in der Nazarethpredigt Jesu: Zur apokalyptischen Tradition Lc 4,16-30', in W. Eltester (ed.), *Jesus in Nazareth* (BZNW, 40; Berlin: de Gruyter, 1972), pp. 38-50; R.C. Tannehill, 'The Mission of Jesus According to Luke IV 16-30', in W. Eltester (ed.), *Jesus in Nazareth* (BZNW, 40; Berlin: de Gruyter, 1972), pp. 51-75; D. Tiede, *Prophecy and History in Luke–Acts* (Philadelphia: Fortress Press, 1980), pp. 19-63. For a summary of recent study and an extensive bibliography, see C.J. Schreck, 'The Nazareth Pericope: Luke 4, 16-30 in Recent Study', in F. Neirynck (ed.), *L'Évangile de Luc: The Gospel of Luke* (BETL, 32; Leuven: Leuven University Press, rev. and enlarged edn, 1989), pp. 399-471.

up reactions to Jesus by characters in Nazareth for comparison with reactions to Jesus in Capernaum.[25] The Nazareth episode divides itself into two parts (4.16-22 and 4.23-29), each half containing action by Jesus and reaction by the synagogue goers.[26] A dramatic chiasm formed by the actions described in 4.16-17 and 4.20 directs the audience's attention to the Scripture reading it encloses (4.18-19).[27]

The Scripture reading by Jesus (Isa. 61.1-2) departs from the LXX in three ways. First, Luke omits 'to heal the broken hearted' (Isa. 61.1) and the harsh words of judgment connected with the day of the Lord (Isa. 61.2b). Secondly, καλέσει (Isa. 61.2a) becomes κηρύξαι (Lk. 4.19). Thirdly, a portion of Isa. 58.6 is inserted between Isa. 61.1 and 61.2a: 'to send the shattered into release'. There are no parallels to inserting one portion of Scripture into another that I am aware of.[28]

25.   For example, the synagogue goers in Nazareth respond to Jesus by calling him 'son of Joseph', whereas the demons in Capernaum respond to Jesus by calling him 'the holy one of God' (Lk. 4.34) and 'the son of God' (4.41).

26.   See Combrink, 'Structure and Significance', pp. 29-30.

27.   D. Hamm, 'Sight to the Blind: Vision as Metaphor in Luke', *Bib* 67 (1986), pp. 457-77 (458-59); J.L. Nolland, *Luke 1–9.20* (WBC, 35A; Dallas: Word Books, 1989), p. 191; Talbert, *Reading Luke*, pp. 54-55; Tiede, *Prophecy and History in Luke–Acts*, p. 35. Tiede's and Hamm's proposed chiasms extend into the scriptural quotation. The foundational insight comes from N.W. Lund, *Chiasmus in the New Testament* (Chapel Hill: University of North Carolina Press, 1942), p. 236. J.S. Siker ('"First to the Gentiles": A Literary Analysis of Luke 4:16-30', *JBL* 111 (1992), pp. 73-90 [77-78]) proposes a second model of the structure of 4.16 and the verses that follow it. That is, that the unit extends through 4.21 and divides into parallel halves, the first half climaxing in the reading beginning with the words 'The Spirit of the Lord is upon me' and the second half climaxing in Jesus' words, 'Today this Scripture has been fulfilled in your hearing'. While this proposal is intriguing, it is less persuasive than the chiastic structure because the parallels Siker points to lack precise verbal correspondence. In other words, word for word parallels are not present.

28.   The frequently mentioned explanation that Isa. 58.6 is connected to Isa. 61.1 by the catchword ἄφεσις does not address the oddity of an interrupted Scripture reading. For proposed thematic and literary reasons for the insertion see Albertz, 'Antrittspredigt', pp. 191-98; Fitzmyer, *Luke I-IX*, p. 533; W. Grundmann, *Das Evangelium nach Lukas* (THKNT, 3; Berlin: Evangelische Verlagsanstalt, 5th edn, 1969), p. 120; D. Hamm, 'Sight to the Blind', p. 459; Lund, *Chiasmus*, pp. 237-38; Prior, *Jesus the Liberator*, pp. 122-23, 130, 132-38, 141, 151; M. Rese, *Alttestamentliche Motive in der Christologie des Lukas* (SNT, 1; Gütersloh: Gütersloher Verlagshaus, 1969), p. 146; K. Stendahl, *The School of St. Matthew*

A challenge to the claim that Luke's authorial audience is familiar with the LXX emerges out of these departures from the LXX in Luke's rendering of Isaiah in Lk. 4.18-19. Could Luke perhaps expect to get away with omitting parts of Isa. 61.1-2 because he did not expect his audience to be familiar with the passage? Or does Luke's intended effect rely in part on the audience's implicit comparison of Isa. 61.1-2 with Luke's citation? Is the insertion of Isa. 58.6 within Isa. 61.1-2 such an oddity that it perhaps suggests that Luke's authorial audience, or even the implied author himself, is relatively ignorant of the LXX?

The typical interpretive view of Luke's editing of Isa. 61.1-2 is expressed by J. Fitzmyer who observes that both 'to heal the broken-hearted' and 'the day of vengeance of our God' are omitted, and then states 'The omission of the former is of little consequence; but the latter is a deliberate suppression of a negative aspect of the Deutero-Isaian message'.[29] Fitzmyer's observation may be correct. Or one might also say that the omitting of the former is a deliberate suppression of a spiritualizing aspect of the Deutero-Isaian message. In any case, the question is: What degree of audience knowledge of the LXX would be necessary to achieve the effect on his audience that Luke is after? There is no simple answer here. If, for example, the latter omission is intended by Luke to signal to his audience that Jesus will not be an avenging agent of God, then Luke's authorial audience must be familiar with the LXX to pick up this signal. On the other hand, if Luke expected his audience to be distressed by the omissions, this would also require LXX competence. Yet there is no textual indication that the authorial audience should be distressed by them, thus there is the possibility that the audience is not distressed because it is unaware that something has been omitted. However, the absence of indications that the authorial audience should be distressed by Luke's free editing does not *necessarily* imply ignorance of the LXX.

and its Use of the Old Testament (Philadelphia: Fortress Press, 1968), p. 96; Tannehill, 'Mission', pp. 66, 70-71; and earlier, E. Klostermann, *Das Lukasevangelium* (HNT, 3; Tübingen: Mohr [Paul Siebeck], 2nd edn, 1929), p. 63. Stendahl (*School of St. Matthew*, pp. 48-50, 216) likens Lk. 4.18 to Mt. 11.10. But the two are only superficially comparable. First, Mt. 11.10 is not set within synagogue worship. Secondly, it is not clear how Mt. 11.10 is related to Exod. 23.20 and Mal. 3.1, but it is certain that in Mt. 11.10 there is no insertion of one text within the other.

29.   Fitzmyer, *Luke I-IX*, p. 532.

If Lk. 4.18-19 were being considered in isolation from the rest of
Luke–Acts, then it would be difficult to conclude whether or not
Luke's authorial audience is familiar with the LXX. But to conclude
from Lk. 4.18-19 that the authorial audience is ignorant of the LXX
would require that Lk. 4.18-19 be isolated even from Lk. 4.25-27,
because grasping the meaning of verses 25-27 quite evidently rests on
being familiar with the LXX stories of Elijah's visit to the widow
Zarephath and Elisha's encounter with Naaman. Therefore, while
recognizing that the Isaiah citation in Lk. 4.18-19 points in ambivalent
directions for constructing Luke's authorial audience, the weight of
evidence when the whole work is taken into account strongly falls in
favor of LXX competence.

There are no textual clues that any of the three departures from the
LXX should be unsettling to Luke's authorial audience. In fact, action
in the narrative points in the opposite direction. The positive response
by onlooking characters in the narrative to the LXX reading and Jesus'
remark following it implies that they sensed nothing unusual about the
reading.[30] The synagogue goers in this scene, not being privy to the

---

30.   Most interpreters consider the first response of the synagogue goers to have
been positive: e.g. Danker, *Jesus and the New Age*, pp. 109-10; C.A. Evans, *Luke*
(New International Biblical Commentary; Peabody, MA: Hendrickson, 1990), p. 71;
Fitzmyer, *Luke I-IX*, pp. 528, 534; Sanders, 'From Isaiah 61', pp. 96-99; E.
Schweizer, *The Good News According to Luke* (trans. D.E. Green; Atlanta: John
Knox, 1984), p. 90; Tannehill, *Narrative Unity*, I, pp. 68-69; Tiede, *Luke*, p. 108.
Others hesitate: e.g. Albertz, 'Antrittspredigt', p. 191; I.H. Marshall, *The Gospel of
Luke: A Commentary on the Greek Text* (New International Greek Testament
Commentary; Grand Rapids: Eerdmans, 1978), pp. 185-86. *Contra* J. Jeremias
(*Jesus' Promise to the Nations* [London: SCM Press, rev. edn, 1967], pp. 44-46),
who bases his interpretation of this scene on the omission of Isa. 61.2b. Jeremias
explains the negative reaction of the people by positing that they were offended by
Jesus' omission of an announcement of God's vengeance. Noteworthy is that in
order to make the people's reaction negative immediately, Jeremias adopts the highly
questionable translation of Lk. 4.22 proposed by B. Violet ('Zum rechten Verständnis
der Nazareth-Perikope Lc 4, 16-30', *ZNW* 37 [1938], pp. 251-71). According to
Violet and Jeremias, ἐμαρτύρουν αὐτῷ means 'they bore witness against him', and
ἐπὶ τοῖς λόγοις τῆς χάριτος ought to be translated 'by the words of [God's] mercy'.
They conclude that the people were astonished that Jesus spoke words of God's
mercy. While eliminating an awkward change of heart on the part of the people, these
esoteric translations presuppose for grammatical reasons an Aramaic tradition underlying this verse. Since 4.22 is incomprehensible apart from the scriptural quotation in
4.18-19, and since the quotation is clearly dependent upon the LXX, an underlying

events observed by the audience, would be less inclined to tolerate departures from Scripture by Jesus than would be the audience, which is aware of Jesus' divine credentials. The absence of a reaction on the second-degree narrative level to the departures suggests that the authorial audience would likewise not be struck by them. It may be cautiously concluded, then, that the changes *qua* changes have no effect at the first-degree narrative level.

This episode contains the first references in Luke–Acts to the poor, the captive, the blind, and the shattered. Therefore, to fill them out the audience must rely on conventions beyond those established to this point within the narrative itself. The thoroughly Septuagintal nature of the opening chapters of Luke's Gospel, including Luke 4, has been argued at length in Chapter 4. The case was made that the rhetoric of the entire Lukan narrative up to and including 4.16-30 directs Luke's authorial audience to concretize the poor, the captive, the blind, and the shattered on the basis of the LXX. At this point, I will simply draw attention to three aspects of 4.16-30 that confirm that the authorial audience is driven by the style and content of Lk. 4.16-30 to the LXX to fill gaps in the text. First, the scene is set in religious space, a synagogue, where the atmosphere exudes reverent attention to Scripture. This is, in a real sense, Scripture's space.

Secondly, the overall form of this episode serves to align it with Scripture. As discussed above in Chapter 4, the episode conforms to what R. Alter has termed 'the paradigmatic biblical story'.[31] All of the elements Alter identifies are packed into the first sentences of the Nazareth episode. (1) The characters are established—Jesus directly and the synagogue goers indirectly by virtue of the immediate setting. (2) The episode is located geographically in Nazarath, and specifically in a synagogue. (3) The phrase 'where he had been brought up' introduces a familial aspect, while a pivotal, explicit reference to family relationships is dramatically postponed. (4) The phrase 'as was his

Aramaic tradition translated into Greek in a manner required for the sense of the sentence proposed by Violet and Jeremias is highly unlikely. For other critiques of Jeremias's proposal, see D. Hill, 'The Rejection of Jesus', pp. 163-65, and J. Nolland, 'Impressed Unbelievers', p. 220.

31.   Alter, *The Art of Biblical Narrative*, p. 80: 'The paradigmatic biblical story starts with a few brief statements that name the principal character or characters, locate them geographically, identify significant family relationships, and in some instances provide succinct moral, social, or physical characterization of the protagonist'.

custom' provides a succinct moral characterization of Jesus: he is a pious Jew. Also, as Alter points out is typical of biblical stories,[32] the salient effects of the episode lie not so much with the actions of one character or the other, but with how characters respond to the situation. The tension and drama of the episode are created by the verses presenting the synagogue goers' responses (4.22, 28-29). Of course, the whole discourse of Jesus in 4.23-27 could be construed as a response to the ambivalent approval his words receive in 4.22.

Thirdly, as was alluded to earlier, these types come to expression out of Scripture. Jesus mentions the poor, the captive, the blind, and the shattered when quoting the LXX. In sum, the authorial audience is guided by the text to read the poor, the captive, the blind, and the shattered as LXX types.

The phrase 'the acceptable year of the Lord' concludes the quotation. It is a highly emotive phrase that recalls scriptural promises of God's dramatic, salvific intrusion into earthly affairs.[33] The final position in the quotation is rhetorically prominent, as A. Strobel suggests,[34] but is not the only position of emphasis. Other interpreters locate the passage's stress near the beginning of the quotation, on 'to announce good news to the poor',[35] or in the middle, on 'sight to the blind'.[36]

The catchword, δεκτός, hooks the second half of the episode to the first half: the acceptable year of the Lord (4.19) finds a prophet not

32. Alter, *The Art of Biblical Narrative*, p. 66.
33. In the past two decades, the Isaiah quote has frequently been said to allude to Jubilee imagery (e.g. Albertz, 'Antrittspredigt', p. 198; Brawley, *Luke–Acts and the Jews*, p. 13; Danker, *Jesus and the New Age*, p. 107; C.F. Evans, *Saint Luke* [TPI New Testament Commentaries; London: SCM Press; Philadelphia: Trinity Press International, 1990], p. 271; Hoyt, 'The Poor', p. 140; B.J. Koet, *Five Studies on Interpretation of Scripture in Luke–Acts* [Studiorum Novi Testamenti Auxilia, 14; Leuven: Leuven University Press/Peeters, 1989], p. 52; Marshall, *Luke*, p. 184; Nolland, *Luke 1-9:20*, p. 197; Strobel, 'Die Ausrufung des Jobeljahrs', pp. 40-41, 50; Tiede, *Luke*, p. 107). Two full-scale studies have pursued this perspective: S. Ringe, *Jesus, Liberation, and the Biblical Jubilee*; R. Sloan, *The Favorable Year of the Lord: A Study of Jubilary Theology in the Gospel of Luke* (Austin, TX: Schola Press, 1977). For an alternative view, see Tannehill, *Narrative Unity*, I, pp. 67-68.
34. Strobel, 'Die Ausrufung des Jobeljahrs', p. 41. So also Sloan, *Favorable Year*, p. 33, and Tannehill, 'Mission', p. 71.
35. Albertz, 'Antrittspredigt', p. 187; Bammel, 'Πτωχός', p. 906; Nolland, *Luke 1-9:20*, p. 196.
36. Hamm, 'Sight to the Blind', pp. 458-59.

acceptable in his hometown (4.24). Jesus illustrates his point with paired references to incidents in the ministries of Elijah and Elisha (4.25-27).[37] As with the Isaiah quotation, the references to Elijah and Elisha invite the audience to recall Scripture.

Characterization. The poor, the captive, the blind, and the shattered are not characters in this scene.[38] They are not present in the synagogue. No discourse is attached to them, no ideology, no action. They are spoken of abstractly. They are distant from the scene in time and space.

The opening comment by the narrator in Lk. 4.16, that Jesus goes to the synagogue on the sabbath day, establishes the setting for this episode and reinforces the audience's impression of Jesus as a pious Jew. The Jewish religious environment of this scene underscores the characterization of Jesus unfolding since Lk. 1.1-4.

In Luke's Gospel, Jesus is divinely fated for greatness even before he is born, and the audience is left with no doubt as to whose son Jesus is. In parallel annunciation scenes (1.5-25 and 1.26-38), John and Jesus are introduced. Juxtaposing the two stories in this way begs the audience to read the second in light of the first. The effect of this upon the audience is to heighten Jesus' grandeur. The angel waxes poetically in praise of John and heralds John's prophetic future (1.14-17). But while John 'will be great in the sight of the Lord' (1.15), Jesus 'will be called the son of the Most High' (1.32). While John 'will bring many of the people of Israel back to the Lord their God' (1.16), Jesus will be given the throne of David and 'will reign over the house of Jacob forever' (1.33). Indeed, the one born to Mary 'will be called the son of God' (1.35).

---

37. For the view that the Elijah and Elisha references in Lk. 4.25-27 in some way foreshadow the church's Gentile mission, see J. Dupont, *Nouvelles études sur les Actes Apôtres* (LD, 118; Paris: Cerf, 1984), p. 506; Esler, *Community*, p. 35; C.A. Evans, 'Elijah/Elisha Narratives', p. 78; Fitzmyer, *Luke I-IX*, pp. 189-90; Juel, *Luke–Acts: The Promise of History*, pp. 30-31; J.T. Sanders, *The Jews in Luke–Acts* (Philadelphia: Fortress Press, 1987), pp. 165-67; Tannehill, *Narrative Unity*, I, p. 71; Tiede, *Prophecy and History in Luke–Acts*, p. 53. For varying alternative views, see Brawley, *Luke–Acts and the Jews*, pp. 11, 26; R.J. Miller, 'Elijah, John, and Jesus in the Gospel of Luke', *NTS* 34 (1988), pp. 611-22 (615); Ringe, *Jesus, Liberation and the Biblical Jubilee*, p. 41.

38. Neither, incidentally, are the widows and lepers of Jesus' short speech (Lk. 4.23-27) characters in the Lukan scene.

Luke also introduces the Holy Spirit early in the narrative and establishes the Spirit's presence in leading characters. John is promised the Holy Spirit (1.15).[39] Mary can anticipate it (1.35). Elizabeth and Zechariah become filled with the Holy Spirit (1.41, 67). Luke reports that the Holy Spirit was upon Simeon (2.25-27). Finally, the Holy Spirit descends upon Jesus at his baptism (3.16; see also 4.1). By the time the audience arrives at 4.16, then, it has witnessed the generous distribution of the Holy Spirit upon pious characters, most recently including Jesus.

Jesus' comment, 'Today this Scripture has been fulfilled in your hearing' (4.21), is not an overt reference to himself.[40] A connection among the LXX quotation, Jesus' reference to the fulfillment of this Scripture, and Jesus' mission is an inference drawn by the first-degree narrative audience on the basis of Luke's entire narrative to this point. On the second-degree narrative level, the synagogue goers know only the action taking place in the immediate episode, plus perhaps unclarified reports about Jesus (Lk. 4.14). Luke's authorial audience, on the other hand, has superior knowledge. It has witnessed everything in the narrative to this point, including the descent of the Spirit upon Jesus. Moreover, Luke's audience has heard Scripture quoted previously in the narrative.

As discussed above in Chapter 4, the scriptural quotation in Lk. 4.18-19 is the fourth instance in the Gospel of a direct quotation from Scripture. On the basis of previous instances, Luke's authorial audience has developed the habit of applying the scriptural passage directly to the narrative situation. But this hermeneutical move by the audience is confined to the first-degree narrative level.

At the second-degree narrative level, Jesus' Scripture reading is simply a reading. At this level, it is no more a self-description of his own personal mission than any scriptural lesson read by a lector would be. The lector reads the prophet's words, not his own. The reading is a *Lesung*, not a *Vorlesung*.

The point is, Jesus does not declare outright that this Scripture is fulfilled in him. Luke's audience supplies the 'in Jesus' aspect by remembering previous narrative action and use of Scripture. Luke's

39. This promise is fulfilled in 1.80.
40. *Pace* Albertz, 'Antrittspredigt', pp. 186-87; Aune, *The New Testament in Its Literary Environment*, p. 132; J. Dupont, 'The Poor and Poverty', p. 35; Sloan, *Favorable Year*, pp. 74, 87.

audience knows that the spirit of the Lord is upon Jesus, and is led to apply Isaiah's words to Jesus in spite of Jesus' oblique and non-personal comment that 'today this Scripture has been fulfilled in your hearing' (4.21).

Jesus' comment in 4.21, answering the onlookers' expectant gaze, is crisp, aurally striking because of the preponderance of long syllables in the sentence, and sufficiently elliptic to allow the audience to use its superior knowledge to reach an understanding of the LXX quotation different from that of the characters. The reading dynamic of 4.16-30 is marked from 4.21 (or perhaps 4.19) by the divergence of the point of view of the audience from the point of view of the synagogue goers. A significant factor in the effect of this episode, therefore, is the presence of dramatic asymmetry between the experience of the audience and the experience of the characters.

The effect is not simply to provide the authorial audience with new data on Jesus, but to begin to create distance between the audience and the synagogue goers. The distance is subtly confirmed and widened by the synagogue goers' response to Jesus in 4.22, even though the response is positive. The clue is the rhetorical question 'This is Joseph's son, isn't it?' Though not a hostile or negative question,[41] it does draw the attention of the audience, who know that Joseph is not Jesus' father.[42] Suddenly, the synagogue goers are cast as unreliable interpreters of the narrative action, and, specifically, unreliable interpreters of Jesus.

Jesus does call for his onlookers to see him in the popular proverb, 'Physician, heal yourself' (4.23).[43] More accurately, Jesus cites this aphoristic maxim after making it explicit at the second-degree narrative level that the applicability of the maxim to Jesus is at issue. Jesus' subsequent reference to Capernaum raises authorial audience expectation that future events in that town will illumine the events in Nazareth.

Thus, the rhetoric of 4.16-22 leads Luke's audience to distance itself from the perspective of the synagogue goers. As a result, it becomes 'natural' for the authorial audience to respond positively to Jesus'

41. Evans, *Luke*, p. 71; Tannehill, *Narrative Unity*, I, p. 68. Cf. Seccombe (*Possessions*, p. 68), who holds that the question is a negative response but not a hostile one in the sense felt by Violet and Jeremias.

42. The fact that Joseph is not Jesus' father has been reinforced in Lk. 3.23.

43. See J.L. Nolland, 'Classic and Rabbinic Parallels to "Physician, Heal Yourself" (Lk IV 23)' *NovT* 21 (1979), pp. 193-209.

references to Elijah and Elisha, and to respond negatively to the synagogue goers' rejection of Jesus.[44] Moreover, the subsequent verses do
not provide good reason for the synagogue goers' hostility toward
Jesus, and their hostile rejection of Jesus on insufficient grounds
further distances Luke's audience from them.[45]

Function of the Character Types. Placed where it is in Luke's narrative, 4.16-30 serves as an introduction to Jesus' ministry. The scriptural quotation stands emphatically in the center of the chiastic structure
of the first half of the scene. The type characters the poor, the captive,
the blind, and the shattered figure prominently in the scriptural
quotation. Therefore, the conclusion is unavoidable that reference to
these character types plays a significant role in defining Jesus on the
basis of his ministry. Moreover, this passage produces the authorial
audience's first and therefore formative encounter with these character
types in Luke's narrative.

As they emerge in Lk. 4.18-19, the poor, the captive, the blind, and
the shattered are provided with no intratextual definition. Luke's
audience supplies the lacking definition by invoking the narrative's
intertext: the LXX. On the basis of its LXX competence, the authorial
audience recognizes the poor, the captive, the blind, and the shattered
as character types destined for divine rescue, that is, rescue by God or
by God's agent. To Luke's audience, Lk. 4.18-19 declares that the poor,
the captive, the blind, and the shattered are recognized to be the promised recipients of Jesus' benefactions. Consequently, Jesus' assigned

44.   Interpreters frequently point to parallels between the rejection of Jesus by
these synagogue goers and the rejection of Paul in the synagogue. The pattern in both
is said to be (1) proclamation by God's representative; (2) rejection of the proclamation by Jews; and (3) the turning of God's representative to the Gentiles.
Rejection in the synagogue is a common theme. But beyond that the parallel is not
perfect. In Lk. 4, Jesus does not turn to the Gentiles after being rejected. In
Capernaum, Jesus is back in a synagogue (4.31). More interestingly, the ostensible
references to the church's Gentile mission, i.e. the stories of Elijah and Elisha, occur
before Jesus is rejected. Cf. Conzelmann, *The Theology of St Luke*, pp. 34-38. In
addition, C.H. Talbert (*Literary Patterns, Theological Themes, and the Genre of
Luke–Acts* [SBLMS, 20; Missoula: Scholars Press, 1974], pp. 16, 18-19) finds
parallels between Lk. 4.16-30 and Acts 2.14-40.

45.   Cadbury, *Making*, p. 334: 'Of course some obscurity may be intentional, or
at least suitable to complex occasions. Mob scenes at Nazareth, Corinth and Ephesus
are not explained as logical performances.'

ministry reveals him scripturally to be God's agent of salvation.

When viewed in light of the whole work of Luke–Acts, αἰχμάλωτος and τεθραυσμένος distinguish themselves from πτωχός and τυφλός in that the former two are not repeated in Luke–Acts and the latter two are. As a result, while in Luke's narrative there are obvious fulfillments of the promises of good news declared to the poor (Lk. 6.20) and of sight to the blind (Lk. 7.21), there is no explicit expression of release for the αἰχμάλωτος and τεθραυσμένος. Indeed, there are no characters in Luke's narrative who are expressly referred to as the αἰχμάλωτος and τεθραυσμένος.

The rescues of Christians from prison in Acts (the apostles in 5.17-41; Peter in 12.1-17; Paul and Silas in 16.19-34) may be reminiscent of divine acts of rescue in the LXX, such as the Exodus.[46] But hearing these episodes as fulfillments of Lk. 4.18 is difficult. Specific verbal links with Lk. 4.18 are lacking and Jesus plays no role in the rescues. Moreover, the narrative is mixed. Not all arrested Christians in Acts are freed. In the introduction to the story of Peter's miraculous release from Herod's prison, we hear that James, the brother of John died at the hands of Herod (12.1-2). Paul, as he pleads his case before Agrippa alludes to the executions of imprisoned Christians (26.10). Moreover, Acts is silent about Paul's own fate.

The repetition of ἄφεσις best explains the insertion of Isa. 58.6 into Isa 61.1-2. Ἄφεσις has already appeared in Luke's Gospel in terms of 'release' from sins: 1.77; 3.3. In fact, apart from the references in Lk. 4.18, ἄφεσις appears in Luke–Acts only in connection with sins: Lk. 5.20; 24.47; Acts 2.38; 5.31; 10.43; 13.38; 26.18. If Luke does indeed use the verbal marker ἄφεσις to correlate αἰχμάλωτος with people in need of release from sin, does Luke, then, make non-literal symbols out of the αἰχμάλωτος and τεθραυσμένος such that they symbolize people 'captive' to sin and 'shattered' by the devil? Not necessarily. The interpreter's question ought to be, 'How does the correlation inform our understanding of Luke's depiction of sin?' Or, better stated from a literary critical perspective, 'How does being associated with the term αἰχμάλωτος characterize characters in Luke's work who need or receive forgiveness?'

Nevertheless, by using Isa. 58.6 to give emphasis by repetition to

46. The language of Acts 5.21 (πᾶσαν τὴν γερουσίαν τῶν υἱῶν Ἰσραὴλ) is, in fact, reminiscent of Exod. 12.21, in which Moses gives Passover instructions to 'the whole council of the sons of Israel' (πᾶσαν γερουσίαν υἱῶν Ἰσραὴλ).

ἄφεσις, Luke entices readers to make mental connections between those who need release from war captivity or oppression and those who need release from sin.[47] Without redefining 'the captive' and 'the oppressed' to be 'the captive to sin' and 'the oppressed by sin', Luke's rhetoric nevertheless borrows from the LXX image of the captive and the shattered to provide an added nuance to the depiction in Luke–Acts of the power of sin. Such a narrative dynamic may be at work when Jesus releases the paralytic from his sins (5.20), in an episode that makes the christological point of Jesus' divine authority.

The parallelism between widows and lepers in the Elijah and Elisha accounts hints that widows and lepers may be comparable to the poor and the blind later in the narrative. Moreover, that Jesus is analogous to Elijah and Elisha in the structure of the discourse suggests to the audience that widows and lepers may share with the poor, the captive, the blind, and the shattered in Jesus' favor if Jesus' ministry indeed manifests God's liberation.

Luke 6.17-26: The Beginning of the Sermon on the Plain

> When he came down with them he stood on a level place, along with a large crowd of his disciples and a large number of people from all Judea and Jerusalem and the coastal areas of Tyre and Sidon. They came to hear him and to be healed from their diseases. And those troubled by unclean spirits were healed, and the whole crowd sought to touch him because power was coming out from him. And he healed them all. And raising his eyes toward his disciples, he said. 'Blessed are the poor, for yours is the kingdom of God. Blessed are those who are hungry now, for you will be satisfied. Blessed are those who cry now, for you will laugh. Blessed are you when people hate you and when they exclude you and reproach and denounce your name as evil on account of the son of man. Rejoice in that day and leap for joy. For, behold, your reward is great in heaven. For their ancestors did the same things to the prophets. But woe to you wealthy, for you have received your consolation. Woe to you who are filled now, for you will hunger. Woe to those laughing now, for you will grieve and cry. Woe, when all people speak well of you. For their ancestors did the same things to the false prophets.

Literary and Rhetorical Features. The Sermon on the Plain (Lk. 6.20-49) immediately follows the episode in which Jesus chooses 12 dis-

---

47. See my discussion of Lk. 15.24 and 15.32 below. The parable of the lost son is fashioned in such a way as to communicate that to be lost in sin is a kind of death.

ciples to be called apostles (6.13). When the scene shifts to the plain (6.17), Jesus is accompanied by a larger crowd of disciples, as well as a throng of other people. The narrator states the throng's purpose in flocking to Jesus: they came to hear Jesus and to be healed by him (6.18). Both aims are realized in this scene, but Jesus' words and healing actions are narrated unequally. Luke briefly summarizes in indirect discourse that healing is taking place (6.18-19). Jesus' words, on the other hand, are recited in direct discourse in the hearing of the audience (6.20-49). The rhetorical effect is to highlight Jesus' speech. But at the same time, Jesus speaks with the credibility of his actions, for 'power was going out from him' (6.19).

The narrative mentions Jesus' auditors four times: 6.20, 27, 39, and 7.1. In 6.20-7.1, the mention of auditors is more a structuring device for Jesus' speech than a precise delimiting of second-degree narrative level addressees. Recall that Luke's authorial audience is a Hellenistic audience, that is, an audience with an ear for well-crafted discourse. Luke 6.20 opens Jesus' sermon and 7.1 closes it. Luke 6.27 marks a shift from epideictic rhetoric to deliberative,[48] and 6.39 a return to epideictic.[49] The references to auditors, therefore, help the authorial audience note the beginning of the sermon, the end of it, and shifts in species of rhetoric within it. When it is recognized that the significance of these references to Jesus' auditors lies in the purpose they serve to structure Jesus' discourse, the pitfall of using the phrase 'And raising his eyes toward his disciples' (6.20a) to over-interpret Jesus' reference to the poor (6.20b) will be avoided. Interpreters over-interpret the passage when they use it to equate the poor and the disciples.

More than any other passage in Luke's Gospel, 6.20 is the storm center of debate about the poor in Luke–Acts because of its central role in efforts to equate the poor of the Lukan beatitudes with the disciples. Yet such efforts fail on several counts. First, there is no change of addressee before 6.24 and the woe to the rich. Secondly, to

48. Kennedy, *New Testament Interpretation*, p. 36: 'The three species [of rhetoric] are judicial, which seeks to bring about a judgment about events of the past; deliberative, which aims at effecting a decision about future action, often in the very immediate future; and epideictic, which celebrates or condemns someone or something, not seeking an immediate judgment or action, but increasing or undermining assent to some value'. See Aristotle, *Rhetoric*, 1.1358a-77b.

49. Kennedy (*New Testament Interpretation*, p. 66) classifies Lk. 6.27-38 as deliberative and the rest of Jesus' speech as epideictic.

reason that the disciples are the poor because they have 'left everything' (5.11) discounts Jesus' admonitions later in the sermon to be generous with one's money (6.30, 32-35), admonitions that express facets of discipleship. Thirdly, consistency requires that if disciples are to be identified as the poor, they must also be identified as those hungry now and those weeping now. Yet in Luke's Gospel, disciples never go hungry or expect to be hungry (see, e.g., Lk. 5.33; 6.1-5; 8.3; 9.3-5, 12-17; 10.3-9; 22.14-38) and may be joyful (10.17; 24.52). Moreover, Jesus himself frequents banquets (5.29; 7.36; 11.37; 14.1) and even develops a reputation for doing so (7.34). In Acts, believers enjoy sufficient sustenance (Acts 2.42-47; 4.32-35). Though interpretations that equate the poor of the Lukan beatitudes with the disciples persist,[50] such interpretations must be considered unpersuasive.

The first seven verses of the Sermon (6.20-26) are balanced in two halves. Each blessing parallels a woe in form and contrasts it in content. The poor (noun) correspond to the wealthy (noun). Participles πεινῶντες and κλαίοντες correspond to ἐμπεπλησμένοι and γελῶντες. The fourth blessing and the fourth woe balance prepositional phrases introduced by ὅταν. The fourth beatitude and fourth woe distinguish themselves from the first three by being longer and more descriptive.

The second outstanding rhetorical feature of these first seven verses is verbal repetition: μακάριοι and οὐαί at the beginning of each blessing and woe respectively;[51] ὅτι in the first three pairs introducing the expressions of reversal of fortunes; ἄνθρωποι in the fourth blessing

---

50.   See Degenhardt, *Evangelist der Armen*, pp. 42-57; Evans, *Saint Luke*, p. 329; Fitzmyer, *Luke I-IX*, p. 631; E. Franklin, *Christ the Lord: A Study in the Purpose and Theology of Luke–Acts* (Philadelphia: Westminster Press, 1975), p. 172; Horn, *Glaube und Handeln*, pp. 123-24, 177-78 (with qualifications); Pilgrim, *Good News to the Poor*, pp. 76-77; Schottroff and Stegemann, *Hoffnung der Armen*, pp. 31-32, 93-95, 101-102, 118; Tannehill, *Narrative Unity*, I, pp. 121-22. On the other hand, Nolland (*Luke 1–9:20*, p. 283) recognizes that renunciation of possessions is not portrayed in Luke–Acts as making oneself poor, and Dupont ('Poor and Poverty', p. 41) states that the beatitudes 'in no way' propose adopting poverty as an ideal way of life. Yet cf. Dupont, 'Poor and Poverty', pp. 44-45, 48-49.

51.   According to Demetrius (*On Style*, 141), anaphora is a characteristic of elegant style. This anaphora gives this portion of Jesus' speech a formal, stately character, and is therefore partly what sets the beatitudes and woes off from the rest of the Sermon.

and woe; and post-positive γὰρ in the fourth blessing and woe introducing clauses recalling the ancestors' practices. These features are easy to identify when the halves of the section are set side by side in two columns.

[20b]Blessed are the poor,
    for yours is
    the kingdom of God.
	[24]But woe to you wealthy,
	    for you have received
	    your consolation.

[21]Blessed are those who are hungry now,
    for you will be satisfied.
Blessed are those who cry now,
    for you will laugh.
	[25]Woe to you who are filled now,
	    for you will hunger.
	Woe to those laughing now,
	    for you will grieve and cry.

[22]Blessed are you when people (ἄνθρωποι) hate you and when they exclude you and reproach and denounce your name as evil on account of the Son of man (ἀνθρώπου).	[26]Woe, when all people (ἄνθρωποι) speak well of you. For (γὰρ) their ancestors did the same things to the false prophets.
[23]Rejoice in that day and leap for joy. For behold, your reward is great in heaven. For (γὰρ) their ancestors did the same things to the prophets.	

The verbal connection between ἄνθρωποι (6.22, 26) and ἀνθρώπου (6.22) is unmistakable in Greek, but difficult to render satisfactorily in English. To Luke's audience, the word play portrays a not too subtle, tragic irony: human beings taking offence at this son of humanity.

This passage contains numerous textual signals to trigger the authorial audience's memory.[52] Here the kingdom of God is announced. Jesus had said that it was necessary for him 'to announce good news of the kingdom of God' (Lk. 4.43). Blessed πτωχοί call to mind the quoted commission 'to announce good news to the poor' (4.18) as well as

---

52. On activities performed by the reader during the reading process described in terms of memory and expectation, see Chapter 3 above.

septuagintal blessings to the poor.[53] The blessing's form is itself embedded in LXX wisdom tradition.[54] Together with the woes, the reversals of fortunes expressed in both halves recall Mary's praise of the Lord's mighty reversals (Lk. 1.51-53), especially her praise that the Lord 'has filled those who are hungry (πεινῶντας) with good things and sent those who are wealthy (πλουτοῦντας) away empty' (1.53).[55]

Rhetorically, the beatitudes begin with a beatitude to which Luke's authorial audience will easily assent. Divine eschatological blessings for the poor are standard fare in the LXX and expected by the audience to be part of Jesus' ministry since Lk. 4.18. By announcing to the poor, 'yours is the kingdom of God', Jesus fulfills the audience's expectation[56]

53. It is precisely these allusions to prior passages in Luke's Gospel and derivatively to Isaiah that enable Dupont ('Introduction aux Beatitudes', *La nouvelle revue théologique* 98 [1976], pp. 97-108 [99-100]) rightly to contend that the kingdom of God of Lk. 6.20 signifies liberation of the oppressed, release of prisoners, recovery of sight to the blind, and leaping ability for the paralyzed.

54. See Ps. 1.1; Prov. 8.34; Dan. 12.12; Tob 13.14; *Pss. Sol.* 4.23; 17.44; 18.6. See also combinations of blessings and woes: Eccl. 10.16-17; Tob. 13.12. Cf. H.D. Betz, 'Eschatology in the Sermon on the Mount and the Sermon on the Plain', *SBLSP* (1985), pp. 343-50 (347): 'The world-view of the SP is Greek throughout, and thus its language, concepts, ideas, and arguments conform to Greek cultural presuppositions'.

55. The characters experiencing reversals of fortunes appear in the Magnificat having a stereotypical quality formally similar to that of the captive, the shattered, the blind, the deaf mute, the lame, lepers, the maimed, the dead, and the poor. Future studies may deem it worthwhile to make in-depth analyses of ὑπερήφανος, δυνάστης, and ταπεινός in the LXX. Ταπεινός, in particular, warrants careful scrutiny. Depending on the context, ταπεινός may refer to one's attitude or deportment before God or other people, i.e. appropriate humility (e.g. Pss. 17.8 [probably]; 33.19; Prov. 3.34; 11.2; 16.2; Sir. 3.20; 10.15; 11.1; 12.5 [probably]; 35.17; Zeph. 2.3; 3.12; Isa. 2.11; 11.4; 26.6; 66.2). Or ταπεινός may refer to one physically abased, sickly, monetarily poor, or simply not among the nobility (e.g. Lev. 27.8 [probably]; 1 Kgdms 18.23; Est. 1.1k [perhaps also pious] Jdt. 9.11; 16.11; Ps 81.3 [probably]; Prov. 30.14; Job 5.11; Sir. 2.4, 5 [perhaps]; 13.21, 22; 29.8; Job 12.21; Amos 2.7; 8.6; Isa. 49.13; 54.11 [of Jerusalem]; Jer. 22.16). In the LXX, it may or may not be favorable to be ταπεινός, again depending on the contextual import of the term. See BAGD, 'ταπεινός', p. 804. For recent studied attempts to tie together thematically the reversals and the scriptural promises to the ancestors expressed in the Magnificat, see G. O'Day, 'Singing Woman's Song: A Hermeneutic of Liberation', *CurTM* 12 (1985), pp. 203-10; Seccombe, *Possessions*, pp. 70-83.

56. That Lk. 6.20 fulfills 4.18, see Albertz, 'Antrittspredigt', p. 200; and Dupont, 'Introduction aux Beatitudes', pp. 99-100.

and vindicates its evaluation of 4.16-21, that is, that the Isaiah passage applies directly to Jesus. Subsequently, Jesus' speech moves toward the beatitude most difficult for the audience to assent to: the blessedness of being denounced on account of Jesus.

The fourfold anaphora beginning each beatitude verbally draws those who suffer because of Jesus into the sphere of salvation occupied by the poor. Consequently, the message to Luke's audience is this: you know from the Scriptures that God saves the poor, and from the events recorded in this narrative that Jesus speaks and acts for God; with the poor in salvation belong also those who follow Jesus. The rhetoric functions to align those who follow Jesus with the divine favor the audience already associates with the poor. The Lukan Jesus further undergirds this fourth blessing with precedent from Israel's scriptural story, wedding his radical agenda to authoritative tradition.

Characterization. As in Lk. 4.18, the poor appear in 6.20 as a type. But further characterization within the beatitudes is more subtle. If we adopt Uspensky's model of four planes of point of view as a lens through which to perceive characterization more clearly, this lens reveals a progression with respect to those to whom blessings are directed. None of those blessed display themselves on a phraseological plane.[57] The spatial positions of the auditors addressed in the scene, while first appearing to suggest a closeness for Jesus and those blessed, send contradictory signals. Those receiving woes are just as proximate to Jesus as those to whom Jesus addresses blessings. Therefore, all of the second-degree narrative level listeners occupy the same spatial perspective vis-à-vis Jesus. Beyond this, the poor cannot be located on a psychological plane or an ideological plane. The descriptions 'being hungry' and 'weeping' respectively, however, depict feelings on the part of these general characters. Being hated and excluded introduces a new psychological and spatial plane for those lastly blessed, and, call it ideology or psychology, clearly the words 'on account of the Son of man' ascribe to them loyalty to Jesus.[58] The effect is a smooth transition from the corresponding woes to admonitions for those who would want to be loyal to Jesus. Yet the focus of characterization is Jesus, for

57. Jesus is the only character who speaks or acts once Luke has summarized the rush for healing (Lk. 6.19).

58. On attachment to Jesus as the distinguishing feature of the fourth beatitude, see Dupont, 'Introduction aux Béatitudes', pp. 101-102.

by word and deed Jesus is confirming to the audience that he is God's anointed representative.

Function of the Character Type. The shift in the nature of Jesus' discourse from 6.20-26 to 6.27-49 is rhetorically significant. Luke 6.20-26 is not exhortation to followers of Jesus about expected behavior. That is, Jesus is not counseling his hearers to be poor any more than to be hungry or weeping or denounced. Rather, the first seven verses of Jesus' speech, led by the announcement of the kingdom to the poor, sharpen the audience's loyalty toward Jesus, prefigure future conflict between Jesus and persons of means, and fashion the eschatological kingdom context for 6.27-49. The first beatitude sets the eschatological tone for the others. It establishes that the hungry and weeping will be full and laughing in the presence of the kingdom of God. Indeed, the first beatitude establishes that all the reversals reveal a divine agenda. Coming between the summary of Jesus' healings and his exhortations, the beatitudes and woes link the healings of 6.18-19 to the kingdom of God before attention shifts from Jesus' benefactions to parenesis. The portion of the sermon that is about conduct, 6.27-49, presupposes the contours of the kingdom established in 6.20-26 and the power and speaking authority of Jesus as God's anointed.

The poor are recipients of God's favor through Jesus. In addition to what has been said above about guiding the audience's evaluation of persons by aligning those who follow Jesus with the divine favor the audience already associates with the poor, once again Luke's audience perceives Jesus in light of LXX convention as God's agent of salvation.

Luke 6.39-40: A Parable about Following

> And he told them a parable. 'It is not possible for a blind person to lead a blind person, is it? They will both fall into a pit, will they not? A disciple is not superior to the teacher. But when fully taught, each will be like his teacher.'

This aphoristic 'parable' (Lk. 6.39) comes in the middle of the Sermon on the Plain (Lk. 6.17-49) and gives us the first instance of third-degree narrative level discourse involving the vocabulary being surveyed in this chapter.[59] The parable is the hypothetical story that Jesus' two

---

59.   The term 'parable' encompasses different forms in the New Testament, including both plotless sayings and brief stories. See J.D. Crossan, *In Parables*, pp. 7-8. Jeremias, *Parables*, p. 20; Tolbert, *Perspectives on the Parables*, pp. 16-17.

questions create: one blind person leads a second blind person, and both of them fall into a pit. The passage returns to second-degree narrative in 6.40 with Jesus' words: 'A disciple is not superior to the teacher'.

Verse 40 applies the parable to discipleship. In the context of Jesus' words in 6.40, the parable shows Jesus' second degree narrative level auditors why it is important that disciples have a competent teacher.[60] A learner cannot be safely taught by someone unlearned. An unlearned teacher has no more competence to teach than a blind person has to serve as a trail guide. The stereotypical incapability of the blind makes the point of the saying. The value promoted by this epideictic rhetoric is allegiance to the proper teacher. By implication, Jesus is the antitype of the blind. Luke's authorial audience would recognize that disciples who choose Jesus to be their teacher are being taught by a teacher who is capable of leading.

Luke 7.11-17: The Son of the Widow of Nain

> And it happened next that he went to a city called Nain. And his disciples and a large crowd went with him. As he approached the gate of the city, behold, someone who died was being carried out—the only son of his mother, and she was a widow. And a sufficiently large crowd was with her. And when the Lord saw her, his heart went out to her and he said to her, 'Do not cry'. And coming forward, he touched the coffin. Those carrying it stopped. And he said, 'Young man, I say to you, arise'. And the dead one sat up and began to speak. And he gave him to his mother. Fear seized them all, and they glorified God saying, 'A great prophet has arisen among us', and 'God has visited God's people'. And this news about him went out into the whole of Judea and all the surrounding region.

---

60. Third-degree narrative level is a hypodiegetic level, i.e. a narrative level below another narrative level. On the various functions of hypodiegetic narratives, see Rimmon-Kenan, *Narrative Fiction*, pp. 92-93. Rimmon-Kenan labels three functions. The hypodiegetic narrative may keep the narrative just above it going 'by the sheer fact of being narrated, regardless (or almost regardless) of their content' (Rimmon-Kenan, *Narrative Fiction*, p. 92). This is the 'actional function'. To illustrate this function, Rimmon-Kenan cites the stories Scheherezade tells the Sultan in *A Thousand and One Nights*: 'the only condition her (Scheherezade's) stories have to fulfill is to sustain the Sultan's attention' (Rimmon-Kenan, *Narrative Fiction*, p. 92). The hypodiegetic narrative may explain the situation or action of the narrative level just above it. This function Rimmon-Kenan labels the 'explicative function'. Thirdly, the hypodiegetic narrative may serve to underscore a theme or motif being expressed at the higher narrative level. Rimmon-Kenan calls this the 'thematic function'. These functions of hypodiegetic narratives may be present individually or in combination.

Literary and Rhetorical Features. The authorial audience recalls Lk. 4.25-26 and would recognize as accurate though incomplete the conclusion expressed by the crowd in 7.16: 'a great prophet has arisen'. The word play on ἐγείρω establishes a connection between what Jesus does and the crowd's accolades. Jesus says to the young man, 'Arise' (ἐγέρθητι, 7.14); the bystanders glorify God with the affirmation that a great prophet 'has arisen' (ἠγέρθη, 7.16). The crowd's acclamation, the first time Jesus is esteemed as a prophet by characters in the narrative, confirms Jesus' comment about finding honor outside of his hometown (4.24).

Characterization and Function of the Character Type. This is the first mention of the dead in Luke–Acts. When he addresses him, Jesus calls the deceased a 'young man'. But beyond this, the text provides no characteristics of the dead man. Luke gives him no personality, no history, no character traits, no attributes other than being dead. He speaks after being resuscitated, but the audience is told nothing of what he says because his point of view is of no concern to the narrative. The fact that he speaks simply confirms that he is alive. The dead young man is resuscitated, ostensibly because of Jesus' sympathy for the man's widowed mother.

The crowd's acclamations characterize Jesus as 'a great prophet' and as the means by which God visits humanity. While a crowd's acclamations may not be reliable, Jesus' act of raising the dead provides Luke's authorial audience with evidence of Jesus' status as God's agent of salvation. That this act is evidence of Jesus' status as God's eschatological agent of salvation is made explicit in the episode that immediately follows this one. This account of the raising of this dead man supplies Luke's audience with a narrative manifestation of one facet of Jesus' answer to the question put to him by John's disciples. When Jesus responds to the question of whether or not he is 'the coming one' (7.19) by pointing to his salvific deeds (7.22), Jesus' list of salvific deeds includes raising the dead.

Luke 7.18-23: Messengers from John

> And John's disciples reported to him about all these things. And summoning at random two of his disciples, John sent them to the Lord to say, 'Are you the coming one, or should we look for another?' When the men came to him, they said, 'John the Baptist sent us to you to say, "Are you the coming one, or should be look for another?"' During that time he healed

many from their diseases and afflictions and evil spirits. And he granted
sight to the many blind. Then answering them, he said, 'Go, report to John
what you saw and heard: the blind see again, the lame walk, lepers are
cleansed, and the deaf mute hear, the dead are raised, the poor are preached
good news. And blessed is the one who is not scandalized by me.'

Literary and Rhetorical Features. The text gives no specific setting to
this episode. The episode is marked off by the close of the previous
episode, the account of the raising of the dead young man of Nain,
with a general statement that news about Jesus spread. The change in
setting at Lk. 7.36 signals a new episode.

The discourse from 7.18 through 7.35 calls attention to John the
Baptist personally and thematically.[61] But the story of John and John's
relationship to Jesus is enmeshed in a second narrative dynamic. The
episode (7.18-35) begins by making an issue of how Jesus relates to
the blind, the lame, lepers, the deaf mute, the dead, and the poor
(7.22) as their rescuer, and ends by making an issue of Jesus' relations
with tax collectors and sinners (7.29, 34) as their friend.

The presence and absence of John's disciples divides this larger
episode (7.18-35) into two parts: 7.18-23, where John's disciples are
in the scene, and 7.24-35, where they are not. The leading interest
of 7.18-23 is signaled by the word-for-word repetition of John's
question.[62] Repetition serves as a rhetorical device to impress upon the
audience the importance of the question for the narrative. Therefore,
what is central to this episode is the question of who Jesus is.

Two further rhetorical devices elicit the audience's reaction to John's
question. First, to the audience's ear σὺ εἶ (7.19) recalls the voice
from heaven at Jesus' baptism, σὺ εἶ ὁ υἱός μου (3.22), and the cries
of exorcized demons, σὺ εἶ ὁ υἱὸς τοῦ θεοῦ (4.41).[63]

Secondly, Luke freezes the action of the story at a significant
moment. In Luke's Gospel, Jesus' answers characteristically follow
immediately upon the questions or requests put to him.[64] In this episode,

61. See A.J. Mattill, *Luke and the Last Things: A Perspective for the
Understanding of Lukan Thought* (Dillsboro, NC: Western North Carolina Press,
1979), pp. 159-64; Sanders, 'From Isaiah 61', p. 100; W. Wink, 'Jesus' Reply to
John: Matt 11:2-6/Luke 7:18-23', *Forum* 5 (1989), pp. 121-28 (123-24).

62. The textual question in Lk. 7.19, 20 concerning ἕτερον and ἄλλον does not
materially affect interpretation.

63. Cf. Lk. 22.67, 70; 23.3, 37.

64. Lk. 5.30-32, 33-39; 6.2-4; 8.9-10; 9.38-41; 10.25-26, 29-35, 40-41; 11.1-

a summary report by the narrator of Jesus' activity (7.21) is inserted
between the question from John's disciples and Jesus' answer. The
narrator literally interrupts the conversation between Jesus and John's
disciples to point out that Jesus has been curing diseases, exorcising
evil spirits, and healing the blind. This rhetorical device not only
reminds the audience of what activity Jesus is engaged in and heightens
the drama of the moment, it invites the audience to answer the question
posed to Jesus before Jesus does, yet answer it in the same manner
Jesus will. During the momentary pause in the conversation, the reader
connects the question by John's disciples to the narrator's reminder of
Jesus' activity. When Jesus himself then makes the same connection
(7.22), the narrative has succeeded in aligning Jesus' and the audience's
points of view. Jesus' mission to the blind, the lame, lepers, the deaf
mute, the dead, and the poor is the definitive content of an affirmative
answer to John's question.

Jesus' answer to John's disciples is compact and aurally striking.
The brevity of each of the six clauses intensifies their forcefulness.[65]
Brevity, rhyming, and rhythm all combine to heighten the stylistic level
of Jesus' discourse and therefore signal special importance to these
words.[66]

All of the benefactions recited in 7.22 have already been bestowed
by Jesus in the narrative except that of the deaf mute hearing.[67] The
first and last benefactions Jesus lists, 'the blind see again' and 'the poor
are preached good news', repeat benefactions promised in Lk. 4.18.[68]

The importance of the echo of 4.18-19 in 7.18-23 can scarcely be
overestimated. It places Jesus' healing and preaching within the context of Isaiah's announcement of 'the acceptable year of the Lord'.
The logic of the narrative may now be seen. In 4.18-19, the audience

4; 12.13-14, 41-53; 13.14-16, 23-30; 17.5-6, 13-14, 20-21, 37; 18.18-20, 26-27,
41-42; 19.39-40; 20.2-4, 33-38; 21.7-9; 22.9-12, 67-69, 70; 23.3, 42-43.

65.   Demetrius, *On Style*, p. 269.

66.   Demetrius, *On Style*, p. 137.

67.   The blind see, Lk. 7.21; the (lame) paralytic walks, 5.17-25; lepers are
cleansed, 5.12-13; the dead are raised, 7.12-15; and the poor are preached good
news, 6.20. Jesus' report of the deaf mute hearing anticipates 11.14.

68.   Worthy of study in the future is whether not repeating in Lk. 7.22 the reference in 4.18 to liberating the captive and the shattered can be related to the narrative
situation, i.e., that the question is put to Jesus on behalf of someone who is captive
whom Jesus does not free. Albertz ('Antrittspredigt', p. 199) states that Luke–Acts
lacks any character clearly corresponding to αἰχμάλωτος.

finds a statement in eschatological terms of what to expect of Jesus'
ministry. The Sermon on the Plain, healings, and resuscitation show
Jesus in the act of carrying out that ministry. The scene with John's
disciples (7.18-23) recaps Jesus' ministry to this point and connects it
to Jesus' reading in the synagogue. Of course, this narrative logic is
available only to Luke's audience, not to characters in the story.[69]

Characterization. Those characterized to greater and lesser extents in
this episode are Jesus, John, Pharisees, lawyers, tax collectors and the
people. Their characterization is organized around two subplots: John's
uncertainty about Jesus, and opposition to John and Jesus by members
of 'this generation' (7.31). The blind, the lame, lepers, the deaf mute,
the dead, and the poor neither speak nor act, except to the extent that
it reflects their healing.

J. Fitzmyer sees in the question to Jesus 'Are you the one who is to
come?' (7.19) an allusion to John's earlier declaration that 'one mightier
than me comes after me'.[70] For Fitzmyer, Jesus rejects the role of
eschatological messenger of God by his answer.[71] R. Brawley disagrees,
stating that Jesus does not reject this messianic designation but 'molds
the reader's understanding of it in terms of his ministry of liberation'.[72]
Brawley contends that Jesus is reforming the reader's understanding
of messiahship and then Jesus is developing his own identity on the
basis of this redefined understanding.[73] Both Fitzmyer and Brawley
are partly correct but miss the rhetorical effect of Jesus' response in
7.22. Luke's authorial audience will recognize the actions that Jesus
summarizes as actions that characterize God's agent of salvation. A
ministry of liberation, to use Brawley's words, is what LXX-competent
readers would expect the messiah to display. Therefore, as Brawley
rightly points out, Jesus' answer does not steer his questioners away
from identifying him as the messiah. However, 7.22 does not mold the
reader's understanding of what it means to be the messiah as much as

---

69.   It is common in secondary literature to recognize that Lk. 7.22 recalls 4.18-
19, but simultaneously to collapse the first- and second-degree narrative levels of
discourse. See, e.g., Albertz, 'Antrittspredigt', p. 200.

70.   Fitzmyer, *Luke I-IX*, p. 66.

71.   Fitzmyer, *Luke I-IX*, p. 66.

72.   R. Brawley, *Centering on God: Method and Message in Luke–Acts* (Literary
Currents in Biblical Interpretation; Louisville: Westminster/John Knox, 1990), p. 49.

73.   Brawley, *Centering on God*, pp. 48-49.

it underscores the audience's image of Jesus as the scripturally-depicted divine agent of salvation. Luke is in the process of reforming his audience's understanding of messiahship, but the issue around which Luke is reforming his LXX-competent authorial audience's understanding of messiahship is the issue of the messiah's relationship to sinners. Luke's LXX-informed authorial audience would not expect the messiah to be a friend of sinners.

Luke 7.23 raises the authorial audience's expectation that some who come into contact with Jesus are and will be further scandalized by Jesus, and assures the audience that Jesus is aware of the opposition his words and actions engender. Almost immediately the audience receives clarification as to the identity of these scandalized, specifically the Pharisees and lawyers (7.30). But Pharisees and lawyers are not scandalized because Jesus bestows benefactions upon the blind, the lame, lepers, the deaf mute, the dead, and the poor. Rather, they are scandalized because Jesus consorts with tax collectors and sinners and discounts religious code (5.21, 30; 6.7; 7.34). Because their 'proofs' from lifestyle are inconsistent, that is, proof that John has a demon is his asceticism and proof that Jesus is ungodly is his 'gluttonism' (7.33-34), the opponents' actual point of contention with John and Jesus is shown to relate to what the two have in common. Both fraternize with tax collectors (3.12-13; 5.30; 7.29, 34).

Function of the Character Types. In Lk. 7.22, the blind, the lame, lepers, the deaf mute, the dead, and the poor are spoken of for the purpose of providing Jesus' answer to John's disciples with persuasive substance. The question to Jesus from John is, in effect, 'Are you the one eschatological prophet mightier than I, whom I announced was coming?'[74] For Jesus to have said 'Yes, I am the coming one' would have been merely an assertion (albeit a reliable assertion as far as Luke's audience is concerned) by Jesus. However, to say 'Go, report to John what you saw and heard: the blind see again, the lame walk, lepers are cleansed, and the deaf mute hear, the dead are raised, the poor are preached good news' has greater persuasive weight and therefore greater rhetorical value because it goes beyond assertion. The rhetorical effect of clustering references to these character types is to

---

74. The question echoes John's announcement in Lk. 3.16: 'The one mightier than I am is coming. I am not fit to loose the straps of his sandals.'

recall both 4.18 and the Septuagintal image of them.[75] As I have argued in Chapter 5, these character types are standard recipients of God's saving activity in the LXX. Therefore, Jesus' answer presupposes that his actions toward these beneficiaries demonstrate both to John at the second-degree narrative level and to his audience at the first-degree narrative level that he is the coming one. To Luke's audience, then, Jesus' words and actions toward the blind, the lame, lepers, the deaf mute, the dead, and the poor confirm him to be God's unique eschatological agent of salvation. Moreover, in LXX-like fashion, clustering references to these character types serves to heighten the magnificence of Jesus' saving action.

Luke 9.7-8: Rumors about Who Jesus Is

> Herod the tetrarch heard of all these things happening and was perplexed because it was being said by some 'John was raised from the dead', by some 'Elijah has appeared', and others 'One of the ancient prophets has arisen'.

Literary and Rhetorical Features. The authorial audience knows first, that John's ministry had divine sanction (Lk. 1.14-17; 76-80; 3.2-6; 7.22-28), and secondly, that Herod is characterized by evil deeds, including the imprisonment of John (3.19-20). At Luke 7, John is still alive. At 9.7, the audience learns that John is dead. At 9.9, the audience learns, from Herod's own mouth, that Herod has executed John.

Characterization and Function of the Character Type. There is nothing novel about this reference to 'the dead'. When he died, John became one of the dead. The character or fate of the dead is not the issue here. The effect of the passage is ominously to foreshadow future interaction between Jesus and Herod. Parallel story lines for Jesus and John began in ch. 1. This parallelism shapes audience expectation as the narrative unfolds. Herod was first introduced in neutral terms (1.5; 3.1). Then Herod turned his attention to John, to John's peril (3.19-

---

75.   D.L. Bock ('Proclamation from Prophecy and Pattern: Luke's Use of the Old Testament for Christology and Mission', in C.A. Evans and W.R. Stegner [eds.], *The Gospels and the Scriptures of Israel* [JSNTSup, 104; Sheffield: Sheffield Academic Press, 1994], pp. 290-91) comments on the fact that Lk. 7.22 answers John's question indirectly by reference to what Jesus does, interpreted in light of the Old Testament.

20). Now the audience learns that Jesus has caught Herod's attention (9.7), that Herod has beheaded John (9.9), and that Herod is attempting to see Jesus (9.9). Audience sympathy moves further toward the dead John and against Herod. But the vignette's overriding effect is what this scene portends for Jesus.

Luke 9.59-60: Jesus' Reply to Delaying Following

> Then he [Jesus] said to another, 'Follow me'. But he said to him, 'Lord, allow me first to go to bury my father'. But he said to him, 'Let the dead bury their own dead. You go and proclaim the kingdom of God.'

Literary and Rhetorical Features. This brief exchange is the second of three exchanges between Jesus and three unnamed characters as Jesus is traveling (Lk. 9.57-62). All three exchanges have to do with following Jesus. The repeated vocabulary of following dominates the section and introduces each exchange: 'I will follow you' (9.57), 'follow me' (9.59), and again, 'I will follow you' (9.61). Yet it is the third exchange that definitively unifies the three, combining as it does distinct elements of each of the preceding two exchanges. The first and third involve persons who, apparently without prompting, volunteer to follow (Lk. 9.57, 61). The second and third focus in parallel fashion on requests to delay briefly before following (9.59: ἐπίτρεψόν μοι. . . πρῶτον; 9.61: πρῶτον δὲ ἐπίτρεψόν μοι).

Characterization and Function of the Character Type. This reference to the dead in 9.60 is striking. To make a point of the urgency of following him, Jesus gives an unreasonable response, amounting to refusal, to a reasonable request by a would-be follower. The would-be follower's request is consistent with scriptural precedent (Gen. 50.4-5; Tob. 4.3). Jesus' response is deliberate hyperbole. The dead can no more bury the dead than the blind can lead the blind. The stereotypical inability of the dead to do anything and Jesus' departure from the conventional norm of etiquette toward the dead give Jesus' response its sharp edge, its shock value.

Luke 11.14: Jesus Casts Out a Demon

> And he was casting out a demon which was causing a person to be deaf mute. And when the demon exited, the deaf mute spoke. And the crowd was amazed.

Literary and Rhetorical Features. The preceding episode (Lk. 11.1-13) concluded with Jesus' promise that the Father will give the Holy Spirit to those who ask. After that episode, the focus shifts to pre-ternatural spirits of a different ilk.

Jesus' exorcism of this demon provides both the immediate occasion for the Beelzebul debate and the interpretive context for Jesus' maxim, 'Any kingdom divided against itself will be ruined, a house divided against itself will fall' (11.17). The 'kingdom' reference verbally ties the Beelzebul debate to the preceding instruction to Jesus' disciples, in which Jesus taught his disciples to seek the Father's kingdom (11.2).

Characterization and Function of the Character Type. Luke is not creating a true character in the deaf mute; that is, the deaf mute is not someone who has choices or displays character through willful actions. Rather, Luke is providing a point of departure for the ensuing debate over the source of Jesus' power. The authorial audience knows that the healing of deaf mutes is a mark of 'the Coming One', God's eschato-logical agent of salvation (7.22). What the deaf mute says after the demon comes out is not pertinent to the story. All that is germane is that he can speak. Here, as with the reference to the widow's dead son speaking (7.15), the notation about speaking simply confirms Jesus' salvific act.

Luke 14.12-24: Jesus the Importunate Dinner Guest

And then he said to the one who had invited him, 'When you hold a lunch or dinner, do not call your friends or your brothers or your relatives or your wealthy neighbors, lest they invite you back and repayment come to you. Rather, when you hold a banquet, call the poor, the maimed, the lame, the blind. And you will be blessed because they are unable to repay you. For you will be repaid at the resurrection of the righteous'. When he heard this, one of the fellow guests said, 'Blessed is whoever will eat bread in the kingdom of God'. But he said to him, 'A certain man held a great dinner, and invited many. And he sent his servant, when it was time for the supper, to say to those invited, "Come, because everything is ready now". But all of them, beginning with the first, began to excuse themselves. The first said to him, "I bought a field and have an obligation to go out to see it. I ask you, have me excused." And another said, "I bought five yoke of oxen and am going to evaluate them. I ask you, have me excused." And another said, "I married a wife, and for this reason cannot come". And the servant returned and reported these things to his lord. Then in a rage, the master of the house said to his servant, "Go

immediately into the streets and alleys of the city and bring the poor and
the maimed and the blind and the lame in here". The servant said, "Lord,
it is as you commanded, and there is still room". And the lord said to the
servant, "Go out to the roads and hedges and compel people to come in,
so that my house may be filled. For I tell you, none of those men who
were invited will taste my dinner."'

Literary and Rhetorical Features. This unit begins with Lk. 14.1,
when the scene moves to the house of a leading Pharisee where Jesus
is 'to eat bread', and extends through 14.24. The meal scene may be
divided into several constituent units: an introduction, 14.1; the sabbath
healing of the man with dropsy, 14.2-5; the parable to those invited,
14.7-11; the parable to the inviting host, 14.12-14; the parable to the
fellow guest at the great dinner, 14.15-24. Only the first of the parables
is labeled a 'parable' in the text (14.7). But the language of 14.12
mirrors that of 14.7-8,[76] and the ἄνθρωπός τις of 14.16 introduces
this story as a parable.[77] It is not that the three parables are of the
same nature. The first two take the form of advice; the third is in the
story form most associated with parables.

Though one would expect the meal setting to provide an atmosphere
of friendliness, at this point in Luke's narrative it portends conflict.
This is the third time Jesus dines with Pharisees.[78] Both of the prior
two episodes have displayed friction between Jesus and the religious
leaders. Indeed, tension between Jesus and the Pharisees and lawyers
enters the present episode immediately with the healing of the man
with dropsy.

Repetitions of key terms guide the audience's understanding of the
discourse of the meal scene and connect the parable of the great dinner
to its immediate narrative setting: 'to eat bread' (14.1, 15), 'those
invited' (14.7, 17, 24), 'dinner' (14.12, 17, 24), and 'the poor, the
maimed, the lame, the blind' (14.13, 21). Since the narrator is speaking
in 14.7, the verbal connection between the lawyers and Pharisees, as
'those invited' to the dinner Jesus is attending, and 'those invited' to
the dinner in the parable is available only to the first-degree narrative
level audience, not to the second-degree narrative level characters

76. Lk. 14.7-8: Ἔλεγεν δὲ πρὸς τοὺς κεκλημένους... ὅταν κληθῇς ὑπό
τινος εἰς γάμους; 14.12: "Ἔλεγεν δὲ καὶ τῷ κεκληκότι αὐτόν ὅταν ποιῇς
ἄριστον ἢ δεῖπνον.

77. See Lk. 10.30; 15.11; 16.1, 19; 19.12.

78. Jesus has dined with Pharisees in 7.36-50 and 11.37-53.

themselves. Repetitions within the parable of the great dinner form a chiastic inclusio: τοῦ δείπνου. . . τοῖς κεκλημένοις (14.17) and τῶν κεκλημένων. . . τοῦ δείπνου (14.24).

Characterization. The poor, the maimed, the lame, and the blind have no personality and do not speak or act. They are referred to, but are not actually in the scene itself. Jesus applies one character trait to them explicitly: they lack the capacity to reciprocate generosity (14.14). This trait accords especially well with the typical image of the poor elicited from the LXX, namely, that the poor do not have the resources to be generous or merciful.[79] The only points of view displayed are those of Jesus and the religious leaders.[80] These opposing points of view advance the ongoing conflict between Jesus and the religious leaders.

There is a sarcastic edge to Jesus' sayings in 14.8-11 and 14.12-14 that moves them from sage advice to thinly-veiled critique. The words of 14.11 to invited lawyers and Pharisees so vividly mimic Ezek. 21.31[81] that Jesus is in effect giving scriptural 'advice' to persons who should not have to hear it, persons for whom such wisdom should already be known and adopted. The saying in 14.11 has an aphoristic quality to it: self-contained, lacking internal context, brief, and rhetorically witty or striking. It appears as though Jesus is (ironically?) inviting the lawyers and Pharisees to be calculating, but saying in effect that if they are going to plot for exaltation they should plot wisely.

Likewise, Jesus' advice in 14.13 is certainly other than simple counsel. To interpret this as sanctified advice to give oneself over to serving humanity rather than seeking rewards is to miss the point. Jesus speaks specifically of a payback. Jesus adopts, at least for the sake of his argument here, the wisdom of calculated hospitality. But Jesus' admonition stings the Pharisee because Jesus implies that the Pharisee has not taken the scriptural path to rewards. What I noted after surveying references to the poor, the blind, and the lame in the LXX was that according to the LXX God-fearing people demonstrate their piety and righteous by their kindness and generosity toward these groups.[82] To exhort the Pharisee host to provide hospitality to them is not merely to dictate a new invitation list. Rather, to exhort the Pharisee

79. See the concluding comments to Chapter 5 above.
80. Powell, 'The Religious Leaders in Luke', pp. 98-100, 104-105.
81. See also Prov. 25.6-7 and Sir. 3.18-20.
82. See Chapter 5 above.

to provide hospitality to these groups is to imply that the Pharisee has overlooked Scripture, specifically, scriptural mandates for generosity to the poor, the blind, and the lame.[83]

Herein lies the cohesion of 14.1-25. The issue of healing on the sabbath (14.2-6) is a matter of scriptural interpretation. Jesus extends the matter of scriptural interpretation into questions of what place to take when invited to a festival and whom to invite to dinner. If the lawyers and Pharisees want the adequacy of their actions adjudicated by Scripture, Jesus accepts those terms, at least for the time being, and critiques them on those terms. Applying Scripture to conduct is the professional arena of the lawyers and Pharisees, but even in their own arena they are bested by Jesus. The episode therefore continues the narrative process of refining and nuancing the characters of Jesus and the religious leaders.

Function of the Character Types. Mention of the poor, the maimed, the blind, and the lame may give an eschatological cast to Lk. 14.13, in light of 4.18-19, 6.20; and 7.22. But other narrative factors confirm that the subsequent parable of the great dinner is eschatological, independent of reference to the character types. The comment by an unidentified guest in 14.15 directs attention to the kingdom of God, picking up on Jesus' reference in 14.14 to the resurrection of the righteous.

In this pericope the types serve a plot function more than a characterization function. In previous passages, these types function in the narrative to reveal and define the character Jesus as God's eschatological agent of salvation. In this passage, the types are employed to give substance to the conflict between Jesus and the lawyers and Pharisees. In 14.13, Jesus is not giving practical advice. He is leveling a criticism on his host's perspective on beneficence in terms Luke's audience unmistakably grasps as a perspective which stands in contrast to Jesus'. In 14.21, the poor, the maimed, the blind, and the lame are among the alternative guests at the great dinner. To the audience, the judgment in

83. On generosity to the poor, see, e.g., Exod. 23.11; Lev. 19.10; 23.22; Deut. 24.19; and Sir. 7.32. On the worthiness of sharing banquets with the poor, see Est. 9.22. In the Old Testament pseudepigrapha, see especially, *T. Job* 17.3. For commands to be courteous or generous to the blind, see Lev 19.14; 21.18; Deut 27.18; 28.29; 2 Kgdms 5.6,8; Job 29.15; Ps. 145.8; Zeph. 1.17; Mal. 1.8; Isa. 29.18; 35.5; 42.7, 16 (perhaps); 59.10; Ep. Jer. 36; Tob. 7.6. On generosity toward the lame, see Job 29.15.

the parable upon the invited who decline to come to the banquet is a transparent judgment upon the invited lawyers and Pharisees listening to the parable.

Luke 15.24 and 15.32: The Lost Son Was Dead

> 'This son of mine was dead and is alive again, was lost and has been found'.
>
> 'This brother of yours was dead and is alive, was lost and has been found'.

Literary and Rhetorical Features. These two verses are lines spoken in Jesus' parable of the prodigal son (15.11-32) by the father to describe this son. The parable of the prodigal son, which we may more aptly refer to as the 'parable of the lost son', is the third of three parables Jesus tells in immediate succession (Lk. 15.3-32).

All three parables are addressed to Pharisees and scribes. All three have to do with something that is lost: the lost sheep (Lk. 15.3-7), the lost coin (Lk. 15.8-10), and the lost son (Lk. 15.11-32). In all three, someone expresses joy upon the recovery of the lost: the man who finds his one lost sheep (Lk. 15.5-6), the woman who finds her lost coin (Lk. 15.9), and the father who receives his lost son (Lk. 15.22-24, 32). These common features bind the three parables together as a rhetorical unit.

Yet the third parable contains significant distinctive features. To begin with, the three lost items are not perfectly parallel. The lost sheep and lost coin cannot be said to be responsible for their lostness. Nor can they find themselves; they must be found. The lost son, on the other hand, 'loses' himself by squandering his share of his father's estate and 'comes to himself' (15.17) when he reaches the depths of his misery. The formal patterns of the three parables are likewise not identical. The first two parables are allegories that intend to depict heavenly joy; this is stated explicitly in comments by Jesus immediately after each of these parables (15.7, 10). When we look at the structure of Jesus' discourse, there is a simple pattern that is followed in both 15.3-7 and 15.8-10:

(a) something is lost
(b) that something is sought
(c) that something is found
(d) the finder rejoices
(e) finder invites others to rejoice with him or her
(f) Jesus applies the parable to joy in heaven at the repentance of sinners

Elements (a) through (e) of the pattern occur in third-degree narrative discourse. Element (f) occurs in second-degree narrative discourse. Stated simply, the third-degree narrative level parables about the lost sheep and lost coin illumine a second-degree narrative level situation: joy in heaven at the repentance of sinners.

Jesus' discourse in 15.11-32 contains elements (a), (c) (though we note that the lost son is not totally passive in the way that the sheep and coin were), (d), and (e). Most significantly, however, the parable of the lost son lacks element (f). That is, the parable of the lost son lacks any similar concluding comment by Jesus that would dictate the parable's application. Instead of a making a concluding comment, Jesus extends the parable. Jesus continues third-degree narrative discourse and adds a second major feature to the parable: the elder son's reaction to the events taking place upon his younger brother's return.

The rhetorical effect of structuring these parables in this manner is to invite Luke's audience to draw conclusions about the third parable and its application from the two preceding parables and from the second-degree narrative situation in which the parables are told. The first two parables, along with Jesus' concluding comments about joy in heaven over repentant sinners, prepare Luke's audience for the father's joy at his lost son's return. By making the finding of the lost sheep and coin occasions for unrestrained joy and celebration, Luke's audience is led to approve of the father's extravagant expressions of joy. After all, the preceding parables and concluding comments establish that the father in the third parable is acting in a heavenly way.

The parables of the lost sheep and the lost coin offer no counterpart to the second half of the parable of the lost son, but it takes little imagination to see how this half of the parable applies to the second-degree narrative situation. The second-degree narrative situation is established in 15.1-2. Jesus 'accepts and eats with' (15.2) tax collectors and sinners who are receptive to his message (15.1; cf. 14.35). Pharisees and scribes disapprove of Jesus' actions (15.2).[84] It is to the

---

84. The description of Jesus' action 'he accepts sinners and eats with them' (Lk. 15.2), comes from the mouths of Pharisees and scribes. From a literary-critical perspective, it is intriguing that Pharisees and scribes give commentary that is undoubtedly reliable even though their evaluation of Jesus' actions is clearly to be rejected by Luke's audience.

grumbling Pharisees and scribes that Jesus then addresses the three parables (15.2). Jesus' allegorical point is unmistakable: the attitudes of the Pharisees and scribes toward sinners and Jesus correspond to the elder son's misguided attitudes toward his younger brother and his father.

Characterization and Function of the Character Type. Our concern here is the term 'dead'. The younger brother is described by the father twice, in parallel verses, as having been 'dead' (15.24, 32). Clearly, the term 'dead' is used here figuratively. But the metaphor defies precise comparison. When did the younger son 'die'? When he expressed his desire to take his portion of the inheritance (Lk. 15.12)? When he left home (15.13a)? When he began squandering his wealth (15.13b)? When he was in dire straits (15.14-16)? And when did the younger son begin to 'live again?' When he 'came to himself' (15.17)? When he got up and went to his father (15.20a)? When his father embraced and kissed him (15.20b)? The parable leaves these questions open.

Whatever the precise comparison, the impact of the metaphor, 'dead', comes from the contrast between dead and alive, which is paralleled by the contrast between lost and found. The twice-spoken confession of the lost son, 'Father, I have sinned against heaven and against you' (15.18-19, 21), is balanced by the twice-spoken affirmation of the father that the younger son 'was dead and is alive, was lost and is found' (15.24, 32).[85] We should avoid romanticizing the lost son. The lost son's confession, which is no doubt to be accepted by Luke's audience as a sincere confession, bears marks of true piety. Yet the lost son is driven to this confession neither by fear nor love of God, nor by remorse over his shabby treatment of his father, nor by guilt feelings about his reckless behavior. As M.A. Tolbert points out, 'It is only after his desires stopped being fulfilled that as the story puts it "he came to himself"'.[86] Thus, his cry, 'Father, I have sinned', is a cry born out of desperation, like the cries of psalmists,[87] and like the cries

---

85. For a detailed presentation of the manner of discourse and the rhetorical style of Lk. 15.11-32, see Tolbert, *Perspectives on the Parables*, pp. 98-100.

86. Tolbert, *Perspectives on the Parables*, p. 102.

87. E.g. Pss. 6.3-5; 9.14, 22; 19.2-3; 21.12; 24.22; 30.10-13; 33.7; 43.24-25; 59.13; 114.1-4; 117.5; 141.2-4.

later in Luke's narrative of lepers, 'Jesus, master, have mercy on us' (17.13), and of the blind man, 'Jesus, son of David, have mercy on me' (18.38, 39). In a sense, the younger son took his own life. But the father gives it back to him. Therefore, in illuminating the second-degree narrative situation, the parable designates sinners as lost and dead. But since God is the salvation of the lost and the dead, by analogy God is the salvation of sinners.

The younger son differs from the dead as the dead are a type character in the LXX in that, at least at the outset, the son has resources to squander and the option to choose between staying in his father's house and leaving. Nevertheless, the parable shows the two to be comparable. To be lost in sin is a kind of death. When the parable is interpreted in its second-degree narrative context, the rhetoric of 'the dead' refines the image of sinners by casting sinners as people in a pitiful state who may nevertheless be reclaimed by God. This image of sinners contrasts sharply with the traditional image of sinners in the Psalms. In the Psalms, sinners are invariably condemned and destroyed by God.[88] We may conclude, then, that the rhetoric of 'the dead' in these passages (15.24, 32) contributes to Luke's broadly-based effort to explain and legitimize Jesus' fraternization with sinners by helping to redefine the status of sinners before God.

Luke 16.19-31: The Rich Man and Lazarus

> There once was a certain rich man. And he attired himself in purple and fine linen, celebrating sumptuously daily. A certain poor man named Lazarus was cast at his door, covered with sores and longing to be filled by what would fall from the rich man's table. But even dogs, when they would come, licked his sores. It happened that the poor man died and was carried by angels to Abraham's bosom. And the rich man died and was buried. And in Hades, lifting up his eyes, beingin torment, he saw Abraham far off, and Lazarus in his bosom. And calling out he said, 'Father Abraham, have mercy on me and send Lazarus to dip the tip of his finger into water and cool my tongue, because I am in agony in these flames'. Abraham said, 'Child, remember that you received your good things during your life, and, correspondingly, Lazarus received bad things. But now, he is consoled here, and you are in agony. In addition to

88. E.g. Pss. 3.8; 9.17-19; 36.12-17, 20, 32; 57.11; 91.8; 118.155; 128.4; 144.20; 145.9; 146.6.

all this, between us and you a great chasm has been established so that those wishing to cross from here to you would not be able, nor may those wishing to do so pass from there to us.' But he said, 'I entreat you, then, father, that you might send him to my father's house, for I have five brothers, so that he may warn them, so they might not also come to this place of torment'. But Abraham said, 'They have Moses and the prophets. Let them heed them.' But he said, 'No, father Abraham, rather, they will repent if someone goes to them from the dead'. But he said to him, 'If they do not heed Moses and the prophets, neither will they be persuaded should someone rise from the dead'.

Literary and Rhetorical Features. This parable concludes a narrative unit, begun in Lk. 16.1 with the parable of the dishonest steward, on uses of money and the kingdom of God.[89] The shift within the parable of the rich man and Lazarus from narrated discourse to predominantly direct discourse suggests that the parable divides itself into two parts: Lk. 16.19-23 and 16.24-31.[90] A second notable literary feature is that there are nine repeated expressions. These two features may easily be seen when the passage is broken up and repeated expressions are underlined. A third literary feature, not recognizable in translation, is the use of exceptional terminology in the opening verses of the parable. In the following representation of the passage, 'ND' and 'DD' distinguish sections of narrated discourse and predominantly direct discourse. Exceptional terminology is identified by footnotes.

89. Pilgrim, *Good News to the Poor*, p. 113; Tiede, *Luke*, p. 289; Tolbert, *Perspectives on the Parables*, p. 61.

90. F. Schneider and W. Stenger ('Die offene Tür und die unüberschreitbare Kluft', *NTS* 25 [1978–79], pp. 273-83), while emphasizing the unity of the parable, speak of the narrated world of Lk. 16.19-23 and the dialogical world of 16.24-31. Since A. Jülicher (*Die Gleichnisreden Jesu* [2 vols.; Tübingen: Mohr (Paul Siebeck), 1910], II, p. 634), commentators typically divide the parable into Lk. 16.19-26 and 16.27-31; see Bultmann, *Synoptic Tradition*, p. 196; Crossan, *In Parables*, pp. 66-67; Evans, *Luke*, pp. 248-49; Fitzmyer, *Luke X-XXIV*, p. 1126; *Horn, Glaube und Handeln*, p. 81; Jeremias, *Parables*, p. 186; Marshall, *Luke*, p. 632; Pilgrim, *Good News to the Poor*, pp. 113-14; Schottroff und Stegemann, *Hoffnung der Armen*, pp. 38-39. Dividing the parable at 16.24 is more in keeping with the formal structure of the parable than is dividing it at 16.27, the latter being based on the interpreter's sense of a thematic change from the theme of reversal to the theme of repentance.

ND: **a**

ND: ¹⁹There once was a *certain* rich man. And he attired himself⁹¹ in purple⁹² and fine linen,⁹³ celebrating sumptuously⁹⁴ daily.

a   b

A *certain poor man* named Lazarus was cast at his door, covered with sores⁹⁵ and longing to be filled by what would fall from the rich man's table. But even dogs, when they would come, licked⁹⁶ his sores.⁹⁷

b   c

It happened that the *poor man died* and was carried by angels to Abraham's
d
bosom.

c

And the rich man *died* and was buried. ²³And in Hades, lifting up his eyes, being

e   **d**

in *torment*, he saw Abraham far off, and Lazarus in his *bosom.*

f

DD: (Rich man) ²⁴And calling out he said, '*Father* Abraham, have mercy on me and send Lazarus to dip the tip of his finger into water and cool my tongue, because I

g

am in agony in these flames'.

(Abraham) ²⁵Abraham said, 'Child, remember that you received your good things during your life, and, correspondingly, Lazarus received bad things. But

g

now, he is consoled here, and you *are in agony*. ²⁶In addition to all this, between us and you a great chasm has been established so that those wishing to cross from here to you would not be able, nor may those wishing to do so pass from there to us.'

91. ἐνεδιδύσκετο: a rare word in the New Testament, occurring in Luke–Acts only here and elsewhere in the New Testament only in Mark 15.17.

92. πορφύραν: a rare word in the New Testament, occurring in Luke–Acts only here and elsewhere in the New Testament only in Mark 15.17, 20 and Rev 18.12. See also, πορφυροῦν in John 19.2, 5; Rev 17.4; 18.16.

93. βύσσον: New Testament *hapax legomenon*; cf. βύσσινος in Rev 18.12, 16; 19.8, 14.

94. λαμπρῷ: New Testament *hapax legomenon*.

95. εἰλκωμένος: New Testament *hapax legomenon*.

96. ἐπέλειχον: New Testament *hapax legomenon*.

97. ἕλκη: a rare word in the New Testament, occurring in Luke–Acts only here and elsewhere in the New Testament only in Rev. 16.2, 11.

f

(Rich man) [27]But he said, 'I entreat you, then, *father*, that you might send him

f

to my *father's* house, [28]for I have five brothers, so that he may warn them, so

e

they might not also come to this place of *torment*'.

h

(Abraham) [29]But Abraham said, 'They have *Moses and the prophets*. Let them heed them.'

f

(Rich man) [30]But he said, 'No, *father* Abraham, rather, they will repent if

i

someone goes to them from *the dead*.'

h

(Abraham) [31]But he said to him, 'If they do not heed *Moses and the prophets*,

i

neither will they be persuaded should someone rise from *the dead*'.

Until Lk. 16.24, the parable is entirely narrated. A close reading reveals the artful manner in which the parallel yet contrasting lives and deaths of 'a certain rich man' and 'a certain poor man' are told. The rich man is introduced first, ἄνθρωπος δέ τις.[98] The paratactic syntax of 16.19 is unassuming, but the unusual vocabulary emphasizes in vividly picturesque eloquence the rich man's opulence. The verbally parallel introduction of the poor man, Lazarus, πτωχὸς δέ τις, encourages Jesus' auditors and Luke's audience to compare the two characters. Likewise, the exceptionally expressive description of Lazarus' circumstances invites comparison with the rich man's circumstances. The deaths of the two are also told in parallel fashion, though in reverse order. The stylized ἐγένετο δὲ with ἀποθανεῖν lengthens the account of Lazarus's death and with ἀπενεχθῆναι creates a sense of one single continuous action encompassing his transport into Abraham's care and protection. Describing Lazarus's death and post-death fate before describing the rich man's strengthens the impact of the abrupt ἀπέθανεν and the especially curt ἐτάφη as reports of the rich man's death and post-death fate.

From 16.24 through 16.31, the parable is entirely in direct discourse except for the parable narrator Jesus' indication of who is

98. On ἄνθρωπος δέ τις as parable introduction, see above the discussion of literary and rhetorical features for Lk. 14.12-24.

speaking. Since narrated discourse creates more narrative distance between the audience and the story and direct discourse diminishes that distance, the audience moves from greater to lesser narrative distance in the second part of the parable.[99] This movement suggests that the emphasis in the parable is to be found in the second part, and pertains to the two speakers: the rich man and Abraham. Yet another dynamic is also at work. The longest uninterrupted portion of the dialogue between Abraham and the rich man is Abraham's opening response (16.25-26), the first half of which is a recapitulation of the circumstances and actions presented in the narrated discourse involving the rich man and poor Lazarus. Since repetition provides emphasis, the reversal of fortunes narrated in the first part of the parable remains significant. Seen as a whole, then, the common element in both literary dynamics is the rich man. Observations about characterization in this parable will confirm that though three characters are present in the parable, the rich man, poor Lazarus, and Abraham, and though other absent characters are mentioned, the five brothers of the rich man, the parable concentrates on the rich man. The rich man's post-death agony is emphasized by the repeated βάσανος (16.23, 28) and ὀδυνάω (16.24, 25).

Characterization. Lazarus has no personality, certainly not piety. In fact, Jesus' terminology in describing the poor man's desire to eat scraps, ἐπιθυμῶν χορτασθῆναι, repeats verbatim Jesus' depiction of the pathetic desire of the lost son (15.16), who had immorally squandered his inheritance. While the description of Lazarus's desire to eat table scraps elicits audience sympathy for Lazarus, it does not imply a psychological or ideological point of view attributable to him. Lazarus is totally passive. He alone of the three featured characters does not speak, and even his earthly action is described as passive: he was cast (ἐβέβλητο) at the rich man's door. The rich man attempts to prompt action by Lazarus, but never addresses Lazarus himself, only Abraham.

---

99. To illustrate relative narrative distances, consider the difference between these two sentences. 'The President proposed that citizens not ask what their country can do for them but rather what they can do for their country.' 'The President said, "Ask not what your country can do for you; ask what you can do for your country".' Aristotle (*Poetics*, 1448a) commented on the distinction between these two manners of discourse. For more on the effects of narrated and direct discourse, see Tolbert, *Perspectives on the Parables*, pp. 75-78.

Interestingly, the phraseology of both Abraham and the rich man connotes closeness,[100] in contrast to the great chasm separating the two. Despite spatial separation, the two display surprisingly consistent points of view: mutual acknowledgment of a familial tie, agreement that the rich man is indeed in agony, and no dispute over the irreversible state of the rich man's situation.[101] They differ, obviously, on the efficacy for the rich man's living brothers of someone rising from the dead.

The rich man's desire that his brothers be prompted to repent (16.30) hints that there was a moral reason for the rich man being consigned to torment, namely, that he is not condemned simply because he is rich, but rather because he did not repent. There is, however, no specific context or action in the parable itself that defines the rich man's sin or justifies the rich man's torment and Lazarus's consolation.[102] The only explicit justification that the parable offers is Abraham's statement of fact that the situations were the reverse in life, that is, the rich man led a sumptuous life and Lazarus suffered a degraded life.

In his narrative, Luke provides a second-degree narrative context for the parable that applies a character trait to the rich man and connects the parable to the action at the second-degree narrative level.[103]

---

100. Abraham and the rich man refer to each other in affectionate familial terms: 'Father Abraham' (Lk. 16.24, 30), 'father' (16.27), and 'child' (16.25).

101. R. Hock ('Lazarus and Micyllus: Greco-Roman Backgrounds to Luke 16:19-31', *JBL* 106 [1987], pp. 447-63 [459]), on the other hand, sees only contrasts when he characterizes the rich man as desperately engaged in bargaining and Abraham as unmoved by the rich man's pleading.

102. So Crossan, *In Parables*, p. 67; Horn, *Glaube und Handeln*, p. 145; Schottroff und Stegemann, *Hoffnung der Armen*, p. 41 (for Lk. 16.19-26). Cf. Hock, 'Lazarus and Micyllus', pp. 453-54, 461.

103. Tolbert (*Perspectives on the Parables*, esp. pp. 48-50, 61) has shown that parable interpretation requires that a context be provided for the parable. Since H. Gressmann (*Vom reichen Mann und armen Lazarus: Eine literargeschichtliche Studie* [Berlin: Königliche Akademie der Wissenschaften, 1918]), an Egyptian folktale about the reversal of fortunes after death for an evil rich man and a virtuous poor man has provided commentators with such a context; see, e.g., Jeremias, *Parables*, p. 183. Bultmann (*Synoptic Tradition*, pp. 196-97) criticizes Gressmann's proposal and cites as background a Jewish legend about a godless woman suffering in hell who sends a message to her living husband to repent. Hock's ('Lazarus and Micyllus') outstanding study of this parable and the history of the parable's interpretation itself further illustrates the need for some extra-parable context out of which to justify the intra-parable condemnation of the rich man. Hock proposes that the con-

This parable is part of Jesus' dialogue with Pharisees, whom Luke, in uniquely direct fashion, has labeled 'lovers of money' (16.14). This labeling prompts the audience to identify the rich man of the parable with the Pharisees of the narrative, and therefore as a lover of money. In the broader context including 16.13, being a lover of money is characterized as having made a choice of money over God, for a person cannot be loyal to both. While the parable text and immediate context do not permit us to conclude with certainty that the rich man's failing is having neglected or mistreated the poor,[104] the context does justify saying at least that the rich man's failing is having chosen money over God.

Part of the issue with the Pharisees is the continuing validity of 'the law and the prophets' (16.16), which echoes in Abraham's references to 'Moses and the prophets' (16.29, 31). The parable insists, in line with 16.17, that not only do the law and the prophets continue to be relevant,[105] but heeding them avoids eschatological judgment, for it means choosing God over money. In its second-degree narrative context, then, the parable underscores the incompatibility of loving money and being faithful to the law and the prophets. Thus when measured against their own standard, namely, fidelity to the law and the prophets, the monetary-minded Pharisees fail.[106]

Function of the Character Types. Lazarus's presence in the parable balances the eschatological scales and heightens the pathos of the scene

text be Cynic views on wealth and poverty, particularly two writings of Lucian of Samosata, Gallus and Cataplus. Hock does not discuss the Lukan context of the parable.

104. Neglect or mistreatment of Lazarus by the rich man is widely appealed to. See, e.g., Crossan, *In Parables*, p. 66; Dupont, *Les Béatitudes* (3 vols.; Paris: Gabalda, 1973), III, pp. 181-82; Evans, *Luke*, p. 248; Fitzmyer, *Luke X-XXIV*, p. 1128; Hock, 'Lazarus and Micyllus', p. 462; Horn, *Glaube und Handeln*, p. 188; R.J. Karris, 'Poor and Rich: The Lukan *Sitz im Leben*', in C.H. Talbert (ed.), *Perspectives on Luke–Acts* (Danville, VA: Association of Baptist Professors of Religion, 1978), p. 122; Marshall, *Luke*, p. 635; Schneider und Stenger, 'Die offene Tür', p. 281; Schweizer, *Good News According to Luke*, p. 262; Seccombe, *Possessions*, pp. 177-81, 185; Tannehill, *Narrative Unity*, I, pp. 131-32.

105. See Tiede, *Luke*, p. 291.

106. Previous interpreters have also related this parable to Jesus' indictment of the Pharisees. See Danker, *Jesus and the New Age*, p. 283; Pilgrim, *Good News to the Poor*, p. 116; Seccombe, *Possessions*, p. 179; Tannehill, *Narrative Unity*, I, pp. 185-86.

by providing contrasting imagery.[107] This poor person's good fortune after death gives the authorial audience a sense of continuity with the rest of the narrative because the audience recalls Jesus' words about eschatological consolation for the poor and woe to the rich (Lk. 6.20, 24). 'The dead' is an impersonal designation for those who have died and simply underscores the eschatological character of the parable.

This parable in its context illustrates this study's contention that 'the poor' and 'the rich' do not function as contrasting ethical designations in Luke's Gospel. While it is appropriate to interpret this parable as a warning not to be like the rich man, it is inconceivable to interpret the parable as exhortation to be like the poor Lazarus. Lazarus has the sympathy of Luke's audience, but he is not its model for lifestyle or behavior.[108]

Luke 17.11-19: The Healing of the Lepers

> And it happened while he was going to Jerusalem that he went through Samaria and Galilee. And as he came to a certain village, ten leprous men met him. They stood at a distance and raised their voices saying, 'Jesus, master, have mercy on us'. When he saw them, he said to them, 'Go, show yourselves to the priests'. And as they were underway, it happened that they were cleansed. Then one of them, when he saw that he was healed, returned, glorifying God with a loud voice. And he fell on his face at his feet, thanking him. And he was a Samaritan. Jesus said in response, 'Ten were cleansed, were they not? Where are the nine? Were none found returning to give glory to God except this foreigner?' And he said to him, 'Get up and go. Your faith has saved you.'

Literary and Rhetorical Features and Characterization. While Lk. 17.11 signals a change in setting from Jesus' dialogues with the Pharisees and with his disciples (15.1-17.10), the break between the healing of the ten lepers and what has preceded it is not great. Jesus' final words to the healed Samaritan leper, 'Your faith has saved you' (17.19), recall the apostles' request that Jesus increase their faith (17.5). In the narrative, Jesus' encounter with the ten lepers is followed by a question from the Pharisees about the kingdom of God (17.20-21) and Jesus' eschatological sayings to his disciples (17.22-37).

---

107. Jeremias, *Parables*, p. 186.

108. This point should be considered before accepting Hock's ('Lazarus and Micyllus', p. 461) proposal that the parable 'as a rhetorical *sygkrisis*. . . praises the poor in the extreme figure of Lazarus'.

Obedience by the lepers to Jesus' command given at a distance recalls leprous Naaman's obedience to Elisha's command through a messenger[109] (4 Kgdms 5.9-14). But there is a still stronger resemblance between Naaman's return (ἐπέστρεψεν, 4 Kgdms 5.15) to Elisha and the Samaritan leper's return (ὑπέστρεψεν, Lk. 17.15) to Jesus after their respective cleansings.

Like a parable,[110] this episode contains elements that give it a fictive air: for example, Jesus repeats in direct discourse (17.18) the report in narrated discourse (17.15) of the healed leper's return;[111] Jesus is journeying, but he seemingly waits for the healed leper's return; the implied criticism of the nine healed lepers who do not return is hardly justifiable if the episode is taken at face value.[112]

The Samaritan would not have to return to Jesus to glorify God,[113] which is what Jesus commends him for. From a strictly narrative perspective, however, face-to-face thanks to Jesus provides suitable grounds for the Samaritan's return to Jesus. Nevertheless, though thanking Jesus is the reason for the Samaritan's return, Luke uses repetition as a literary device to give precedence to the fact that the returning Samaritan glorified God. The narrator reports in 17.15 that the one healed leper returned (ὑπέστρεψεν) glorifying God (δοξάζων τὸν θεόν); Jesus comments in a rhetorical question that only one leper has returned (ὑποστρέψαντες) to give glory to God (δοῦναι δόξαν τῷ θεῷ). By repeating the narrator's report as he does, Jesus confirms that what this Samaritan leper did was appropriate. Moreover, this repetition has the effect of highlighting the actions of returning and glorifying God over against other actions in the episode, such as going to the priests, as all the lepers initially set out to do, or falling at Jesus'

109. Tiede, *Luke*, p. 297.

110. E.E. Ellis (*The Gospel of Luke* [NCB; Grand Rapids: Eerdmans, rev. edn, 1981], p. 208) calls this episode a 'real-life parable'.

111. This technique of repeating in direct discourse something presented in narrated discourse appears in the parable of the rich man and Lazarus (Lk. 16.19-25) and the parable of the widow and the judge (18.2,4).

112. There are three especially puzzling aspects to this episode. First, why does Jesus criticize the nine other healed lepers for not returning? By continuing their trip to the priests, they are doing precisely what Jesus directed them to do. Secondly, what is the nature of the healed Samaritan's faith? Thirdly, what does it mean that the healed Samaritan is 'saved'? A full discussion of these issues would take us beyond the scope of this study, but their presence underscores how 'parable-like' this episode is.

113. Tannehill, *Narrative Unity*, I, p. 119.

feet and thanking Jesus, as the Samaritan leper does. One result is that even though the Samaritan thanks Jesus, an atypical action in Luke's Gospel, God remains the focus of praise expressed by the one healed, a characteristic of Lukan healing episodes.

This is the third episode in Luke's Gospel involving a Samaritan or Samaritans. In 9.52-55, Jesus intends to journey to a Samaritan village, but changes his plans when the village refuses to receive him. In the parable of the Good Samaritan (10.30-35), the Samaritan traveler is the one, in contrast to the priest and Levite, who shows mercy to the man robbed and beaten.

Samaritans are outsiders. This perspective is reflected in Luke's narrative, in that the forceful impact of the parable of the Good Samaritan and of the account of the healing of the lepers derives from the Samaritan's status as a religious and social outsider.[114] Still, in the narrative world of Luke's Gospel, there is no expressed or implied condemnation of contact between Jews and Samaritans. Jesus' intention to go to a Samaritan village appears to be routine, and there is no controversy attached to it per se. Moreover, Jesus' Jewish messengers go without objection to the village. Indeed, James and John seek retribution because the inhospitality of the Samaritan village, that is, for their rebuff of cordial contact. Likewise, contact between the Samaritan and the (Jewish?) victim and contact between the Samaritan and the (Jewish?) innkeeper receive no comment in the parable. The parable does, however, sharply contrast the Samaritan, who would not be expected to respond correctly to the situation, and the priest and Levite, who would be expected to respond correctly to the situation. No issue is made in 17.11-19 of the fact that Jewish and Samaritan lepers congregated together, assuming that the other lepers were Jewish, or of the fact that Jesus interacts with the healed Samaritan, even though Jesus' Pharisaic opponents are directly at hand (17.20-21).

Earlier references to lepers as stated recipients of Jesus' healing power incline the audience's sympathy toward suffering lepers in general. Yet the audience's sympathy for the returning healed leper is not left to inference. It is secured by Jesus' commendation of him. Subsequently, another aspect of the rhetoric of this episode appears.

114. Commentators universally point to the heightened effect that Lukan texts involving Samaritans have because of the Samaritans' status as outsiders. See, e.g., Danker, *Jesus and the New Age*, p. 222; Johnson, *Luke*, pp. 175, 260; Talbert, *Reading Luke*, p. 121; Tannehill, *Narrative Unity*, I, p. 119; Tiede, *Luke*, p. 297.

As Tannehill points out, the audience is 'told that he is a Samaritan only after they have received a positive impression of the leper through a strong depiction of his gratitude'.[115]

In a rhetorical grand stroke, this episode combines in one character a character type the authorial audience would recognize as a standard beneficiary of Jesus' beneficence, namely, the leper, and a character category that is synonymous with outsider, namely, the Samaritan.[116] This combination elicits contrasting emotions from Luke's audience: sympathy and apprehension.[117]

Three expressions repeat earlier expressions in the Gospel. The cry of the lepers, ἐλέησον ἡμᾶς (17.13), echoes the cry of the rich man agonizing in Hades to Abraham in the parable of the rich man and Lazarus (16.24) and pleas of psalmists.[118] In Lk. 5.12, a leprous man fell on his face (πεσὼν ἐπὶ πρόσωπον) before Jesus, asking him for healing. Here (17.16), the healed leper falls on his face before Jesus, thanking him for healing. Jesus' parting words to the Samaritan former leper, ἡ πίστις σου σέσωκέν (17.19), are identical to Jesus' parting words to the forgiven woman in the Pharisee's house (7.50) and the healed woman with the twelve-year flow of blood (8.48).[119] Of these three, the third is the most striking.

Word-for-word repetitions serve 'in larger narrative units, to sustain a thematic development and to establish instructive connections between seemingly disparate episodes'.[120] Clearly, there is a common thread signaled by Jesus' words, 'your faith has saved you', running through the episodes of the forgiven woman (7.36-50), the healed woman (8.43-48), and the healed Samaritan leper (17.11-19), connecting these characters. But the thread is not an abstract theme such as 'faith', nor is it a narrowly defined, technical concept of 'salvation'.

115. Tannehill, *Narrative Unity*, I, p. 119. See also Tannehill, *Narrative Unity*, I, p. 93.

116. With a similar insight, Tannehill (*Narrative Unity*, 1 p. 119) speaks of this episode attacking the stereotype of the Samaritan by combining a positive characteristic, gratitude, with the negative stereotype.

117. Analogous emotions might be evoked in an American audience of the 1990s by the expression 'illegal alien infant'.

118. Pss. 6.3; 9.14; 24.16; 25.11; 26.7; 29.11; 30.10; 40.5, 11; 50.3; 55.2; 56.2; 85.3, 16; 118.58, 132; 122.3.

119. Jesus repeats this pronouncement again in 18.42 to the man healed of blindness.

120. Alter, *The Art of Biblical Narrative*, p. 94.

Rather, it is found in a consistent characteristic of these unnamed individuals: their desire for contact with Jesus. In each particular circumstance, the character's actions demonstrate that being in Jesus' presence is more valuable than being in compliance with social or religious norms. To the Samaritan leper, returning to Jesus is more pressing than fulfilling the implied directive of Lev. 13.49.[121]

Healing occurs within the sphere of salvation, and Jesus is the locus of salvation. That this basic message is the force of Lk. 17.11-19 is confirmed by the episode's placement immediately before a question from Pharisees to Jesus, the subject matter of which is the presence of the kingdom of God. The juxtaposition of these two episodes highlights the central failure of the Pharisees to recognize that salvation, that is, the kingdom of God, is present in Jesus.

Function of the Character Type. The typal nature of lepers as standard recipients of Jesus' beneficence serves to make the beginning of the encounter predictable in a manner satisfying to the audience. Specifically, the audience anticipates that the exchange will result in healings, as it does. This typal quality fades into the background as the plot shifts to the contrast between the one returning leper and the other nine. As the lone returning leper takes on character traits and definition—namely gratefulness, piety, and identification as a Samaritan—these take precedence over the initial typal image and govern the effect of the episode.

Luke 18.22: Instructions to the Rich Ruler

> Jesus listened and said to him, 'You lack yet one thing. Sell everything, whatever you have, and distribute to the poor, and you will have a treasure in heaven. And come, follow me.'

The characters in this episode (Lk. 18.18-30) are Jesus, the rich ruler, and those who overhear the conversation between Jesus and the ruler, including Peter and other disciples. This passage exposes the difficulty an interpreter would have sustaining throughout Luke's Gospel the image of 'the poor' as a metaphor for a religious ideal. If 'the poor' is a consistent reference to Jesus' ideal disciples, for example, then in effect Jesus commands the ruler to turn his assets over to the disciples and then become a disciple himself, thus sharing according to need in

121. Similarly, Danker, *Jesus and the New Age*, p. 290.

the newly-distributed resources. Clearly, such a reading is forced, even if intriguing in light of the sharing of possessions in Acts, and it domesticates Jesus' uncompromising demand to the ruler. The narrative emphasizes abandonment of possessions now to follow Jesus, compared with eschatological abundance.[122] To domesticate Jesus' command to the ruler would be to mute the shock expressed by those who overheard: 'Who, then, can be saved?' (18.26).

'The poor' as a typical term serves to give Jesus' command a certain moral legitimacy. Making the poor the potential beneficiaries of the ruler's assets at least eliminates controversy over where the assets would go.[123] The authorial audience knows of God's desire for beneficence toward the poor. The poor, then, would be judged by Luke's audience to be scripturally appropriate recipients.

Luke 18.35-43: Jesus Heals a Blind Man

> And it happened while he was approaching Jericho that a certain blind man was sitting by the road begging. When he heard the crowd passing by he asked what was happening. They reported to him that Jesus of Nazareth was coming by. And he shouted saying, 'Jesus, Son of David, have mercy on me.' And those going by in front rebuked him, to silence him. But he cried out more loudly, 'Son of David, have mercy on me.' Jesus stopped and ordered that he be brought to him. When he approached, he asked him, 'What do you want me to do for you?' He said, 'Lord, [do something] so that I will see.' And Jesus said to him, 'See again. Your faith has saved you.' And immediately he saw, and he followed him, glorifying God. And all the people, when they saw this, gave praise to God.

Literary and Rhetorical Features and Characterization. This episode is bordered by shifts in the narrative setting signaled in Lk. 18.35 and 19.1. Yet repetitions and allusions harken back to earlier points in the narrative.

The blind man's persistent entreaty matches that of the widow in Jesus' parable of the widow and the judge (18.2-5). When healed, the blind man follows (ἠκολούθει, 18.43) Jesus. This term recalls Jesus' invitation to the rich man to follow (ἀκολούθει, 18.22) him.

The healing of the blind man exhibits several formal parallels to the

---

122. Reference to abundance in this present age as well as in the age to come does not come until Lk. 18.30.

123. See the discussion below of the poor widow's temple offering in Lk. 21.1-4.

parable-like healing of the ten lepers (17.11-19): (1) the episodes take place as Jesus is approaching a village (17.12) or city (18.35); (2) the lepers' cry, 'Jesus, master' (17.13), corresponds to the blind man's cry, 'Jesus, son of David' (18.38); (3) the substance of requests is 'Have mercy on us/me' (17.13; 18.38, 39); (4) a healed one glorifies God (17.15; 18.43); (5) Jesus says, 'Your faith has saved you' (17.19; 18.42).

The prominent rhetorical features of this passage are first, verbal repetition and secondly, emphasis through direct discourse. Both can be easily observed when the verses are arranged according to direct and narrated discourse.

ND: [35]And it happened while he was approaching Jericho that a certain blind man was sitting by the road begging. [36]When he heard the crowd passing by he asked what was happening. [37]They reported to him that Jesus of Nazareth was coming by.

DD: [38]And he shouted saying, 'Jesus, *Son of David, have mercy on me*'.

ND: [39]And those going by in front rebuked him, to silence him.

DD: But he cried out more loudly, '*Son of David, have mercy on me*'.

ND: [40]Jesus stopped and ordered that he be brought to him.

DD: When he approached, he asked him, [41]'What do you want me to do for you?'

DD: He said, 'Lord, [do something] so that I *will see again*'.

DD: [42]And Jesus said to him, '*See again*. Your faith has saved you.'

ND: [43]And immediately he *saw again*, and he followed him, glorifying God. And all the people, when they saw this, gave praise to God.

The opening narration sets the stage for the entire episode and introduces the characters who will be involved: Jesus, the blind man, and the crowd. The first half of the episode consists of opening narration, the blind man's plea for mercy, narration of the crowd's rebuke, and the blind man's repeated plea.

Jesus' numerous previous healings lead Luke's audience to expect another healing here. But the blind man's rhetoric signals that there is more being communicated here than simply another healing. The blind man's plea is forceful and direct: 'Jesus, Son of David, have mercy on me'. It is highly evocative in content as well as in style. 'Son of David' recalls not only the prediction of the angel to Mary: 'The Lord God will give him the throne of his father David' (Lk. 1.32), but also the LXX hope for an ideal king, a royal messiah. 'Have mercy on me' echoes the plea of the lepers (Lk. 17.13) and, like that prior plea, evokes an image of cries of psalmists. There is no reason for the

The Blind, the Lame, and the Poor

rebuke of the blind man by those going by.[124] In the narrative, though, the rebuke serves as the occasion for the blind man's persistence and as the opportunity for repetition of the messianic acclamation of Jesus. The blind man's persistence is not an end in itself in the narrative, though Jesus has recently encouraged his disciples to pray persistently (18.1). Rather, the word-for-word repetition of 'Son of David, have mercy on me' underscores the importance of what the blind man persistently asserts. The episode is not just about the blind man's faith. It is also about who Jesus is. The blind man pleads to Jesus for deliverance from his affliction in a manner carefully crafted to imitate the psalmists' pleas to God for deliverance from affliction and to cast Jesus—Son of David—as the scripturally appropriate object of his plea.

The second half of the episode is Jesus' conversation with the blind man, framed by two pieces of narration. The outstanding feature in the second half is the repeated ἀναβλέπω. The blind man asks that he *see again* (Lk. 18.41); Jesus gives the command, '*See again*' (18.42); and the narrator reports that immediately the blind man could *see again* (18.43). This almost monotonous repetition of the term ἀναβλέπω ensures that the audience will recall 4.18 and 7.22 and recognize this episode as further fulfillment of Jesus' messianic calling.

Function of the Character Type. The typal image of the blind leads the audience to anticipate a healing when he is introduced. This expectation is fulfilled, but, as in the case of the story of the ten lepers, Luke adds a new twist to a predictable event. The blind man takes initiative, or seems to.

That this blind man steps out of the conventional role of actee, though in keeping with conventional passivity he is brought by others to Jesus, suggests that the world does not operate in traditional ways in the presence of Jesus. The blind man's persistence is exemplary, but not purely so. The scene makes a christological point that is sharpened by the atypical action of the blind man.

Later in the narrative, the disciples shout acclamations of Jesus' messianic kingship (19.38). When Pharisees object to Jesus, requesting that he rebuke (ἐπιτίμησον) his disciples, Jesus replies that if his dis-

---

124. The suggestion (Evans, *Luke*, p. 278) that the blind man's outburst would have struck those accompanying Jesus as impertinent or dangerous lacks support from the text. There is similarly no reason for the disciples' rebuke of those bringing infants to Jesus (Lk. 18.15).

ciples were silent the stones would cry out (κράξουσιν, 19.39-40), the point being that Jesus' kingship cannot but find expression. The healing of the blind man in Luke 18 anticipates this point. Immediately prior to the episode of the blind man healed, the audience observes Jesus' third passion prediction and is told that the disciples understand nothing of this (18.31-34). But if the disciples do not yet understand, even the blind cry out (ἔκραζεν), despite being rebuked (ἐπετίμων) to be silent (18.39).

'Blind' does not equal 'pious'. Likewise, 'seeing' does not equal coming to faith, for the blind man has confidence in Jesus before Jesus restores his sight.[125] Rather, the man's blindness makes his faith more remarkable and intensifies the contrast between him and the rich ruler (18.18-25). From a rhetorical standpoint, it is captivating to read the paradox of a blind man with insight.

Luke 19.8: Zacchaeus's Response to Jesus' Visit

> But Zacchaeus stood up and said to the Lord, 'Behold, half of my belongings, Lord, I will give to the poor. And if I have cheated anyone, I will pay them back fourfold.'

The poor function in Lk. 19.8 as they have functioned in 18.22. In short, the poor are impersonal, non-controversial objects of generosity. The authorial audience would not question the godliness of Zacchaeus's promise. Indeed, promising lavish generosity to the poor would gain for Zacchaeus the authorial audience's approval.[126]

Luke 20.34-38: Jesus' Response to the Sadducees' Question About Marriage in the Coming Age

> And Jesus said to them, 'The sons of this age marry and are given in marriage. But those deemed worthy to attain to that [coming] age and to

125. Cf. D. Hamm's ('Sight to the Blind', pp. 457-77) attempt to push 'seeing' terminology into symbolism for a deeper vision of who Jesus is. Hamm's discussion of the Jericho beggar ('Sight to the Blind', pp. 462-63) does not prove his case because the blind man identifies Jesus as 'Son of David' before he 'sees' and before 'seeing' terminology is introduced into the story.

126. R.C. Tannehill ('The Story of Zacchaeus as Rhetoric: Luke 19.1-10', *Semeia* 64 [1993], pp. 201-11 [203]) rightly points out that the allotting of one half of his goods to the poor does not imply a limit to Zacchaeus's giving up of his wealth. The context may well imply that the other half is what is needed for Zacchaeus to make fourfold restitution to those he has cheated.

the resurrection of the dead there neither marry nor are given in marriage.
For they cannot still die, for they are like angels and are sons of God,
being sons of the resurrection. That the dead are raised, even Moses
revealed in the account of the bush, inasmuch as he speaks of the Lord as
"the God of Abraham and the God of Isaac and the God of Jacob". God is
not the God of the dead, but of the living, for all live to God.'

Literary and Rhetorical Features. These are the last references in
Luke's Gospel to the dead before Jesus' death. With the sole exception
of the aphoristic 'let the dead bury their own dead' (Lk. 9.60), every
reference to the dead has something to do with rising from the dead
or coming to life again. The dead young man sits up (7.15). Raising
the dead is listed as a mark of the messianic 'Coming One' (7.22).
Herod wonders if John is raised from the dead (9.7). The lost son was
dead, but is alive again (15.24, 32). The rich man wants Lazarus to
rise from the dead (16.30, 31). Here in Luke 20 as well, the dead are
discussed in light of resurrection.

The narrative context consists of swelling opposition to Jesus (19.47;
20.19, 20) as he teaches in the temple (19.47; 20.1). The chief priests,
scribes, elders, and their agents (20.1, 20) have examined Jesus for the
purpose of trapping him. Now the Sadducees take their turn at Jesus
(20.27-33).

Characterization and Function of the Character Type. Ostensibly, the
Sadducees' question about whose wife the seven-times married woman
would be in the resurrection assumes resurrection. The audience knows
that the question is contrived, however, because the narrator describes
the Sadducees as 'those who say there is no resurrection' (20.27). The
second part of Jesus' response (20.37-38), confronts the Sadducees'
point of view directly.

The Sadducees and Jesus are a conflict looking for a place to happen.
'The dead' provide that place. Or more precisely stated, 'the dead'
serve as the vehicle for a narrative expression of conflict between
Jesus and the Sadducees.

Luke 21.1-4: The Poor Widow

Looking up, he saw those who were putting their offerings into the collection box. They were wealthy. Then he saw a certain needy widow put two
small coins there. And he said, 'Truly I say to you, this poor widow put

in more than all the others. For all the others put in offerings out of what they had left over, but she, out of her inadequate means, put in all the assets she had.'

Literary and Rhetorical Features. This episode is set within a long day for Jesus in the Temple. The day begins in Lk. 20.1, 'One day, as he was teaching the people in the Temple. . . ' and ends with the conclusion of Jesus' apocalyptic discourse in 21.36. This day is set within a larger section of the Gospel (19.45-20.38) that features the Temple. The section begins with Jesus entering the Temple and driving out the merchants there (19.45-46). The summary statement of Lk. 21.37-38 echoes 19.47-48 in sketching Jesus' Temple routine such that ἦν διδάσκων τὸ καθ᾽ ἡμέραν ἐν τῷ ἱερῷ (19.47) and ἦν δὲ τὰς ἡμέρας ἐν τῷ ἱερῷ διδάσκων (21.37) form a roughly chiastic *inclusio*, rounding off the section. This highly charged religious setting adds a level of complexity to the unfolding story. How Luke's audience feels about the Temple affects its evaluation of words and actions in the narrative.

In Luke's Gospel, the Temple initially is the sacred space of the righteous and devout persons Zechariah (1.5-9), Simeon (2.25), and Anna (2.36-37). Mary and Joseph practice their piety in the Temple (2.22-38). God is worshiped in the Temple. The boy Jesus speaks of it as his 'Father's house' (2.49). After the devil's temptation on the parapet of the Temple (4.9), however, no mention is made of the Temple until Jesus tells the parable of the Pharisee and the tax collector (18.9-14). In this parable, the Temple, by association with the Pharisee, begins to be associated with phony religiosity, for humble piety is expressed by the tax collector 'standing far off' (18.13). In 19.46, the audience learns that the Temple has become a 'den of robbers'. Even though Jesus teaches in the Temple daily when he reaches Jerusalem (19.47), the Temple is the locus of corrupt religious leaders and contention between them and Jesus (19.47; 20.1, 19, 20, 27).[127] In sum, the portrait of the Temple painted for the audience before Luke 21 is neither wholly positive nor wholly negative, but ambivalent.

Jesus' observations about those putting offerings into the Temple collection box, including the poor widow, follow harsh words from Jesus about scribes, who 'devour widows' houses' (20.47), and pre-

---

127. Though in Acts Jesus' followers frequent the Temple for prayer, the Temple is still a site of contention. See Acts 3.1–4.4; 5.12-18, 25-26; 21.27-30.

cede Jesus' ominous words predicting the destruction of the Temple adorned with precious stones and votive offerings (21.5-6). Thus these verses, 21.1-4, hook neatly into Jesus' prior teaching through the word 'widow(s)' and into his subsequent teaching by reference to the Temple.[128]

Characterization. Standard interpretation of this episode views the widow's action as exemplary and Jesus' words as commending her.[129] A close reading of the text, however, reveals that Jesus speaks no words of praise for the poor widow or her action.

A.G. Wright takes the absence of praise of the widow's action as an opening for understanding Jesus' comments about her gift as a lament, rather than as praise.[130] Jesus condemned the scribes for devouring

128. The connection between Lk. 21.1-4 and 21.5-6 is not one of precise verbal repetition. But Luke's authorial audience would have had little trouble associating the collection box (21.1) with the Temple (21.5) and the offerings (21.1, 2) with the ornateness of the Temple (21.5). See 2 Esd. 22.44; 23.4-7; 2 Macc. 3.4-6; 5.17-21.

129. Comments vary somewhat, but focus on the contrast between the poor widow and the wealthy givers in terms of the attitude of the giver, the relative value of the gift compared to the giver's resources, or both. G.B. Caird (*The Gospel of Saint Luke* [The Pelican New Testament Commentaries; Harmondsworth: Penguin Books, 1963], p. 227) contrasts the 'self-forgetful' widow with the 'self-important' scribes. Danker (*Jesus and the New Age*, p. 327-28) speaks of the widow's 'true devotion' in contrast to 'ostentatious religion', 'genuine beneficence' in contrast to 'niggardliness', 'faith that transcends material security', and total commitment to God. Ellis (*Luke*, p. 238) refers to the widow as 'truly pious' and locates the teaching of the passage in moral and eschatological judgment upon hypocritical piety in contrast to the moral and eschatological value of true piety. C.A. Evans (*Luke*, p. 306) says that the widow's gift is superior because it entailed 'significant personal hardship'. According to C.F. Evans (*Saint Luke*, p. 728), the story teaches that the rich cannot really give at all, 'but only the poor can give, since their giving involves the expenditure of themselves'. Marshall (*Luke*, p. 750) says that 'the lesson [is] that what matters is not the amount that one gives but the amount that one keeps for oneself', so that by giving all she possessed the widow 'expressed her faith in God to provide for her needs'. Schweizer (*Good News According to Luke*, p. 309) simply concludes that 'much or little does not matter, only whether the gift comes from abundance or poverty'. Seccombe (*Possessions*, p. 185 n. 230) says the woman is 'highly praised' for her tiny contribution because it 'represents a real and total engagement with God'.

130. A.G. Wright, 'The Widow's Mites: Praise or Lament? A Matter of Context', *CBQ* 44 (1982), pp. 256-65. Wright treats both the Markan and Lukan contexts of this episode. Much of his treatment of Mark has to do with connecting the pericope of the widow's mites (Mark 12.41-44) with the *corban* pericope (7.10-13). The

the houses of widows (20.47), that is, for stripping widows of their livelihood. Now the poor widow gives up her livelihood. Says Wright, 'Her religious thinking has accomplished the very thing that the scribes were accused of doing'.[131] For Wright, this means that the poor widow has been caught up in a value system propagated by the religious leaders that motivates her to self-destructive action. Moreover, since the destruction of the Temple is coming, 'the final irony of it all' is that her gift is also a waste.[132]

Wright does not comment on whether the contrasting gifts of the wealthy givers are correspondingly praiseworthy. In fact, the point of comparison between the two classes of givers drops out of Wright's analysis. D. Tiede's nuanced interpretation balances both this point of comparison and Wright's compelling challenge to traditional interpretation. The widow's giving is superior to that of the wealthy; indeed, she 'may be virtuous'.[133] Her sacrifice is superior to their shallow generosity, but the injustice of the whole system prevents this from being an example story. According to Tiede, 'Jesus may ask his disciples to abandon their wealth to serve God rather than mammon (see 16.1-31), but he does not endorse any religious value system which supports wealthy institutions or clergy at the expense of poor widows'.[134]

Function of the Character Type. The audience's sympathy for the poor widow adds pathos to the narrative critique of the wealthy religious leaders. The narrative presents her as a foil to the shallow and devious scribes, but not as a paradigm for discipleship, for her virtue is tragic. Here—in the only instance in Luke's Gospel in which a character labeled 'poor' acts—her action paradoxically underscores how vulnerable and dominated by outside forces the poor one is.

---

absence of the *corban* pericope in Luke's Gospel does not, in Wright's thinking, make the point there less valid. Wright's proposal is adopted by Fitzmyer (*Luke X-XXIV*, p. 1321), cautiously raised as a possibility by C.A. Evans (*Luke*, p. 306-307), and adapted by Tiede (*Luke*, pp. 354-55). See also Danker's (*Jesus and the New Age*, p. 328) caution against exploiting this passage for stewardship purposes, noting that Jesus does not praise the widow's actions.

131. Wright, 'The Widow's Mites', p. 262.
132. Wright, 'The Widow's Mites', p. 263.
133. Tiede, *Luke*, p. 354.
134. Tiede, *Luke*, p. 355.

Luke 24.5: The Question From the Men in the Tomb

> While they [the women] were terrified and bowed their faces to the
> ground, they [the two men] said to them, 'Why do you seek the living one
> among the dead?'

And Luke 24.46: Jesus' Exegesis

> And he said to them, 'Thus it is written that the Messiah would suffer and
> rise from the dead on the third day.'

The term 'the dead' has the same function in each of these last two
references to the dead in Luke's Gospel. The location of the scene in
Lk. 24.5, in a tomb, suggests that 'among the dead' means 'among
corpses'. Beyond the intense aura of dead bodies the setting provides,
'the dead' as a typical term carries no notions of personality or point
of view. It is a morally neutral reference to an impersonal type.

The question from the men in the tomb (24.5) is purely rhetorical.
As the men in the tomb go on to say to the women, Jesus is not one of
the dead. The one who raised others (7.22) has been raised (24.6).

Luke 24.46 is part of Jesus' post-resurrection instruction to 'the
eleven and those with them' (Lk. 24.33) in Jerusalem. While the
unspecified Jerusalem setting here lacks the intense aura the tomb
provided in 24.5, 'the dead' is again an impersonal designation of the
general type. It describes what Jesus was, but is no longer.

Chapter 7

ACTS AND THE CAPTIVE, THE SHATTERED, THE BLIND,
THE DEAF MUTE, THE LAME, LEPERS, THE MAIMED,
THE DEAD, AND THE POOR

Of the nine terms investigated in the Gospel of Luke, six do not
appear at all in the Acts of the Apostles: αἰχμάλωτος, θραύειν,
κωφός, λεπρός, ἀνάπηρος, and πτωχός. Of the remaining three, only
νεκρός occurs with any frequency, and it is mentioned quite often:
seventeen times.[1] Χωλός and τυφλός appear only three times and
once, respectively.[2]

The opening two chapters of Acts illustrate how literary patterning
may be employed as a rhetorical device to fashion the authorial audience's expectations regarding future events in the narrative. These
chapters in Acts, especially ch. 2, also point to the dominant function
of 'the dead' in Acts. As C.H. Talbert[3] and R.C. Tannehill[4] have noted,
in Tannehill's words, 'both the mission of Jesus and the mission of the
apostles begin with prayer and the coming of the Spirit, followed by
an inaugural speech that relates the coming of the Spirit to the new
mission through a Scripture quotation'.[5] Moreover, as Tannehill says,
'the importance of the quotation from Isaiah in Lk. 4.18-19 suggests
that we should look closely at the quotation from Joel in Acts 2.17-21

1.   Acts 3.15; 4.2, 10; 5.10; 10.41, 42; 13.30, 34; 17.3, 31, 32; 20.9; 23.6;
24.21; 26.8, 23; 28.6.
2.   Χωλός: Acts 3.2; 8.7; 14.8. Τυφλός: Acts 13.11.
3.   Talbert, *Literary Patterns*, pp. 15-19.
4.   Tannehill, *Narrative Unity*, II, p. 29.
5.   Tannehill, *Narrative Unity*, II, p. 50. The parallels Tannehill points to are not
perfect parallels. For example, in the case of Jesus the coming of the Spirit and the
inaugural speech with the scriptural quotation are separated by the temptation of Jesus
in the wilderness. Nevertheless, the pattern is evident enough to raise the question of
what effect its recurrence in Acts would have had on the authorial audience of Luke–
Acts.

to see whether it has similar importance'.[6] Tannehill concludes that
the quotation does have similar importance: 'The Joel quotation, like
the Isaiah quotation in Lk. 4.18-19, provides important clues to the purpose that gives events in the story their meaning, thereby providing a
guide to understanding the narrative'.[7] For our purposes, it is sufficient to point out the value the Joel quotation in Acts has for Luke's
characterization of the apostles in Acts. Already in the opening chapters
of the Gospel, Luke's audience developed the habit of dissolving the
hermeneutical distance between the scriptural quote and the narrative
situation. Thus, the authorial audience would apply the quote from
Joel in Acts directly to the second-degree narrative situation, as they
applied the quote from Isaiah in the Gospel directly to the situation in
the Nazareth synagogue. Luke's audience would interpret the Joel
quotation in part as a statement of the future ministry of the eleven.
What will that ministry be? In short, the apostles will prophesy (Acts
2.17-18), summoning their hearers to acknowledge Jesus as the risen
Lord and Christ, for 'whoever calls upon the name of the Lord shall
be saved' (2.21). It will be argued in succeeding paragraphs that the
dominant function of references in Acts to the dead corresponds to
characterization of the apostles as prophets who declare Jesus' resurrection from the dead.

Almost half of the occurrences of νεκρός (eight of seventeen) are
in passages that say that Jesus was raised from 'the dead': Peter declares
that God raised Jesus from the dead in Acts 3.15, 4.10, and 10.40-41;
Paul testifies that God raised Jesus from the dead (13.30; 34; 17.31)
and that Jesus rose from the dead (17.3; 26.23). Peter and Paul pro-
fess that Jesus was raised as the Scriptures, specifically Moses and the
prophets (Acts 26.22-23), foretold would be the destiny of the messiah.
These references echo in form and in function the words of the post-
resurrection Jesus (Lk. 24.26-27, 44-46) and the announcement by the
two men in the tomb (Lk. 24.5-7). Thus, these references in Acts to
the dead continue and expand two thematic threads that rose to prominence in the Gospel after Jesus' resurrection:[8] first, God raised Jesus

---

6.   Tannehill, *Narrative Unity*, II, p. 29.
7.   Tannehill, *Narrative Unity*, II, p. 32.
8.   C.F.D. Moule commented almost thirty years ago on features of Lukan discourse that point to Jesus' resurrection as the pivotal moment in the narrative.
Speaking of when and by whom Jesus is referred to as ὁ κύριος, Moule stated
('Christology of Acts', pp. 160-61): 'It is not always stated that until the resurrection

from the dead; and secondly, Jesus' destiny fulfills Scripture.

Another six of the seventeen occurrences of νεκρός in Acts are in passages that refer to the general resurrection of the dead.[9] These references in Acts to the dead approximate Jesus' usage of the term in his comment in response to the Sadducee's hypothetical question about whose wife the seven-times married woman would be in the resurrection: 'Those deemed worthy to attain to that [coming] age and to the resurrection of the dead there neither marry nor are given in marriage' (Lk. 20.34). In Acts, however, the general resurrection of the dead is explicitly associated with Jesus: priests and the captain of the temple and Sadducees are annoyed because Peter and John proclaim that in Jesus there is resurrection from the dead (4.2); Peter declares Jesus to be ordained by God to be judge of the living and the dead (10.42); Athenians at the Areopagus scoff at the mention of the resurrection of the dead (17.32) when Paul speaks of Jesus' having been raised from the dead (17.31); and reference to God's ability to raise the dead introduces Paul's recital of his encounter with the risen Jesus on the road to Damascus (26.8).[10]

Two of the seventeen references in Acts that mention νεκρός occur in episodes that are unlike anything in the Gospel. The first episode is stunning for its deadly harshness. The young men who buried Ananias, who was struck dead for engaging in deceptive practices, come back

---

this (i.e., references to Jesus as Lord) is, with very rare exceptions, confined (on the lips of men) to passages in which the evangelist is himself as the narrator alluding to Jesus. . . But as soon as his narrative reaches the post-resurrection period, both in the Gospel and Acts, it is immediately different. In Lk. 24.34 and from the beginning of Acts onwards, the disciples themselves are represented as doing precisely what they do not do in the Gospel before the resurrection: they freely apply the term κύριος to Jesus.' Moule makes similar observations regarding differences between pre- and post-resurrection uses of the terms 'prophet' for Jesus, 'Son of man', 'Savior', and υἱός ('Christology of Acts', pp. 161-65). Moule concluded ('Christology of Acts', p. 165): 'The common factor behind the contrasts that have been described is, of course, the consciousness of the resurrection as making a decisive vindication of Jesus'.

9.   Acts 4.2; 10.42; 17.32; 23.6; 24.21; 26.8.

10.   The exceptions to this practice in Acts of associating the general resurrection of the dead with Jesus are Acts 23.6 and 24.21. In Acts 23.6, Paul cleverly instigates a dispute between his Pharisee opponents on the one hand and his Sadducee opponents on the other hand by making reference to the resurrection of the dead. In Acts 24.21, Paul recounts his statement of 23.6 during his trial before the governor Felix.

inside to discover Ananias's wife and co-conspirator, Sapphira, also dead (5.10). In the second episode, Paul, having been bitten by a viper, is expected by onlookers to swell up and drop dead, but he does not (28.6).

Finally, νεκρός appears is one episode in which a follower of Jesus raises a dead person (Acts 20.7-12). Young Eutychus fell asleep during Paul's sermon and tumbled from his window perch three floors up. When Eutychus is lifted up, he is dead (20.9). Whereas Jesus raised the dead with a word (Lk. 7.14; 8.54), Paul's technique of lying on top of the corpse mimics the examples of Elijah (3 Kgdms 17.21) and Elisha (4 Kgdms 4.34).[11] The raising of Tabitha by Peter (Acts 9.36-41) more closely resembles the raising of Jairus's daughter by Jesus (Lk. 8.41-2, 49-56), for Peter raises her with a word (Acts 9.40);[12] but Peter does not order the people on hand to tell no one about the miracle (cf. Lk. 8.56). In any case, the resuscitation of Eutychus demonstrates the prophetic power of Paul, just as the resuscitation of Tabitha demonstrates Peter's prophetic power.

The power residing in the prophet becomes evident in references in Acts to the lame. All three references speak of healings. At the Temple gate, Peter and John meet a man lame from birth (Acts 3.2). Peter declares to him, 'In the name of Jesus Christ of Nazareth, walk' (3.6). The man walks, and he and the onlookers respond with praise to God (3.8-9). This healing episode (3.1-10) creates the occasion for Peter to preach about Jesus (3.12-26) and becomes the point of departure for a series of events continuing through 4.22. The unfolding events serve to emphasize that the formerly lame man was healed through Jesus (3.16; 4.7-10).

The second reference to the lame in Acts comes in a summary statement (8.7) of healings by Philip as he preached the word and proclaimed Christ in Samaria (8.4-13). The third reference, in 14.8, recalls the reference in 3.2 verbatim: τις ἀνὴρ... χωλὸς ἐκ κοιλίας

---

11. Haenchen, *Acts*, p. 585. Cf. Tannehill, *Narrative Unity*, II, pp. 249-50.

12. See Tannehill's (*Narrative Unity*, II, p. 126) list of similarities between the accounts of the raising of dead persons by Elijah, Elisha, Jesus, and Peter. It is noteworthy that Tannehill does not mention that Elijah and Elisha stretched themselves out over the corpses. Taking nothing away from the similarities between the four episodes involving Elijah, Elisha, Jesus, and Peter, the act by the prophet of lying on the corpse is an outstanding feature of the LXX stories. This feature is present in the raising of Eutychus (Acts 20.10).

μητρὸς αὐτοῦ. Paul interrupts his speech when he notices that the lame man who is listening has sufficient faith to be healed (14.9). This healing becomes the catalyst for an appeal by Paul to the crowds to repent and turn to the living God (14.15-17).

Whereas all three references in Acts to someone who is lame occur in the context of healing, the lone mention of τυφλός occurs in the context of conflict and denunciation. Paul condemns Elymas the magician to temporary blindness (13.11). The episodes involving Elymas, who is struck blind, and Ananias and Sapphira, who are struck dead, are hardly designed to elicit audience sympathy for the blind Elymas and the dead Ananias and Sapphira. Thus, there is a distinct contrast between the connotations associated with the terms νεκρός and τυφλός in Acts 5.10 and 13.11 and the connotations for these terms drawn from the lxx and conventionally applied to narrative situations in the Gospel (Lk. 4.18; 7.11-17; 7.22; 14.13, 21; 18.35-43).

In Acts, the apostles have the power to heal and to afflict. This brief survey of νεκρός, χωλός, and τυφλός has found the terms used with varying connotations and rhetorical effects. In sum, however, it may be said that the function of 'the dead', 'the lame', and 'the blind' in Acts is to assist in characterizing the apostles as prophets who announce Jesus' resurrection from the dead and display the power of God's Spirit and Jesus' name through miraculous deeds.[13]

13. See S.R. Garret's (*The Demise of the Devil: Magic and the Demonic in Luke's Writings* [Minneapolis: Augsburg–Fortress, 1989], esp. pp. 102-103) discussion of the authority of those in Acts who faithfully call upon Jesus' name to triumph over the forces of the devil.

Chapter 8

SUMMARY OF ARGUMENTS AND CONCLUSIONS

Chapter 1 began with this question: 'Why are the blind, the lame, the poor, and the deaf so prominent in the Gospel of Luke and all but absent in the Acts of the Apostles?' Pursuing this question prompted numerous other questions, such as, 'How do the blind, lepers, the poor, and the deaf, as well as those groups mentioned with them, function in Luke's narrative?' and, in order to understand how these narrative characters function, 'Who are the blind, lepers, the poor, the deaf mute, the captive, the shattered, the lame, the maimed, and the dead in Luke–Acts?' To this adheres the question 'What is the nature of ancient characterization?' Since intratextual characterization of these character groups is so scanty, I have argued that interpreters are compelled to concretize these character groups on the basis of extra-textual information. Consequently, the question was asked, 'What denotative and connotative definitions for these character groups do extra-textual resources provide?' From this point, the need to concretize the blind, the lame, the poor, and the others[1] from extra-textual resources prompted the question, 'What extra-textual resources are available and applicable to the study of these character groups in Luke–Acts?' Then, to provide the methodological means by which to sift through the myriad of extra-textual resources available to the interpreter of Luke–Acts, I asked the question, 'In what extra-textual direction does Luke's narrative itself direct Luke's audience?' Then, to answer the question of where the narrative directs the audience it was necessary to ask, 'How do readers read?' and, finally, 'What sort of audience does Luke–

---

1. Rather than type out 'the captive, the shattered, the blind, the deaf mute, the lame, lepers, the maimed, the dead, and the poor' each time I would refer to them, I have frequently used 'the blind, the lame, the poor, and the others' as a short-hand way of referring to the entire grouping.

Acts presuppose?' A satisfactory answer to the primary question could not be given until the other questions had been resolved. These other questions had to be addressed beginning with the last one.

A survey of the history of research revealed problems with focusing almost exclusively on the poor; problems with concretizing the poor on the basis of socio-religious contexts; problems with relating conclusions about the poor drawn from the Gospel to Acts; failure to address in a systematic fashion the issue of the linguistic and literary competence of Luke's intended audience; and failure to consider seriously the nature of ancient characterization. These shortcomings of previous studies called for a new study along different lines.

I chose to address the issues involved in this study from a literary-critical perspective. There should be no doubt by this point that the literary-critical approach followed here is committed to treating Luke–Acts in a historically-appropriate manner as an ancient writing; that is, I attempted to read Luke–Acts according to the linguistic and literary conventions that would have been in place when the narrative was written.

As a quick way to summarize the arguments made in the study, let me review the list of questions the study brought out and answer them briefly.

(1)   'What sort of audience does Luke–Acts presuppose?' This study argued that Luke–Acts presupposes an audience that is not familiar with Hebrew terminology, but is familiar with the LXX.

(2)   'How do readers read?' The essential points are as follows. Reading is a temporal experience of discovery. Readers read sequentially: prior episodes provide the context for subsequent episodes. Readers build consistency into the narrative as they progressively integrate perspectives and actions depicted by the text. Readers also build consistency by concretizing textual indeterminacies (filling in the 'gaps') with information drawn from their extra-textual repertoire. In addition, ancient readers read aloud. They were hearers with ears attuned to conventions of rhetoric.

(3)   'What extra-textual resources are available and applicable to the study of these character groups in Luke–Acts?' I have pointed out that the Lukan interpreter must sift through the

pool of information available from the first century and decide which resources are most appropriate for Lukan exegesis. Extra-textual resources abound, such as epigraphical material, archeological finds, Qumran documents, and the extant writings of various Graeco-Roman authors. I have argued that the LXX is an especially applicable extra-textual resource for the Lukan interpreter because the authorial audience of Luke–Acts is presumed by the implied author to be familiar with the LXX.

(4)   'In what extra-textual direction does Luke's narrative itself direct Luke's audience?' I have sought to demonstrate that the narrative itself prompts Luke's audience to concretize the blind, the lame, the poor, and the others on the basis of the LXX. Moreover, I have argued that the rhetoric of the opening chapters of the Gospel establish a strong intertextual relationship between Luke–Acts and the LXX, such that characters such as Zechariah, Mary, Simeon, Anna, John, and Jesus are cast as biblical characters.

(5)   'What denotative and connotative definitions to these character groups does the LXX provide?' The survey of every instance of αἰχμάλωτος, θραύειν, τυφλός, κωφός, χωλός, λεπρός, ἀνάπηρος, νεκρός, and πτωχός in the LXX led to the conclusion that these figures are character types. In addition, these figures align themselves together in a constellation of character types, all displaying common stereotypical features. The blind, the lame, the poor, and the others are typically anonymous, powerless, vulnerable, and a-responsible. In addition, and most significantly, these character types are standard, conventional recipients of God's saving action.

(6)   'What is the nature of ancient characterization?' Ancient characterization is illustrative, rather than representational. Therefore, ancient characters typically act in stylized, conventional ways. They lack the depth and complexity of modern characters. Ancient characters reveal their moral stature, or lack of moral stature, by their actions. That is, the honorable or dishonorable, pious or impious nature of character is revealed by what the character chooses to do and chooses not to do.

(7)   'Who are the blind, the lame, the poor, and the others in Luke–
       Acts?' For the most part, they are character types.[2] They lack
       the capacity that morally responsible ancient characters have
       to choose a course of action and reveal their character by their
       choices. Specifically, they display neither piety nor impiety,
       neither moral character nor immoral character. As character
       types, they conform to their LXX stereotype: they are typi-
       cally anonymous, powerless, vulnerable, and a-responsible.

(8)   'How do these character types function in Luke's narrative?'
       Predominantly, they function christologically by directing
       the audience's cognitive and attitudinal perceptions of Jesus
       and characters who interact with Jesus. Broadly speaking, the
       earthly Jesus is the eschatological agent of God, whose
       ministry and fate express in narrative form God's end-time
       intervention to restructure the world. In the Gospel, especi-
       ally in the formative first reference to them in Luke 4.18,
       these character types serve to define Jesus on the basis of his
       beneficent acts.[3] Jesus does not identify with the blind, the
       lame, the poor, and the others,[4] Jesus heals, blesses, and saves
       them.[5] Jesus' benefactions toward the blind, the lame, the
       poor, and the others characterize Jesus scripturally for Luke's
       intended audience. The fact that Jesus saves these character
       types as only God or God's agent in the LXX can do confirms
       his status as God or God's agent. In other words, his saving
       acts toward the blind, the lame, the poor, and so on charac-
       terize Jesus as God's unique eschatological agent of salvation.
       Just as God is the appropriate addressee for the psalmist's
       pleas, Jesus is the appropriate addressee for the pleas of the
       lepers (17.13) and the blind man (18.39) because Jesus' pre-
       sence is the presence of the kingdom of God. Moreover, Jesus'
       earthly presence is proleptically eschatological. Only while
       Jesus is bodily present can it be said that 'the kingdom of God
       is among you' (10.9; 11.20; 17.21). Those who experienced
       Jesus' presence before his ascension experienced the kingdom

2.   Lk. 4.18; 6.20, 39; 7.15, 21, 22; 11.14; 14.12-24; 16.19-31; 18.22; 19.8;
20.35, 38; 24.5, 46.
3.   Lk. 4.16-30; 6.20; 7.11-17, 22; 11.14; 17.11-19; 18.35-43.
4.   In fact, Jesus sets himself up as the antitype of the blind in Lk. 6.39-40.
5.   Lk. 4.18; 5.12-13, 17-25; 6.20; 7.21, 22; 11.14; 17.11-19; 18.35-43.

of God for a time. To use banquet imagery, they enjoyed a foretaste of the eschatological feast. The kingdom will come again when Jesus, taken away from his followers into heaven, comes again in the same way. In Acts, the kingdom is preached, but not present (Acts 8.12; 14.22; 19.8; 20.25; 28.23, 31).

To be sure, Jesus' divine identity has already been disclosed to the audience before the blind, the lame, the poor, and so on are introduced into the narrative from Lk. 4.16 through 7.22. But knowing how character types function rhetorically in the reading process helps us to see how Luke's use of the blind, the lame, the poor, and others is persuasive. Before Jesus' entrance into the synagogue in Nazareth, the voices of the angels (1.32-35; 2.11) and the divine voice from the cloud (3.22) attest directly to who Jesus is. In Iser's terminology, there are few gaps in these attestations for the audience to fill in. Luke 4.16-30 and 7.22 testify less directly to who Jesus is. The character types in the quotation from the prophet Isaiah and in Jesus' response to John's disciples introduce gaps into the text that require the audience to invest itself in the construction of the text's meaning. When the audience fills the gaps by concretizing the character types by means of its LXX competence, the audience has the satisfaction of completing the narrative. This satisfaction functions rhetorically. By using its own familiarity with the LXX to make the gap-filling connections with the LXX that characterize Jesus as God's eschatological agent of salvation, the audience is in a position to say to itself, 'Jesus is attested to by angels, by the Father, by Scripture, and by me'. The desire to be consistent with oneself has enormous persuasive force. Therefore, the audience that has identified Jesus as God's eschatological agent of salvation in part through its own efforts will want to see its judgment confirmed in and by future episodes. Future episodes do indeed confirm the audience's judgment.

Even in third-degree narrative level passages referring to the blind, the lame, the poor, and so on—passages that are not about Jesus' beneficence—the discourse relative to the character types underscores Jesus' eschatological status. In the parables of the great dinner (14.16-24) and the lost son

(15.11-32), together with the parables of the lost sheep (15.4-6) and lost coin (15.8-9), and the rich man and Lazarus (16.19-31), Jesus creates images of the kingdom of God or the heavenly realm. Each of these parables, as third-degree narrative level discourse, serves to interpret the second-degree narrative level situation. In the process of interpreting the second-degree narrative situation through the parables, Jesus speaks authoritatively through the parables about present joy in heaven (15.7, 10) over sinners reclaimed through repentance and about what the unseen heavenly future promises to be like (14.15-24; 16.19-31). Thus, the parables that mention the poor, the maimed, the blind, the lame, and the dead rhetorically accentuate Jesus' status as divine agent for the kingdom of God because they display the authoritative insight into the kingdom possessed by Jesus.[6]

---

6.   It may be a fruitful avenue of further study to explore whether there is a christological explanation for the absence of parables in Acts. But a full discussion of Jesus as the teller of parables in Luke's Gospel is beyond the scope of this study. M. Parsons and R. Pervo (*Rethinking the Unity of Luke and Acts* [Minneapolis: Fortress Press, 1993], p. 51) appeal to the fact that the followers of Jesus do not speak in parables in Acts as testimony against the premise that the Gospel and Acts form a unified narrative. Parsons and Pervo do not, however, explore other possible explanations for the uniqueness of Jesus' parable discourse in Luke and Acts. The authors argue throughout *Rethinking the Unity of Luke and Acts* that we ought to question the notion that the Gospel and Acts are a unity from beginning to end. They contend that the hyphenated title 'Luke–Acts' ought to be retired, that the Gospel and Acts are best described as separate, self-contained narratives, and that Acts 'is thus best understood as a sequel rather than a second chapter or simple continuation' (p. 123). *Rethinking the Unity of Luke and Acts* came into my hands too late to be incorporated into this study. But a few brief comments about the approach of this study as it relates to the thesis of the book by Parsons and Pervo are in order. Several factors indicate that the authorial audience of Acts is expected be familiar with the Gospel. First, in Acts 1.1, the narrator makes a direct reference to the Gospel, and refers to it as 'the first book'. Secondly, characters appear in Acts whose presence and role in Acts would be baffling to Luke's audience if the audience had not heard of them in the Gospel (e.g., John and baptism by him [Acts 1.5; 10. 37; 11.16. 18.25; 19.1-5], the eleven remaining apostles who are mentioned by name [1.13], and Judas, together with the story of his sedition [1.16]). Thirdly, the references in Acts to Jesus' trial and execution (2.23; 3.13-15; 4.27-28; 5.30; 7.52; 10.39; 13.27-29; 26.23) are brief and lacking crucial details as to how exactly these events came to be, such as how Jesus' suffering and death could be at the same time both planned by God and the act of 'lawless' persons

Once we begin to sense how the blind, the lame, the poor, and so on function rhetorically, it becomes evident that lumping the blind, the lame, the poor, and others together with sinners and tax collectors into one overall category of 'oppressed and excluded people' obscures how rhetorically distinct the two groups are. The LXX-competent audience would approach the respective groups quite differently. It would be predisposed to be sympathetic toward the blind, the lame, the poor, and so on. On the other hand, the sinner in the LXX is accursed: God destroys sinners. The LXX-competent audience would be predisposed to antipathy toward sinners and expect godly persons in Luke–Acts to avoid and condemn sinners.

In Luke's Gospel, however, Jesus is found associating with and expressing God's favor toward the lame, the blind, and the others, *and* toward sinners. Jesus fulfills the authorial audience's expectation that the 'coming one' will be the divine deliverer of the blind, the poor, and the lame. But the sinner is also the object of Jesus' mission. The responses of religious leaders to these two poles of Jesus' ministry reflect the predisposition of the Gospel of Luke's LXX-competent authorial audience. Jesus is never criticized for associating with or being beneficent toward the blind, the deaf mute, the lame, lepers, the dead, or the poor. Grumbling elicited by Jesus' healings is not over healings per se, but over healing on the sabbath.[7] The lame, the blind, and the others are not scorned by religious leaders or the people, at least not openly. On the other hand, Jesus does receive criticism for fraternizing with sinners and tax collectors.[8] Whatever else they are in Luke's Gospel, sinners and tax collectors are the recipients of the hostility of religious leaders.[9]

(2.23). Since the authorial audience of Acts is expected to have heard the Gospel, the arguments by Parsons and Pervo have no direct effect on an audience-oriented, sequential analysis of the Gospel and Acts.

7. Lk. 6.6-11; 13.10-17; 14.1-6.
8. Lk. 5.29-32; 7.36-50; 15.1-2. See also 19.1-7.
9. E.P. Sanders (*Jesus and Judaism* [Philadelphia: Fortress Press, 1985]) is engaged in historical Jesus research, and a discussion of his methods and conclusions is beyond the scope of this study because historical Jesus research is not germane to this study. Nevertheless, Sanders argues for a decisively negative connotation for the

It is a task of Luke's narrative to undermine the LXX-nourished, traditional rejection of sinners. By shaping the audience's attitudes favorably toward Jesus and unfavorably toward the religious leaders, the narrative persuades the audiencethat God seeks the salvation of sinners, not their destruction. To undermine the conventional LXX antipathy toward sinners, Luke employs the other LXX convention: divine beneficence toward the lame, the blind, and so on. Jesus must have credibility in the eyes of the LXX-competent audience in order for this audience to be persuaded to change its attitude toward sinners. Jesus' beneficence toward the lame, the blind, and the others contributes to the requisite credibility because it scripturally establishes his credentials as God's eschatological agent of salvation. Because the convention of God's beneficence toward the blind, the lame, the poor, and so on is applied to Jesus, Jesus carries LXX-based credentials solid enough to permit him, without losing credibility in the eyes of Luke's audience, to undermine the LXX condemnation of sinners. Thus, Jesus has the authority in Luke's narrative to represent

word 'sinner' and for drawing a distinction between 'sinners' and 'economically impoverished' persons. Thus, there are parallels between his findings and the assessment of 'sinners' proposed in this study. I will simply quote selectively from *Jesus and Judaism* to illustrate his argument.

> The word ['sinners'] in English versions of the Bible translates the Greek word ἁμαρτολοί. Behind ἁμαρτολοί stands, almost beyond question, the Hebrew word *resha'im* (or the Aramaic equivalent). The Semitic languages have other words which are used in parallel with *resha'im*, but it is the dominant term. *Resha'im* is virtually a technical term. It is best translated 'the wicked', and it refers to those who sinned willfully and heinously and who did not repent (p. 177).
>
> Jesus saw his mission as being to 'the lost' and the 'sinners': that is, to the wicked. He was doubtless also concerned with the poor, the meek and the downtrodden, and in all probability he had a following among them. The *charge* against him was not that he loved the *'amme ha-arets*, the common people. If there was a conflict, it was about the status of the *wicked*. It is a mistake to think that the Pharisees were upset because he ministered to the ordinarily pious common people and the economically impoverished (p. 179).

David A. Neale (*'None but the Sinners': Religious Categories in the Gospel of Luke* [JSNTSup, 58; Sheffield: Sheffield Academic Press, 1991]), in his own historical study, expands on Sanders' observation. Neale's analysis of the LXX, as well as of other Jewish texts, leads him to conclude that the term 'sinners' refers to unrepentent enemies of God (Neale, *'None but the Sinners'*, p. 97).

God's point of view on sinners even if this point of view is, ironically, at odds with Scripture. The audience's changing perspective on tax collectors accompanies its changing perspective on sinners.

Moreover, by aligning God's favor with sinners, the narrative succeeds in overcoming a major potential problem for Luke's LXX-competent reader: the fact that Jesus died in a manner befitting a sinner. By the time in the narrative that Jesus is crucified, he is established as God's agent of salvation. Death on a cross cannot counter this, not only because of what the audience has come to know about Jesus, but also because of what the audience has come to learn from Jesus about God's attitude toward sinners, the epitome of cursed ones. Consequently, the authorial audience will not be alienated from this one who is executed in the manner of one accursed.[10]

Jesus does not become one of the blind, the lame, the poor, and the others. But by hanging on the tree, he does become like the sinner: ostensibly cursed. Yet just as the tax collector, whom the narrative constructs to be equivalent to the sinner, went home justified (δεδικαιωμένος, 18.14), so Jesus goes to the Father righteous (δίκαιος, 23.47), ironically declared so by a centurian. Thus, by the end of Luke's Gospel, the rhetoric of the narrative makes credible within the world of the narrative the exaltation of the crucified Jesus to Lord.

(9) 'Why are the blind, the lame, the poor, and so on so prominent in the Gospel and all but absent in Acts?' The answer may be stated briefly: the christological function of these character types in the Gospel does not fit the status of Jesus in Acts. The blind, the lame, the poor, and the others virtually disappear in Acts because in Acts Jesus is no longer God's earthly eschatological agent of salvation. In Acts, Jesus is the risen and ascended Lord;[11] a new christological situation is

10. See Deut. 21.22 and Acts 5.30.

11. As C.F.D. Moule said ('The Christology of Acts', in Keck and Martyn (eds.), *Studies in Luke–Acts*, pp. 159-85 [179]), 'More consistently than in any other New Testament writing, Acts presents Jesus as exalted and, as it were, temporarily 'absent', but 'represented' on earth in the meantime by the Spirit (except that, undeniably, in the vision of Acts 18.10 Jesus says ἐγώ εἰμι μετὰ σοῦ)'.

present. Parallels between Jesus' earthly ministry and the ministries of the apostles exist.[12] Nevertheless, the apostles are not characterized by programmatic ministries to the captive, the shattered, the blind, the deaf mute, the lame, lepers, the maimed, the dead, and the poor—various healing episodes in Acts notwithstanding—because theapostles are not 'the coming one'.[13]

12. See, e.g., Lk. 5.17-26 and Acts 3.1-10; Lk. 6.19 and Acts 5. 16; Lk. 7.11-17 and Acts 9.36-43; 20.7-12. For lists of such parallels, see O'Toole, *Unity*, pp. 62-94.

13. No attempt has been made in this study to conduct an exhaustive study into the rhetorical techniques used by Luke to direct his audience to the LXX. Avenues for further study in this vein include study into the rhetorical effects of angelophanies, of the testimony of Spirit-filled prophets and prophetesses, and of genealogies. It may also be fruitful to explore further the rhetoric of applying one LXX convention to Jesus in order to provide Jesus with sufficient scripturally-based credibility to violate another LXX convention.

Appendix

Table 1. *Distribution in LXX of Terms Surveyed*

In table 1, A = αἰχμάλωτος; B = θραύειν; C = τυφλός; D = κωφός; E = χωλός; F = λεπρός; G = ἀνάπηρος; H = νεκρός; I = πτωχός.

	A	B	C	D	E	F	G	H	I
Gen.								×	
Exod.	×	×	×	×					×
Lev.			×	×	×	×		×	×
Num.	×	×				×		×	
Deut.		×	×		×			×	×
Josh.									
Judg.								×	
Ruth									×
1 Kgdms		×						×	×
2 Kgdms		×	×		×	×		×	×
3 Kgdms								×	
4 Kgdms						×		×	×
1 Chron.									
2 Chron.		×				×		×	
1 Esd.									
2 Esd.									
Est.	×								×
Jdt.		×						×	
Tob.	×						×	×	×
1 Macc.	×								
2 Macc.		×					×	×	
3 Macc.		×		×					
4 Macc.								×	
Pss.			×	×				×	×
Odes									
Prov.								×	
Eccl.								×	
Cant.									
Job	×		×		×				×

	A	B	C	D	E	F	G	H	I
Wis.				×				×	
Sir.								×	×
Pss. Sol.		×							×
Hos.									
Amos	×								×
Mic.									
Joel									
Obad.									
Jon.									
Nah.	×								
Hab.				×					×
Zeph.		×							
Hag.									
Zech.									
Mal.			×		×				
Isa.	×	×	×	×	×			×	×
Jer.		×						×	×
Bar.								×	
Lam.								×	
Ep. Jer.	×		×					×	×
Ezek.	×	×						×	×
Sus.									
Dan.									
Bel									

Table 2. *Distribution in Old Testament Pseudepigrapha of Terms Surveyed*

In table 2, A = αἰχμάλωτος; B = θραύειν; C = τυφλός; D = κωφός; E = χωλός; F = λεπρός; G = ἀνάπηρος; H = νεκρός; I = πτωχός.

Old Testament pseudepigraphical works in which the terms surveyed do not appear are not listed.

	A	B	C	D	E	F	G	H	I
1 Enoch								×	
T. Abr.							×		
T. XII Patr.	×		×		×			×	×
Jos. Asen.	×	×	×	×				×	×
Gk. Apoc. Ezra								×	
T. Job							×	×	
Ep. Arist.	×								
Sib. Or.			×	×				×	
Liv. Prop.						×		×	
Apoc. Ezek.		×		×					
Ps.-Phoc.			×						×
Dem. Chr.	×								
Theod.	×								
Ezek. Trag.			×					×	
Anon. Frag.									×
Anon. Hist.		×							

BIBLIOGRAPHY

Abrams, M.H., *The Mirror and the Lamp: Romantic Theory and the Critical Tradition* (London: Oxford University Press, 1953).

Achtemeier, P.J., '*Omne verbum sonat*: The New Testament and the Oral Environment of Late Western Antiquity', *JBL* 109 (1990), pp. 3-27.

Ackroyd, P.R., 'Exile', in *Harper's Bible Dictionary* (ed. P.J. Achtemeier; San Francisco: Harper & Row, 1985), pp. 287-88.

Adams, H. (ed.), *Critical Theory Since Plato* (New York: Harcourt Brace Jovanovich, 1971).

Albertz, R., 'Die "Antrittspredigt" Jesu im Lukasevangelium auf ihrem alttestamentlichen Hintergrund', *ZNW* 74 (1983), pp. 182-206.

Alter, R., *The Art of Biblical Narrative* (New York: Basic Books, 1981).

—'How Convention Helps Us Read: The Case of the Bible's Annunciation Type-Scene', *Prooftexts* 3 (1983), pp. 115-30.

Argyle, A.W., 'The Greek of Luke and Acts', *NTS* 20 (1974), pp. 441-45.

Aristotle, *The Art of Rhetoric* (trans. J.H. Freese; LCL; Cambridge, MA: Harvard University Press, 1926).

—*Nicomachean Ethics* (trans. Martin Ostwald; The Library of Liberal Arts; Indianapolis and New York: Bobbs-Merrill, 1962).

—*The Poetics* (trans. W. Hamilton Fyfe; LCL; Cambridge, MA: Harvard University Press, rev. edn, 1932).

Aune, D.E, *The New Testament in Its Literary Environment* (Library of Early Christianity, 8; Philadelphia: Westminster Press, 1987).

Austin, J.L., *How to Do Things With Words* (Oxford: Oxford University Press, 1962).

Baily, R., *Biblical Perspectives on Death* (Overtures to Biblical Theology, 5; Philadelphia: Fortress Press, 1979).

Balogh, J. 'Voces paginarum', *Philologus* 82 (1927), pp. 84-109, 202-31.

Bammel, E., 'Πτωχός', *TDNT*, VI, pp. 885-915.

Barrett, C.K., *Luke the Historian in Recent Study* (London: Epworth, 1961).

Bartsch, H.-W., *Wachet aber zu jeder Zeit!Entwurf einer Auslegung des Lukasevangeliums* (Hamburg: Herbert Reich Evangelischer Verlag, 1963).

Beardslee, W.A., *Literary Criticism of the New Testament* (Guides to Biblical Scholarship; Philadelphia: Fortress Press, 1970).

Beavis, M.A., *Mark's Audience: The Literary and Social Setting of Mark 4.11-12* (JSNTSup, 33; Sheffield: JSOT Press, 1989).

Berger, K., *Exegese des Neuen Testaments: Neue Wege vom Text zur Auslegung* (Uni-Taschenbücher, 658; Heidelberg: Quelle & Meyer, 2nd edn, 1984).

—*Formgeschichte des Neuen Testaments* (Heidelberg: Quelle & Meyer, 1984).

—'Hellenistische Gattungen im Neuen Testament', in H. Temporini and W. Haase (eds.)

Aufstieg und Niedergang der Römischen Welt: Geschichte und Kultur Roms im Spiegel der Neueren Forschung (Berlin: de Gruyter, 1984), II, 25.2, pp. 1031-432.

Bergquist, J.A., '"Good News to the Poor": Why Does this Lucan Motif Appear to Run Dry in the Book of Acts?', *Trinity Seminary Review* 9 (1987), p. 18-27.

Betz, H.-D., 'Eschatology in the Sermon on the Mount and the Sermon on the Plain', *SBLSP* (1985), pp. 343-50.

—*Galatians: A Commentary on Paul's Letter to the Churches in Galatia* (Hermeneia; Philadelphia: Fortress Press, 1979).

Beyer, K., *Semitische Syntax im Neuen Testament* (2 vols.; Göttingen: Vandenhoeck & Ruprecht, 1962).

Blass, G., and A. Debrunner, *A Greek Grammar of the New Testament and Other Early Christian Literature* (trans. and rev. R.W. Funk; Chicago: University of Chicago Press, 1961).

Bock. D.L., 'Proclamation from Prophecy and Pattern: Luke's Use of the Old Testament for Christology and Mission', in C.A. Evans and W.R. Stegner (eds.), *The Gospels and the Scriptures of Israel* (JSNTSup, 104; Sheffield: Sheffield Academic Press, 1994), pp. 290-91.

Booth, W.C., '"Preserving the Exemplar": Or, How Not to Dig Our Own Graves', *Critical Inquiry* 3 (1977), pp. 407-24.

—*The Rhetoric of Fiction* (Chicago: University of Chicago Press, 2nd edn, 1983).

Brawley, R.L., *Centering on God: Method and Message in Luke–Acts* (Literary Currents in Biblical Interpretation; Louisville: Westminster/John Knox, 1990).

—*Luke–Acts and the Jews: Conflict, Apology, and Conciliation* (SBLMS, 33; Atlanta: Scholars Press, 1987).

Brenton, C.L.C., *The Septuagint with Apocrypha: Greek and English* (London: Samuel Bagster & Sons, 1851; repr.; Peabody, MA: Hendrickson, 1986).

Bultmann, R., *Form Criticism: Two Essays on New Testament Research* (trans. and ed. F.C. Grant; New York: Willett, Clark, 1934).

—*History of the Synoptic Tradition* (trans. John Marsh; New York: Harper & Row, rev. edn, 1963).

—*Theology of the New Testament* (trans. K. Grobel; 2 vols.; New York: Charles Scribner's Sons, 1951, 1955).

Burnette, F.W., 'Characterization and Reader Construction of Characters in the Gospels', *Semeia* 63 (1993), pp. 3-28.

Burton, E., *Some Principles of Literary Criticism and their Application to the Synoptic Problem* (The Decennial Publications, 5; Chicago: University of Chicago Press, 1904).

—*Syntax of the Moods and Tenses in New Testament Greek* (Chicago: University of Chicago Press, 2nd rev. edn, 1893).

Busse, U., *Das Nazareth-Manifest Jesu: Eine Einführung in das lukanische Jesusbild nach Lk 4,16-30* (SBS, 91; Stuttgart: Katholisches Bibelwerk, 1977).

Cadbury, H.J., *The Book of Acts in History* (New York: Harper; London: A. & C. Black, 1955).

—'Luke: Translator or Author?', *American Journal of Theology* 24 (1920), pp. 436-55.

—*The Making of Luke–Acts* (New York: Macmillan, 1927; repr.; London: SPCK, 1961).

—*The Style and Literary Method of Luke* (Harvard Theological Studies, 6; Cambridge, MA: Harvard University Press, 1920).

Caird, G.B., *The Gospel of Saint Luke* (The Pelican New Testament Commentaries; Harmondsworth: Penguin Books, 1963).

Carroll, J.T., 'Luke's Portrayal of the Pharisees', *CBQ* 50 (1988), pp. 604-21.

Cassidy, R.J., *Jesus, Politics, and Society: A Study of Luke's Gospel* (Maryknoll: Orbis Books, 1978).

Cassidy, R.J., and P.J. Scharper (eds.), *Political Issues in Luke–Acts* (New York: Orbis Books, 1978).

Charlesworth, J.H. (ed.), *The Old Testament Pseudepigrapha* (2 vols.; Garden City, NY: Doubleday, 1983, 1985).

Chatman, S., 'Characters and Narrators: Filter, Center, Slant, and Interest-Focus', *Poetics Today* 7 (1986), pp. 189-204.

—*Story and Discourse: Narrative Structure in Fiction and Film* (Ithaca, NY: Cornell University Press, 1978).

Clarke, W.K.L., 'The Use of the Septuagint in Acts', in F.J.F. Jackson and K. Lake (gen. eds.), *The Beginnings of Christianity, Part I, The Acts of the Apostle. II. Prolegomena II; Criticism* (London: Macmillan, 1920–33; repr.; Grand Rapids: Baker Book House, 1979), pp. 66-105.

Clements, R.E., 'History and Theology in Biblical Narrative', *HBT* 4–5 (1982–83), pp. 45-60.

Combrink, H.J.B., 'The Structure and Significance of Lk 4:16-30', *Neotestamentica* 7 (1973), pp. 27-47.

Conzelmann, H., *The Theology of St Luke* (trans. G. Buswell; New York: Harper & Row, 1960).

Craddock, F.B., 'Luke', in *Harper's Bible Commentary* (ed. J.L. Mays; San Francisco: Harper & Row, 1988), pp. 1010-43.

Crossan, J.D., *In Parables: The Challenge of the Historical Jesus* (New York: Harper & Row, 1973).

Culler, J., *Structuralist Poetics: Structuralism, Linguistics, and the Study of Literature* (Ithaca, NY: Cornell University Press, 1975).

Culpepper, R.A., *Anatomy of the Fourth Gospel: A Study in Literary Design* (Foundations and Facets; Philadelphia: Fortress Press, 1983).

Danker, F.W., *Jesus and the New Age: A Commentary on St Luke's Gospel* (Philadelphia: Fortress Press, rev. edn, 1988).

—*Luke* (Proclamation Commentaries; Philadelphia: Fortress Press, 2nd edn, 1987).

Darr, J., 'Glorified in the Presence of Kings: A Literary-Critical Study of Herod the Tetrarch in Luke–Acts' (PhD dissertation, Vanderbilt University, 1987).

—*On Building Character: The Reader and the Rhetoric of Characterization in Luke–Acts* (Literary Currents in Biblical Interpretation; Louisville: Westminster/John Knox, 1992).

Dawsey, J., *The Lukan Voice: Confusion and Irony in the Gospel of Luke* (Macon, GA: Mercer University Press, 1986).

Degenhardt, H.-J., *Lukas: Evangelist der Armen. Besitz und Besitzverzicht in den lukanischen Schriften: Eine traditions- und redaktionsgeschichtliche Untersuchung* (Stuttgart: Katholisches Bibelwerk, 1965).

Deissmann, G.A., *Biblical Studies: Contributions Chiefly from Papyri and Inscriptions to the History of the Language, the Literature, and the Religion of Hellenistic Judaism and Primitive Christianity* (trans. A. Grieve; Edinburgh: T. & T. Clark, 1909).

—*Light from the Ancient East* (trans. L.R.M. Strachan; London: Hodder & Stoughton, 1910).

—*The Philology of the Greek Bible: Its Present and Future* (trans. L.R.M. Strachan; London: Hodder & Stoughton, 1908).

DeMaria, R., Jr, 'The Ideal Reader: A Critical Fiction', *Publications of the Modern Language Association of America* 93 (1978), pp. 463-74.

Demetrius, *On Style* (trans. W. Hamilton; LCL, 199; Cambridge, MA: Harvard University Press, 1932).

Denis, A.-M., with Y. Janssens and CETEDOC, *Concordance Grecque des Pseudepigraphes d'Ancien Testament: Concordance, Corpus des textes, Indices* (Louvain-la-Neuve: Université Catholique de Louvain, Institute Orientaliste, 1987).

Detweiler, R., 'After the New Criticism: Contemporary Methods of Literary Interpretation', in *Orientation by Disorientation: Studies in Literary Criticism and Biblical Literary Criticism Presented in Honor of William A. Beardslee* (ed. R.A. Spencer; Pittsburgh Theological Monograph Series, 35; Pittsburgh: Pickwick, 1980), pp. 3-23.

Detweiler, R. (ed.), *Reader-Response Approaches to Biblical and Secular Texts* (Semeia, 31; Atlanta: Scholars Press, 1985).

Dibelius, M., *James: A Commentary on the Epistle of James* (trans. and rev. H. Greeven; Hermeneia; Philadelphia: Fortress Press, 1976).

—*From Tradition to Gospel* (trans. B.L. Woolf; New York: Charles Scribner's Sons, 1935).

—*Jesus* (Philadelphia: Westminster Press, 1949).

Dodd, C.H., *The Parables of the Kingdom* (New York: Charles Scribner's Sons, rev. edn, 1961).

Donahue, J., 'Tax Collectors and Sinners', *CBQ* 33 (1971), pp. 39-61.

—'Two Decades of Research on the Rich and the Poor in Luke–Acts', in D. Knight and P. Paris (eds.), *Justice and the Holy* (Scholars Press Homage Series; Atlanta: Scholars Press, 1989), pp. 129-44.

Dupont, J., *Les Béatitudes* (3 vols.; Paris: Gabalda, 1973).

—*Études sur les Actes des Apôtres* (LD, 45; Paris: Cerf, 1967).

—'Introduction aux Beatitudes', *La nouvelle revue théologique* 98 (1976), pp. 97-108.

—*Nouvelles études sur les Actes Apôtres* (LD, 118; Paris: Cerf, 1984).

—'The Poor and Poverty in the Gospel and Acts', in *Gospel Poverty: Essays in Biblical Theology* (trans. M.D. Guinan; Chicago: Franciscan Herald, 1977).

Ellis, E.E., *The Gospel of Luke* (NCB; Grand Rapids: Eerdmans, rev. edn, 1981).

Eltester, W., 'Israel im lukanischen Werk und die Nazarethperikope', in *idem* (ed.), *Jesus in Nazareth* (BZNW, 40; Berlin: de Gruyter, 1972), pp. 76-147.

Esler, P.F., *Community and Gospel in Luke–Acts: The Social and Political Motivations of Lucan Theology* (SNTSMS, 57; Cambridge: Cambridge University Press, 1987).

Evans, C.A., *Luke* (New International Biblical Commentary; Peabody, MA: Hendrickson, 1990).

—'Luke's Use of the Elijah/Elisha Narratives and the Ethic of Election', *JBL* 106 (1987), pp. 75-83.

Evans, C.F., *Saint Luke* (TPI New Testament Commentaries; London: SCM Press; Philadelphia: Trinity Press International, 1990).

Fish, S., 'Interpreting the *Varorium*', *Critical Enquiry* 2 (Spring 1976), pp. 465-85 (reprinted in Tompkins [ed.], *Reader-Response Criticism*, pp. 164-84).

—'Literature in the Reader: Affective Stylistics', *New Literary History* 2 (1970), pp. 123-62. Reprinted in J. Tompkins (ed.), *Reader Response Criticism: From Formalism to Post-Structuralism* (Baltimore: The Johns Hopkins University Press, 1980), pp. 70-100.

Fitzmyer, J., *Essays on the Semitic Background of the New Testament* (London: Chapman, 1971).

—*The Gospel According to Luke I-IX* (AB, 28; Garden City, NY: Doubleday, 1981).

—*The Gospel According to Luke X-XXIV* (AB, 28A; Garden City, NY: Doubleday, 1985).

Forster, E.M., *Aspects of the Novel* (New York: Harcourt, Brace & World, 1927).

Fowler, R., *Let the Reader Understand: Reader-Response Criticism and the Gospel of Mark* (Minneapolis: Fortress Press, 1991).

—'Who is "the Reader" in Reader-Response Criticism?', *Semeia* 31 (1985), pp. 5-23.

Franklin, E., *Christ the Lord: A Study in the Purpose and Theology of Luke–Acts* (Philadelphia: Westminster Press, 1975).

Frei, H.W., *The Eclipse of Biblical Narrative* (New Haven: Yale University Press, 1974).

Frein, B.C., 'Narrative Predictions, Old Testament Prophecies and Luke's Sense of Fulfillment', *NTS* 40 (January 1994), pp. 22-37.

Fuller, R.H., *A Critical Introduction to the New Testament* (Naperville, IL: Allenson, 1966).

Garrett, S.R., *The Demise of the Devil: Magic and the Demonic in Luke's Writings* (Minneapolis: Augsburg–Fortress, 1989).

Gehman, H.S., 'The Hebraic Character of Septuagint Greek', *VT* 1 (1951), pp. 81-90.

Gelin, A., *The Poor of Yahweh* (trans. K. Sullivan; Collegeville, MN: The Liturgical Press, 1964).

Genette, G., *Narrative Discourse: An Essay in Method* (trans. Jane E. Lewin; Ithaca, NY: Cornell University Press, 1980).

Gibson, W., 'Authors, Speakers, Readers, and Mock Readers', *College English* 11 (1950), pp. 265-69. Reprinted in *Reader Response Criticism: From Formalism to Post-Structuralism* (edited J. Tompkins; Baltimore: The Johns Hopkins University Press, 1980), pp. 1-6.

Goldingay, J., *Models for Interpretation of Scripture* (Grand Rapids: Eerdmans; Carlisle: The Paternoster Press, 1995).

Goulder, M.D., *Luke: A New Paradigm* (JSNTSup, 20; 2 vols.; Sheffield: JSOT Press, 1989).

—*Type and History in Acts* (London: SPCK, 1964).

Grant, F.C., *The Economic Background of the Gospels* (London: Oxford University Press, 1926; repr.; New York: Russell & Russell, 1973).

Grant, M., *The Ancient Historians* (New York: Charles Scribner's Sons, 1970).

Gressmann, H., *Vom reichen Mann und armen Lazarus: Eine literargeschichtliche Studie* (Berlin: Königliche Akademie der Wissenschaften, 1918).

Grundmann, W., *Das Evangelium nach Lukas* (THKNT, 3; Berlin: Evangelische Verlagsanstalt, 5th edn, 1969).

Haenchen, E., *The Acts of the Apostles: A Commentary* (trans.R.McL. Wilson; Philadelphia: Westminster Press, 1971).

Hamm, D., 'Sight to the Blind: Vision as Metaphor in Luke', *Bib* 67 (1986), pp. 457-77.

Hanhart, R., 'Die Bedeutung der Septuaginta', *ZTK* 81 (1984), pp. 395-416.

Hatch, E., *Essays in Biblical Greek* (Oxford: Oxford University Press, 1889).

Hatch, E., and H.A. Redpath, *A Concordance to the Septuagint and the Other Greek Versions of the Old Testament* (2 vols.; Grand Rapids: Baker, 1987).

Hauch, F., *Die Stellung des Urchristentums zu Arbeit und Geld* (BFCT, 2.3; Gütersloh: Gerd Mohn, 1921).

Hauerwas, S., 'The Politics of Charity in Luke', *Int* 31 (1977), pp. 251-62.

Heard, W., 'Luke's Attitude toward the Rich and the Poor', *Trinity Journal* 9 (1988), pp. 47-80.

Heil, J.P., 'Blindness', in *Harper's Bible Dictionary* (ed. P.J. Achtemeier; San Francisco: Harper & Row, 1985), pp. 135-36.

Hendrickson, G.L., 'Ancient Reading', *Classical Journal* 25 (1929), pp. 182-96.

Hengel, M., *Eigenhum und Reichtum in der früken Kirche* (Stuttgart: Calwer Verlag, 1973); ET *Property and Riches in the Early Church: Aspects of a Social History of Early Christianity* (trans. J. Bowden; London: SCM Press; Philadelphia: Fortress Press, 1974).

Hill, D., *Greek Words and Hebrew Meanings* (Cambridge: Cambridge University Press, 1967).

—'The Rejection of Jesus at Nazareth (Luke iv 16-30)', *NovT* 13 (1971), pp. 161-80.

Hock R., 'Lazarus and Micyllus: Greco-Roman Backgrounds to Luke 16:19-31', *JBL* 106 (1987), pp. 447-63.

Hofheinz, W.C., 'An Analysis of the Usage and Influence of Isaiah Chapters 40-66 in the New Testament' (PhD dissertation, Columbia University, 1964).

Holladay, C.R., 'Biblical Criticism', in *Harper's Bible Dictionary* (ed. P.J. Achtemeier; San Francisco: Harper & Row, 1985), pp. 129-33.

Hollenbach, P., 'Defining Rich and Poor Using Social Sciences', in K.H. Richards (ed.), *SBLSP* 26 (Atlanta: Scholars Press, 1987), pp. 30-63.

Holman, C.H., *A Handbook to Literature* (ed. W.F. Thrall and A. Hibbard; Indianapolis: Bobbs-Merrill, 4th edn, 1980).

Holtz, T., *Untersuchungen über die alttestamentlichen Zitate bei Lukas* (TU, 104; Berlin: Akademie Verlag, 1968).

Holtzmann, H.J., *Lehrbuch der historisch-kritischen Einleitung in das Neue Testament* (Freiburg: Mohr [Paul Siebeck], 3rd edn, 1892).

Hoppe, L.J., *Being Poor: A Biblical Study* (Good News Studies, 20; Wilmington: Michael Glazier, 1987).

Horace, *Satires, Epistles and Ars Poetica* (trans. H.R. Fairclough; LCL; Cambridge, MA; Harvard University Press, rev. edn, 1936).

Horn, F.W., *Glaube und Handeln in der Theologie des Lukas* (Göttinger Theologische Arbeiten, 26; Göttingen: Vandenhoeck & Ruprecht, 1983).

Horsley, G.H.R., *New Documents Illustrating Early Christianity*. V. *Linguistic Essays* (NSW, Australia: Macquarrie University Press, 1989).

Horton, F.L., Jr, 'Reflections on the Semitisms of Luke–Acts', in C.H. Talbert (ed.), *Perspectives on Luke–Acts* (Danville, VA: Association of Baptist Professors of Religion, 1978), pp. 1-23.

Hoyt, T., Jr, 'The Poor in Luke–Acts' (PhD dissertation, Duke University, 1975).

Ingarden, R., *The Cognition of the Literary Work of Art* (trans. R.A. Crowly and K.R. Olsen; Evanston: Northwestern University Press, 1973).

Iser, W., *The Act of Reading: A Theory of Aesthetic Response* (Baltimore: The Johns Hopkins University Press, 1978).

—*The Implied Reader: Patterns of Communication in Prose Fiction from Bunyan to Beckett* (Baltimore: The Johns Hopkins University Press, 1974).

Jacoby, H., *Neutestamentliche Ethik* (Königsberg: Thomas & Oppermann, 1899).

Jakobson, R., 'Closing Statement: Linguistics and Poetics', in T.A. Sebeok (ed.), *Style in Language* (Cambridge, MA: Technology Press, 1960), pp. 350-77.

Jeremias, J., *Jesus' Promise to the Nations* (London: SCM Press, rev. edn, 1967).

—*The Parables of Jesus* (trans. S.H. Hooke; New York: Charles Scribner's Sons, 2nd rev. edn, 1972).

Johnson, L.T., *The Gospel of Luke* (Sacra Pagina, 3; Collegeville, MN: The Liturgical Press, 1991).

—*The Literary Function of Possessions in Luke–Acts* (SBLDS, 39; Missoula, MT: Scholars Press, 1977).

Josephus, *Antiquities* (LCL, 5; Cambridge, MA: Harvard University Press, 1934).

Juel, D., *Luke–Acts: The Promise of History* (Atlanta: John Knox, 1983).

Jülicher, A., *Einleitung in das Neue Testament* (Grundriss der Theologischen Wissenschaften, 3.1; Tübingen: Mohr [Paul Siebeck], 6th edn, 1921).

—*Die Gleichnisreden Jesu* (2 vols.; Tübingen: Mohr [Paul Siebeck], 1910).

Kähler, M., *The So-called Historical Jesus and the Historic Biblical Christ* (trans. C. Braaten; Philadelphia: Fortress Press, 1964).

Karris, R.J., *Luke, Artist and Theologian: Luke's Passion Account as Literature* (Theological Inquiries; Mahwah, NJ: Paulist Press, 1985).

—'Poor and Rich: The Lukan *Sitz im Leben*', in C.H. Talbert (ed.), *Perspectives on Luke–Acts* (Danville, VA: Association of Baptist Professors of Religion, 1978), pp. 112-25.

Käsemann, E., *Essays on New Testament Themes* (trans. W.J. Montague; London: SCM Press, 1964; repr.; Philadelphia: Fortress Press, 1982).

—*Jesus Means Freedom* (trans. F. Clarke; Philadelphia: Fortress Press, 1969).

—'What I have Unlearned in 50 Years as a German Theologian' (trans. S.J. Roth), *Currents in Theology and Mission* 15 (August 1988), pp. 325-35.

Kautzky, K., *Der Ursprung des Christentums: eine historische Untersuchung* (Stuttgart: Dietz, 1908).

Keck, L.E., 'Armut—III. Neues Testament', *Theologische Realenzyklopädie* (ed. G. Krause and G. Mueller; Berlin: de Gruyter, 1976-90), pp. 76-80.

—'Poor', *IDBSup*, pp. 672-75.

—'The Poor Among the Saints in the New Testament', *ZNW* 56 (1965), pp. 100-29.

Keck, L.E., and J.L. Martyn (eds.), *Studies in Luke–Acts: Essays in Honor of Paul Schubert* (Nashville: Abingdon Press, 1966).

Kelber, W.H., *Mark's Story of Jesus* (Philadelphia: Fortress Press, 1979).

Kennedy, G.A., *Classical Rhetoric and Its Christian and Secular Tradition from Ancient to Modern Times* (Chapel Hill: University of North Carolina Press, 1980).

—*New Testament Interpretation through Rhetorical Criticism* (Chapel Hill: University of North Carolina Press, 1984).

Kennedy, H.A.A., *Sources of New Testament Greek or the Influence of the Septuagint on the Vocabulary of the New Testament* (Edinburgh: T. & T. Clark, 1895).

Kermode, F., *The Genesis of Secrecy: On the Interpretation of Narrative* (Cambridge, MA: Harvard University Press, 1979).

Kingsbury, J., *Conflict in Luke: Jesus, Authorities, Disciples* (Minneapolis: Augsburg–Fortress, 1991).

—*Jesus Christ in Matthew, Mark and Luke* (Proclamation Commentaries; Philadelphia: Fortress Press, 1981).

—*Matthew as Story* (Philadelphia: Fortress Press, 1986).

Klein, R.W., *Textual Criticism of the Old Testament: The Septuagint after Qumran* (Guides to Biblical Scholarship; Philadelphia: Fortress Press, 1974).

Klostermann, E., *Das Lukasevangelium* (HNT, 3; Tübingen: Mohr [Paul Siebeck], 2nd edn, 1929).

Knott, J.R., Jr, 'Paradise Lost and the Fit Reader', *Modern Language Quarterly* 45 (June 1984), pp. 123-43.

Koch, R., 'Die Wertung des Besitzes im Lukasevangelium', *Bib* 38 (1957), pp. 151-69.

Koester, H., *Introduction to the New Testament* (2 vols.; Hermeneia Foundations and Facets; Philadelphia: Fortress Press, 1982).

Koet, B.J., *Five Studies on Interpretation of Scripture in Luke–Acts* (Studiorum Novi Testamenti Auxilia, 14; Leuven: Leuven University/Peeters, 1989).

Kraft, R.A., 'Septuagint: Earliest Greek Versions', *IDBSup*, pp. 811-15.

Krentz, E., *The Historical-Critical Method* (Guides to Biblical Scholarship; Philadelphia: Fortress Press, 1975).

Krieg, M., *Todesbilder im Alten Testament* (ATANT, 73; Zürich: Theologischer Verlag, 1988).

Krodel, G., *Acts* (Proclamation Commentaries; Philadelphia: Fortress Press, 1981).

Kugel, J., 'On the Bible and Literary Criticism', *Prooftexts* 1 (1981), pp. 217-36.

Kümmel, W.G., *The New Testament: The History of the Investigation of Its Problems* (trans. S.M. Gilmour and H.C. Kee; Nashville: Abingdon Press, 1972).

Kurz, W.S., *Reading Luke–Acts: Dynamics of Biblical Narrative* (Louisville: Westminster/ John Knox Press, 1993).

Kuschke, A., 'Arm und Reich im Alten Testament mit besonderer Berücksichtigung der nachexilischen Zeit', *ZAW* 57 (1939), pp. 44-57.

Kysar, R., *John, the Maverick Gospel* (Atlanta: John Knox, 1976).

Lanser, S.S., *The Narrative Act: Point of View in Prose Fiction* (Princeton, NJ: Princeton University Press, 1981).

Lee, J.A.L., *A Lexical Study of the Septuagint Version of the Pentateuch* (SBLSCS, 14; Chico, CA: Scholars Press, 1983).

Leitch, T.M., *What Stories Are: Narrative Theory and Interpretation* (University Park: Pennsylvania State University Press, 1986).

Leitch, V.B., 'A Primer of Recent Critical Theories', *College English* 39 (October 1977), pp. 138-52.

Lentricchia, F. and T. McLaughlin, *Critical Terms for Literary Study* (Chicago: University of Chicago Press, 1990).

Liu, P., 'The Poor and the Good News: A Study of the Motif of "Euangelizesthai Ptochois" in Isaiah and Luke–Acts' (PhD dissertation, Fuller Theological Seminary, 1985).

Lohse, E., 'Das Evangelium für die Armen', *ZNW* 73 (1982), pp. 51-64.

Longinus, *On the Sublime* (trans. W. Hamilton; LCL, 199; Cambridge, MA: Harvard University Press, 1932).

Longus, *Daphnis and Chloe* (trans. G. Thornley; rev. and augmented J.M. Edmonds; LCL; London: Heinemann; New York: Putnam's Sons, 1916).

Lotman, J., *The Structure of the Artistic Text* (Ann Arbor: Michigan Slavic Contributions, 1977).

Lund, N.W., *Chiasmus in the New Testament* (Chapel Hill: University of North Carolina Press, 1942).

McCartney, E.S., 'Notes on Reading and Praying Audibly', *Classical Philology* 63 (1948), pp. 184-87.

Mack, B., *Rhetoric and the New Testament* (Guides to Biblical Scholarship; Minneapolis: Augsburg–Fortress, 1990).

McKnight, E.V. (ed.), *Reader Perspectives on the New Testament* (Semeia, 48; Atlanta: Scholars Press, 1989).

Maddox, R.L., *The Purpose of Luke–Acts* (Studies of the New Testament and its World; Edinburgh: T. & T. Clark, 1982).

Maier, J. 'Armut—IV: Judentum', *Theologische Realenzyklopädie* (ed. G. Krause and G. Mueller; Berlin: de Gruyter, 1976–90), pp. 80-85.

Mailloux, S., 'Interpretation', in F. Lentricchia and T. McLaughlin (eds.), *Critical Terms for Literary Study* (Chicago: University of Chicago Press, 1990), pp. 121-34.

—*Interpretive Conventions: The Reader in the Study of American Fiction* (Ithaca, NY: Cornell University Press, 1982).

—'Reader-Response Criticism?', *Genre* 10 (1977), pp. 413-31.

Malina, B., 'Interpreting the Bible with Anthropology: The Case of the Rich and the Poor', *Listening* 21 (1986), pp. 148-59.

—*The New Testament World: Insights from Cultural Anthropology* (Atlanta: John Knox, 1981).

—'Wealth and Poverty in the New Testament and its World', *Int* 41 (1987), pp. 354-67.

Marrou, H.I., *A History of Education in Antiquity* (London and New York: Sheed & Ward, 1956).

Marshall, I.H., *The Gospel of Luke: A Commentary on the Greek Text* (New International Greek Testament Commentary; Grand Rapids: Eerdmans, 1978).

Mattill, A.J., *Luke and the Last Things: A Perspective for the Understanding of Lukan Thought* (Dillsboro, NC: Western North Carolina Press, 1979).

Mays, J.L. (gen. ed.), *Harper's Bible Commentary* (San Francisco: Harper & Row, 1988).

Mealand, D.L., *Poverty and Expectation in the Gospels* (London: SPCK, 1980).

Meierding, P., 'Jews and Gentiles: A Narrative and Rhetorical Analysis of the Implied Audience in Acts' (ThD dissertation, Luther Northwestern Theological Seminary, Mineapolis, 1992).

Metzger, B.M., *A Textual Commentary on the Greek New Testament: A Companion Volume to the United Bible Societies' Greek New Testament* (London: United Bible Societies, 3rd edn, 1975).

Michel, D., 'Armut—II: Altes Testament', *Theologische Realenzyklopädie* (ed. G. Krause and G. Mueller; Berlin: de Gruyter, 1976-90), pp. 72-76.

Miller, R.J., 'Elijah, John, and Jesus in the Gospel of Luke', *NTS* 34 (1988), pp. 611-22.

Minear, P., 'Luke's Use of the Birth Stories', in Keck and Martyn (eds.), *Studies in Luke–Acts*, pp. 111-30.

Moessner, D.P., *Lord of the Banquet: The Literary and Theological Significance of the Lukan Travel Narrative* (Minneapolis: Fortress Press, 1989).

Moltman, W.E., *The Women Around Jesus* (New York: Crossroad, 1982).

Morgenthaler, R., *Statistik des Neutestamentlichen Wortschatzes* (Zürich: Gotthelf, 1958).

Moscato, M.A., 'Current Theories Regarding the Audience of Luke–Acts', *CurTM* 3 (1976), pp. 355-61.

Mott, S.C., 'Poor', *Harper's Bible Dictionary* (ed. P.J. Achtemeier; San Francisco: Harper
& Row, 1985), pp. 807-808.

Moule, C.F.D., *An Idiom Book of New Testament Greek* (Cambridge: Cambridge
University Press, 2nd edn, 1959).

—'The Christology of Acts', in Keck and Martyn (eds.), *Studies in Luke–Acts*, pp. 159-85.

Moulton, J.H., W.F. Howard and N. Turner, *A Grammar of New Testament Greek*
(4 vols.; Edinburgh: T. & T. Clark, 1976).

Moxnes, H., *The Economy of the Kingdom: Social Conflict and Economic Relations in
Luke's Gospel* (Overtures to Biblical Theology; Philadelphia: Fortress Press, 1988).

Moyise, S., *The Old Testament in the Book of Revelation* (JSNTSup, 115; Sheffield:
Sheffield Academic Press, 1995).

Neale, D.A., *'None but the Sinners': Religious Categories in the Gospel of Luke*
(JSNTSup, 58; Sheffield: Sheffield Academic Press, 1991).

Neusner J., *From Politics to Piety: The Emergence of Pharisaic Judaism* (Englewood
Cliffs: Prentice–Hall, 1973).

—*What is Midrash?* (Guides to Biblical Scholarship; Philadelphia: Fortress Press, 1987).

Nickelsburg, G.W.E., *Jewish Literature between the Bible and the Mishnah: A Historical
and Literary Introduction* (Philadelphia: Fortress Press, 1981).

—'Riches, the Rich, and God's Judgment in I Enoch 92-105 and the Gospel according to
Luke', *NTS* 25 (1978–79), pp. 324-44.

Nolland, J.L., 'Classic and Rabbinic Parallels to "Physician, Heal Yourself" (Lk IV 23)',
NovT 21 (1979), pp. 193-209.

—'Impressed Unbelievers as Witnesses to Christ (Luke 4:22a)', *JBL* 98 (1979), pp. 219-29.

—*Luke 1–9:20* (WBC, 35A; Dallas: Word Books, 1989).

—'Words of Grace (Luke 4,22)', *Bib* 65 (1984), pp. 44-60.

Nunn, H.P.V., *A Short Syntax of New Testament Greek* (Cambridge: Cambridge University
Press, 5th edn, 1956).

Oakman, D.E., *Jesus and the Economic Questions of his Day* (Studies in the Bible and
Early Christianity, 8; Lewiston, NY: Edwin Mellen, 1986).

O'Day, G., 'Singing Woman's Song: A Hermeneutic of Liberation', *CurTM* 12 (1985),
pp. 203-10.

Ong, W., 'The Writer's Audience is Always a Fiction', *Publications of the Modern
Language Association of America* 90 (1975), pp. 9-21.

Osiek, C., *Rich and Poor in the Shepherd of Hermas: An Exegetical-Social Investigation*
(CBQMS, 15; Washington DC: The Catholic Biblical Association of America, 1983).

O'Toole, R.F., 'Activity of the Risen Jesus in Luke–Acts', *Bib* 62 (1981), pp. 471-98.

—*The Unity of Luke's Theology: An Analysis of Luke–Acts* (Good News Studies, 9;
Wilmington, DE: Michael Glazier, 1984).

Parsons, M., and R. Pervo, *Rethinking the Unity of Luke and Acts* (Minneapolis: Fortress
Press, 1993).

Perelman, C., *The Realm of Rhetoric* (trans. W. Kluback; Notre Dame: University of Notre
Dame Press, 1982).

Perelman, C., and L. Olbrechts-Tyteca, *The New Rhetoric: A Treatise on Argumentation*
(trans. J. Wilkinson and P. Weaver; Notre Dame: University of Notre Dame Press,
1969).

Perrin, N., *Rediscovering the Teaching of Jesus* (New York: Harper & Row, 1967).

—'The Evangelist as Author: Reflections on Method in the Study and Interpretation of the
Synoptic Gospels and Acts', *BR* 17 (1972), pp. 5-18.

—*Jesus and the Language of the Kingdom* (Philadelphia: Fortress Press, 1976).

Petersen, N.R., *Literary Criticism for New Testament Critics* (Guides to Biblical Scholarship; Philadelphia: Fortress Press, 1978).

—'Literary Criticism in Biblical Studies', in R.A. Spencer (ed.), *Orientation by Disorientation: Studies in Literary Criticism and Biblical Literary Criticism Presented in Honor of William A. Beardslee* (Pittsburgh Theological Monograph Series, 35; Pittsburgh: Pickwick Press, 1980), pp. 25-50.

Pilgrim, W.E., *Good News to the Poor: Wealth and Poverty in Luke–Acts* (Minneapolis: Augsburg, 1981).

Piwowarczyk, M.A., 'The Narrative and the Situation of Enunciation: A Reconsideration of Prince's Theory', *Genre* 9 (1976), pp. 161-77.

Ploeg, J. van der, 'Les Pauvres d'Israel et leur Pieté', *Old Testament Studies* 7 (1950), pp. 242-70.

Plato, *Crito* (trans. H.N. Fowler; LCL, 36; Cambridge, MA: Harvard University Press, 1914).

Powell, M.A., 'The Religious Leaders in Luke: A Literary Critical Study', *JBL* 109 (1990), pp. 93-110.

—'The Religious Leaders in Matthew: A Literary Critical Approach' (PhD dissertation, Union Theological Seminary in Virginia, 1988).

—*What Are They Saying About Luke?* (New York: Paulist Press, 1989).

—*What is Narrative Criticism?* (Guides to Biblical Scholarship; Minneapolis: Augsburg–Fortress, 1990).

Pratt, M.L., *Toward A Speech Act Theory of Literary Discourse* (Bloomington: Indiana University Press, 1977).

Prior, M. *Jesus the Liberator: Nazareth Liberation Theology (Luke 4.16-30)* (The Biblical Seminar, 26; Sheffield: Sheffield Academic Press, 1995).

Rabinowitz, P., 'Truth in Fiction: A Reexamination of Audiences', *Critical Inquiry* 4 (1977), pp. 121-41.

Rahlfs, A., *Ani und Anaw in den Psalmen* (Göttingen: Dieterichsche Verlagsbuchhandlung, 1892).

—(ed.), *Septuaginta* (Stuttgart: Deutsche Bibelgesellschaft, 1979 [1935]).

Reeves D., 'Studies in the Ethics of Luke' (PhD dissertation, Harvard University, 1971).

Reicke, B., 'Jesus in Nazareth: Lk 4, 14-30', in H. Balz und S. Schulz (eds.), *Das Wort und die Wörter* (Festschrift G. Friedrich; Stuttgart: Kohlhammer, 1973), pp. 47-55.

Rese, M., *Alttestamentliche Motive in der Christologie des Lukas* (SNT, 1; Gütersloh: Gütersloher Verlagshaus, 1969).

Reumann, J., *Jesus in the Church's Gospel: Modern Scholarship and the Earliest Sources* (Philadelphia: Fortress Press, 1968).

Rhoads, D., 'Narrative Criticism and the Gospel of Mark', *JAAR* 50 (1982), pp. 411-34.

Rhoads, D., and D. Michie, *Mark as Story: An Introduction to the Narrative of a Gospel* (Philadelphia: Fortress Press, 1982).

Richard, E., *Acts 6:1-8:4: The Author's Method of Composition* (SBLDS, 41; Missoula, MT: Scholars Press, 1978).

Riffaterre, M., 'Intertextual Representation: On Mimesis as Interpretive Discourse', *Critical Inquiry* 11 (September 1984), pp. 141-62.

—*Semiotics of Poetry* (Bloomington: Indiana University Press, 1978).

Rimmon-Kenan, S., *Narrative Fiction: Contemporary Poetics* (London: Methuen, 1983).

Ringe, S., *Jesus, Liberation, and the Biblical Jubilee: Images for Ethics and Christology* (Overtures to Biblical Theology; Philadelphia: Fortress Press, 1985).

—*Luke* (Westminster Bible Companion; Louisville: Westminster/John Knox, 1995).

Robbins, V.K., *Jesus the Teacher: A Socio-Rhetorical Interpretation of Mark* (Philadelphia: Fortress Press, 1984).

Robertson, A.T., *A Grammar of the Greek New Testament in the Light of Historical Research* (Nashville: Broadman, 1934).

Robinson, D., 'Reader's Power, Writer's Power: Barth, Bergonzi, Iser, and the Modern-Postmodern Period Debate', *Criticism* 28 (Summer 1986), pp. 307-22.

Sanders, E.P. *Jesus and Judaism* (Philadelphia: Fortress Press, 1985).

Sanders, J.A., 'From Isaiah 61 to Luke 4', in J. Neusner (ed.), *Christianity, Judaism, and Other Greco-Roman Cults* (Leiden: Brill, 1975), I, pp.75-106.

Sanders, J.T., *The Jews in Luke–Acts* (Philadelphia: Fortress Press, 1987).

—'The Pharisees in Luke–Acts', in D.E. Groh and R. Jewett (eds.), *The Living Text: Essays in Honor of Ernest W. Saunders* (New York: University Press of America, 1985), pp. 141-88.

Sankey, P.J., 'Promise and Fulfillment: Reader-Response to Mark 1.1-15', *JSNT* 58 (1995), pp. 3-18.

Sattler, W., 'Die Anawim im Zeitalter Jesu Christi', in *Festgabe für A. Jülicher* (Tübingen: Mohr, 1927), pp. 1-15.

Schmidt, T., *Hostility to Wealth in the Synoptic Gospels* (JSNTSup, 15; Sheffield: JSOT Press, 1987).

Schneider, F., and W. Stenger, 'Die offene Tür und die unüberschreitbare Kluft', *NTS* 25 (1978–79), pp. 273-83.

Schneider, J., *Die Taufe im Neuen Testament* (Stuttgart: Kohlhammer, 1952).

Scholes, R., and R. Kellogg, *The Nature of Narrative* (London: Oxford University Press, 1966).

Schottroff, L., and W. Stegemann, *Jesus von Nazareth: Hoffnung der Armen* (Stuttgart: Kohlhammer, 3rd edn, 1990 [1978]).

Schreck, C.J., 'The Nazareth Pericope: Luke 4, 16-30 in Recent Study', in F. Neirynck (ed.), *L'Évangile de Luc: The Gospel of Luke* (BETL, 32; Leuven: Leuven University Press, rev. and enlarged edn, 1989), pp. 399-471.

Schubert, P., 'The Structure and Significance of Luke 24', in W. Eltester (ed.), *Neutestamentliche Studien für Rudolf Bultmann* (BZNW, 21; Berlin: Töpelmann, 1954), pp. 165-86.

Schüssler Fiorenza, E., *In Memory of Her: A Feminist Theological Reconstruction of Christian Origins* (New York: Crossroad, 1983).

Schweizer, E., *The Good News According to Luke* (trans. D.E. Green; Atlanta: John Knox, 1984).

Searle, J.R., *Intentionality* (Cambridge: Cambridge University Press, 1983).

—*Speech Acts: An Essay in the Philosophy of Language* (Cambridge: Cambridge University Press, 1969).

Seccombe, D., *Possessions and the Poor in Luke–Acts* (SNTU, Series B, 6; Linz: A. Fuchs, 1983).

Sedgwick, W.B., 'Reading and Writing in Classical Antiquity', *Contemporary Review* 135 (January–June 1929), pp. 93-94.

Sevenster, J.N., *Do You Know Greek? How Much Greek Could the First Jewish Christians Have Known?* (NovTSup, 19; Leiden: Brill, 1968).

Siker, J.S., ' "First to the Gentiles": A Literary Analysis of Luke 4:16-30', *JBL* 111 (1992), pp. 73-90.

Sloan, R., *The Favorable Year of the Lord: A Study of Jubilary Theology in the Gospel of Luke* (Austin, TX: Schola Press, 1977).

Sparks, H.F.D. (ed.), *The Apocryphal Old Testament* (Oxford: Oxford University Press, 1984).

Stegemann, W., *The Gospel and the Poor* (trans. D. Elliott; Philadelphia: Fortress Press, 1984).

Stendahl, K., *The School of St. Matthew and its Use of the Old Testament* (Philadelphia: Fortress Press, 1968).

Strobel, A., 'Die Ausrufung des Jobeljahrs in der Nazarethpredigt Jesu: Zur apokalyptischen Tradition Lc 4,16-30', in W. Eltester (ed.), *Jesus in Nazareth* (BZNW, 40; Berlin: de Gruyter, 1972), pp. 38-50.

Suleiman, S.R., 'Introduction: Varieties of Audience-Oriented Criticism', in Suleiman and Crosman (eds.), *The Reader in the Text*, pp. 3-45.

Suleiman, S.R. and I. Crosman (eds.), *The Reader in the Text: Essays on Audience and Interpretation* (Princeton, NJ: Princeton University Press, 1980).

Swete, H.B., *An Introduction to the Old Testament in Greek* (rev. R.R. Ottley; Cambridge: Cambridge University Press, 1914; repr.; Peabody, MA: Hendrickson, 1989).

Talbert, C.H., *Literary Patterns, Theological Themes, and the Genre of Luke–Acts* (SBLMS, 20; Missoula, MT: Scholars Press, 1974).

—*Reading Luke: A Literary and Theological Commentary on the Third Gospel* (New York: Crossroad, 1982).

—*What is a Gospel? The Genre of the Canonical Gospels* (Philadelphia: Fortress Press, 1977).

Tannehill, R.C., 'Literature, the New Testament as', *Harper's Bible Dictionary* (ed. P.J. Achtemeier; San Francisco: Harper & Row, 1985), pp. 564-67.

—'The Mission of Jesus According to Luke IV 16-30', in W. Eltester (ed.), *Jesus in Nazareth* (BZNW, 40; Berlin: de Gruyter, 1972), pp. 51-75.

—*The Narrative Unity of Luke–Acts: A Literary Interpretation* (Foundations and Facets: New Testament; 2 vols.; Philadelphia: Fortress Press, 1986, 1990).

—'The Story of Zacchaeus as Rhetoric: Luke 19.10', *Semeia* 64 (1993), pp. 201-11.

Tetlow, E., *Women and Ministry in the New Testament* (New York: Paulist Press, 1980).

Thackeray, H. St J., *A Grammar of the Old Testament in Greek According to the Septuagint*. I. *Introduction, Orthography and Accidence* (Cambridge: Cambridge University Press, 1909).

Theophrastus, *The Characters* (ed. and trans. J.M. Edmonds; LCL; London: Heinemann; New York: Putnam's Sons, 1929).

Thompson, C., *The Septuagint Bible, the Oldest Version of the Old Testament* (ed., rev., and enlarged C.A. Muses; Indian Hills, CO: Falcon Wing's Press, 1954).

Tiede, D.L., *Luke* (Augsburg Commentary on the New Testament; Minneapolis: Augsburg, 1988).

—*Prophecy and History in Luke–Acts* (Philadelphia: Fortress Press, 1980).

Tolbert, M.A., *Perspectives on the Parables: An Approach to Multiple Interpretations* (Philadelphia: Fortress Press, 1979).

—*Sowing the Gospel: Mark's World in Literary-Historical Perspective* (Minneapolis: Fortress Press, 1989).

Tompkins, J.P., 'An Introduction to Reader-Response Criticism', in *idem* (ed.), *Reader-Response Criticism*, pp. ix-xxvi.

—'The Reader in History: The Changing Shape of Literary Response', in Tompkins (ed.), *Reader-Response Criticism*, pp. 201-32.

Tompkins, J.P. (ed.), *Reader Response Criticism: From Formalism to Post-Structuralism* (Baltimore: The Johns Hopkins University Press, 1980).

Turner, N., *Grammatical Insights into the New Testament* (Edinburgh: T. & T. Clark, 1965).

Tyson, J.B., *Images of Judaism in Luke–Acts* (Columbia, South Carolina: University of South Carolina Press, 1992).

Uspensky, B., *A Poetics of Composition: The Structure of the Artistic Text and Typology of a Compositional Form* (trans. V. Zavarin and S. Wittig; Berkeley: University of California Press, 1973).

Via, D.O., *The Parables: Their Literary and Existential Dimension* (Philadelphia: Fortress Press, 1967).

Violet, B., 'Zum rechten Verständnis der Nazareth-Perikope Lc 4, 16-30', *ZNW* 37 (1938), pp. 251-71.

Voelz, J.W., 'The Language of the New Testament', in H. Temporini and W. Haase (eds.), *Aufsteig und Niedergang der Römischen Welt: Geschichte und Kultur Roms im Spiegel der Neueren Forschung* (Berlin: de Gruyter, 1984), II.25.2, pp. 893-977.

Vorster, W.S., 'The Reader in the Text: Narrative Material', *Semeia* 48 (1989), pp. 21-39.

Wächter, L., *Der Tod im Alten Testament* (Arbeiten zur Theologie, 2.8; Stuttgart: Calwer Verlag, 1967).

Wellek, R., 'The New Criticism: Pro and Contra,' *Critical Inquiry* 4 (1978), pp. 611-24.

Wellek, R., and A. Warren, *Theory of Literature* (New York: Harcourt, 1949).

Wilder, A., *The Bible and the Literary Critic* (Minneapolis: Augsburg-Fortress, 1991).

—*Early Christian Rhetoric: The Language of the Gospel* (Cambridge, MA: Harvard University Press, 1971).

Wimsatt, W., Jr, and C. Brooks, *Literary Criticism: A Short History* (2 vols.; Chicago: University of Chicago Press, 1957).

Wink, W., 'Jesus' Reply to John: Matt 11:2-6/Luke 7:18-23', *Forum* 5 (1989), pp. 121-28.

Wissmann, H., 'Armut—I: Religionsgeschichtlich', *Theologische Realenzyklopädie* (ed. G. Krause and G. Mueller; Berlin: de Gruyter, 1976-90), pp. 69-72.

Wolff, E., 'Der intendierte Leser', *Poetica* 4 (1971), pp. 141-66.

Wright, A.G., 'The Widow's Mites: Praise or Lament? A Matter of Context', *CBQ* 44 (1982), pp. 256-65.

Wright, D.P., 'Leprosy', *Harper's Bible Dictionary* (ed. P.J. Achtemeier; San Francisco: Harper & Row, 1985), pp. 555-56.

Ziesler, J.A., 'Luke and the Pharisees', *NTS* 25 (1979), pp. 146-57.

INDEXES

INDEX OF REFERENCES

OLD TESTAMENT

JOURNAL FOR THE STUDY OF THE NEW TESTAMENT
SUPPLEMENT SERIES